Major J. R. Hillkirk
Kenworthy Hall
Northenden, Cheshire
1893.

CRIMINAL LIFE:

REMINISCENCES

OF

FORTY-TWO YEARS AS A POLICE OFFICER.

BY

SUPERINTENDENT BENT.

———

JOHN HEYWOOD,
DEANSGATE AND RIDGEFIELD, MANCHESTER;
1, PATERNOSTER BUILDINGS,
LONDON.

INTRODUCTION.

I was born at Eccles, of parents in a humble station in life, on the 3rd of February, 1828, but my early associations of the town noted for its celebrated cakes were not of a pleasant character. At seven years of age I commenced to work in a silk mill. The hours of labour at that time were long, as the Factory Acts, with their beneficent provisions as regards juveniles, were not then in operation, and children were often subjected to very bad treatment, and even severe punishment, at the hands of the overlookers, who used to walk about with a strap, and no matter how small the neglect of work on the part of a child might be, used it unsparingly. Scores of times I have had "wheals" on my arm about the thickness of my finger from this ill-usage.

After reaching the age of nine years we went to live in Salford, my father being at that time a member of the "Old Watch" in Manchester, so that if not born in the police force I may be said to have been nurtured in it. My father wore, I recollect even now, a low crowned hat with a yellow band, had numbers nightly painted on his coat with ochre, and he used to cry the hours through the night.

To this day I can well remember him telling my mother what I thought was a laughable story of a comrade who had just joined the watch. When he was told that he would be required to call out the hours he asked my father, who was on the next beat to him, how he should go on, as he had no watch.

"Well," was the reply, "you will be at one side of the canal, and I shall be at the other, and when you hear me call the hour all you have to do is to call the same as me."

Thinking the man understood what he meant, they went to their respective beats, and when my father called out, "Past ten o'clock, and a fine moonlight night," he expected, of course, that his comrade across the canal would make use of the same words; but his surprise may be judged when the other responded with the words, "Same here."

On the 7th of November, 1848, when I was approaching my twenty-first birthday, I joined the Lancashire Constabulary at the headquarters in Preston, having a short time previously entered the married state.

I remained at Preston for about five weeks as a recruit, when I was sent to the headquarters of the Manchester Division, which were then at Pendleton; and in about three months from that time I was removed to Croft's Bank, Barton-upon-Irwell, where I was stationed until the 16th of April, 1858.

In July, 1849, I was promoted to the rank of second-class constable, and in July, 1850, attained the first-class rank. In 1852 I received the merit badge, and in 1858 was promoted to the rank of sergeant, and sent to Longsight. Just at this time there were many cases of undetected crime at Newton Heath and Failsworth, and being fortunate enough to recover a large quantity of property that had been stolen from that district, at the expiration of two months I was selected to take charge of Newton Heath section, where I remained until 1863. In 1860 I was again promoted to the class of merit, and in 1863 was promoted to the rank of inspector. In that capacity I took charge of the Prestwich subdivision, which then included Harpurhey, Moston, Blackley, Higher and Lower Crumpsall, Great and Little Heaton, Prestwich, Pendlebury, Swinton, Clifton, Eccles, Barton, Worsley, Irlam, and Cadishead.

On the 16th of April, 1868, I was promoted to the rank of superintendent, and assumed the command of the Manchester Division.

When I left Croft's Bank, in 1858, the inhabitants of that district presented me with a watch, a small purse of money, and a testimonial, which ran as follows: "Presented by a few of the inhabitants of Davyhulme, Croft's Bank, Barton-upon-Irwell, and neighbourhood, to Mr. James Bent, county police constable, as a token of their esteem and respect for the very efficient manner in which he has performed his duties in the district for upwards of eight years." On leaving Newton Heath, the inhabitants of that place presented me with a gold chain, a purse of gold, and an illuminated address, which ran as follows: "Presented to Mr. Inspector James Bent, by the inhabitants of Newton Heath, as a token of respect and esteem for his meritorious services as sergeant of police during a period of five years." In 1875 the county magistrates of the Manchester Division presented me with a silver tea and coffee service and a purse containing £75, the plate bearing the following inscription: "Presented by the magistrates of the Manchester Division of the county of

Lancaster to Mr. Superintendent Bent, in recognition of faithful and valued services during twenty-five years."

Having had a severe attack of illness in May, 1884, and at the same time received an anonymous letter, evidently written with the intention of causing me annoyance and trouble, the members of the police force under my command presented me with a sympathetic address in the following terms: "We, the undermentioned officers and men of the Manchester, Division of the Lancashire Constabulary, having heard with deep regret and indignation that you have lately received an anonymous letter making imputations and aspersions on your character as superintendent of this division, which we know to be utterly without foundation, respectfully beg to repudiate the foul sentiments expressed in the letter, and to express our utter abhorrence of the dastardly conduct of the writer in making such false and base statements. Having had the honour of serving under you—many of us for a long term of years—we can, and do, unanimously testify from our own personal experience that no man in this division has ever experienced anything from your hand but justice, impartiality, and leniency. We gratefully tender you our sincere thanks, not only for practical help and guidance, so often and so readily given us by you, but for many privileges and benefits you have been the means of obtaining for this division. And while expressing our deep and heartfelt sympathy with you in your long-continued and painful illness, we sincerely hope and trust that you may long be spared, in restored health, to continue many years at the head of the Manchester Division of the County."

PREFACE.

HAVING had a lengthened and varied experience as a police officer, in all the grades of the service, from third-class constable to superintendent, it has frequently been suggested by my friends that I should write and publish my reminiscences. To these requests I have at last acceded, with the result that this work is now given to the world. My career in the force has been an exceedingly eventful one, and the recollections which I have recorded of crime and its detection and punishment, of dangers encountered and overcome, and of incidents both of a humorous and sorrowful nature, will, I trust, be found interesting to the general reader. This much is certain, that my memoirs afford a reliable insight into the duties, the risks, and the inner workings of police life of which the public at large can have very little idea.

PREFACE.

Instead of arranging the contents of the book in chronological order, I have aimed at the classification of different incidents and adventures, captures and discoveries, in groups of subjects, an arrangement which will, I think, be found to be acceptable to my readers. It will be seen that I have written in a plain style, without any attempt at literary ornamentation, this undoubtedly being the most suitable plan for the cases dealt with and the materials used.

Your faithful servant,

JAMES BENT.

Old Trafford Police Station,
January, 1891.

CONTENTS.

CHAPTER I.
Desperate Struggle with an Escaped Convict.. 1

CHAPTER II.
Racecourse Gaming 9

CHAPTER III.
How to Deal with Brutal Husbands 19

CHAPTER IV.
Troubles with the Colliers, &c.... 25

CHAPTER V.
Larceny Incidents 35

CHAPTER VI.
Capture of Escaped Prisoners 69

CHAPTER VII.
Horrible Burning with Red-hot Irons... ... 75

CHAPTER VIII.
Offences Against Infants... 81

CHAPTER IX.

ROBBERIES BY DOMESTIC SERVANTS... 89

CHAPTER X.

BURGLARIES AND HOUSEBREAKINGS 101

CHAPTER XI.

EVENTS AND CASES—GRAVE AND GAY 126

CHAPTER XII.

BEERHOUSE OFFENCES 151

CHAPTER XIII.

POLICE EXPERIENCES AND PLEASANTRIES.—THE STORY OF A WHISTLE, &c. 155

CHAPTER XIV.

TALES OF TIMIDITY 175

CHAPTER XV.

FEMININE ATTEMPTS AT EXTORTION... 187

CHAPTER XVI.

MISCELLANEOUS PHASES OF DRUNKENNESS... ... 197

CHAPTER XVII.

SWINDLERS 208

CHAPTER XVIII.

PAWNBROKERS 214

CHAPTER XIX.

GARROTTERS 220

CHAPTER XX.

SCUTTLERS 223

CHAPTER XXI.
THE HARPURHEY MURDER ... 227

CHAPTER XXII.
THE MURDER OF CONSTABLE COCK ... 235

CHAPTER XXIII.
THE MOSTON MURDER ... 244

CHAPTER XXIV.
THE ATHERTON MURDER ... 247

CHAPTER XXV.
THE MAPP CASE ... 256

CHAPTER XXVI.
POLICE COURT WITTICISMS ... 261

NOTE ... 271

APPENDIX.
OLD TRAFFORD POLICE SOUP KITCHEN ... 273

CRIMINAL LIFE.

CHAPTER I.

DESPERATE STRUGGLE WITH AN ESCAPED CONVICT.

IN August, 1860, when I was stationed at Newton Heath as a sergeant, I received information that a convict named Jack Robinson, *alias* " Lord Raglan," had escaped from Dartmoor Gaol, where he was undergoing a sentence of twenty years' penal servitude He was a notorious thief, who had been tried for murder, but the evidence not being sufficient, his conviction was for robbery only, the watch of the murdered man having been found in his possession. Robinson's mother kept a small beerhouse down Culcheth Brow, Newton Heath, and as I had been told that he had been seen in the neighbourhood with a five-chambered revolver ready charged, and had sworn that if any policeman went near him, with a view to his recapture, he would shoot him dead, I at once concluded that he would be found at his former home. I then resolved to attempt his arrest, and was not dissuaded by the fact that I was advised by my friends not to go near him, as I was not likely to come away alive.

Consequently, I adhered to my resolution to try what I could do, and about two o'clock in the morning after I had received the intelligence I met one of my constables—the only one I could find, as it happened—and acquainted him with the position of affairs. I pointed out to him that this Robinson was a desperate fellow, and would, no doubt, use his revolver upon either of us if he got the chance. All the same, I added that I was determined to try to apprehend him, and if he was game enough to accompany me, I should not ask him to tackle the ruffian himself, if he would only prevent others from attacking me.

I further said to my subordinate, "I have told you all. If you would rather not go, say so now. Do not deceive me. I will never name the matter to anybody, but if you go with me you must make up your mind to stand by me. There is a reward of £20 offered," I added, "and if I succeed in securing our man, I will divide it with you."

"All right, sergeant," was the reply, "I will go with you."

Having ascertained that the officer had his handcuffs and staff all right, we started for Culcheth Brow and Robinson's mother's beerhouse. I found it to be a low building—two houses having, in fact, been made practically into one, with a view to bringing the rateable value up to a sufficient sum for a licence. There were several holes and places round about, including a calf-cote, and knowing that a ferocious dog was kept somewhere on the premises, in order to prevent my steps being heard I got down on my hands and knees and went into this outhouse to see if Robinson was concealed there, but on emerging from it I found that my subordinate was in such a state of nervous excitement that he could not keep quiet, and in fact was shaking all over like an aspen leaf.

"Keep your spirits up," I whispered to him. "You shall have all the reward if we can catch Robinson. Do not be frightened. I will tackle him, and you can keep his friends from setting on me."

As I had found nothing in the calf-cote or in any of the other places round about, by way of a ruse I sent the constable to knock at the front door, in order to ask if they had any company in the house, whilst I went round and put my ear against the back door. I could hear the constable knock at the front door, and immediately afterwards someone appeared to fall or jump out of bed, and directly after that I could hear the sister of the man we were after talking to the constable. I ran round the gable end of the house and showed an arm and part of my body, and then ran round again to the other end and repeated the process, with the view, of course, of impressing upon them that the police were present in force. I then heard the convict's sister say to the constable—

"You are a fresh one, and, by God, if I had a gun, I would shoot you dead."

Thereupon I stepped from my place, and proceeding to the front, where my man was, saluted her with, "Oh, Jane, is that you?"

Her answer was, "Oh, sergeant, there are five or six of you."

Seeing that I had deceived her as to our numbers, I said, "You must let me in, Jane"; and further noticing that the constable was in a state of trembling timidity, I asked him to go to the back door, and give me immediate notice if he saw anybody stir. In the meantime I remained at the front entrance, and in the course of a few seconds Robinson's brother came and opened it. I had expected a shot every moment through the door.

"What do you want, sergeant?" demanded the brother.

My reply was, "I want your Jack."

"He is not here," said he.

"Fetch me a candle, and let me look," was my response.

"We have not a candle in the house," replied he.

"You are bound," I returned, "to have a candle in the house to show the police through whenever they think proper to call."

"Well, go into this room," said the brother, pointing to a door in the lobby on my left, "and I'll go upstairs and see if I can find one."

The place being dark, and believing that the man I wanted was in the room indicated, I put my stick against the door and said, in a loud voice "I am a policeman, and if either man, woman, or child comes out of this room until a candle is brought, I will knock their brains out."

A few minutes afterwards Robinson's brother came downstairs with a lighted candle, and offered it to me. "Go in first yourself," I said. He opened the door, and went into a rather long room, under the window of which there was an old sofa with a print valance hanging down. I walked towards this sofa and lifted up the valance with my stick, and there I saw Robinson on his hands and knees. His hair was cut short, he had an incipient moustache, and he wore a convict's shirt and socks, while in his hand he clasped a cane, such as one could buy for a penny, but which had fixed at one end a lump of lead about the size of a duck's egg. Taking him altogether, I never saw a worse or more dangerous-looking man in all my life. Feeling that I could take him without using my stick, I put it down, and got hold of an ankle in each hand, holding him face downwards, and drew him from under the couch, saying, "Jack, I want you." I had not the slightest idea that he would be able to use his life-preserver—which, to me, on the occasion, was nearly proving my life-taker—for immediately after he struck me a blow under the left eye, raising a lump which quickly became nearly as big as my fist. As Robinson was a strong man, of greater height than myself, and knowing that his brother and sister and a woman were behind me, I dared not leave hold of his feet. Perceiving my difficulty, he struck me another severe blow with the same weapon on the crown of the head, inflicting a wound from which the blood flowed freely, blinding me entirely. Just at this moment my subordinate came in, and I remember that he also got a blow on the head. The sister of the convict called out to his brother, who was standing there—

"Dod, fetch the poker, and knock his brains out. He shan't take him."

All the while I continued drawing Robinson from the room, as I thought that if I could get him out of the house I should know what to do with him; but as soon as the brother turned round to fetch the poker, the sister and another woman, who had come downstairs, got behind me, and tumbled me head over heels over the convict. I recovered myself at once, and, after a severe struggle, again succeeded in getting hold of his ankles, and continued to draw him towards the passage, when the brother came downstairs armed with a poker, with which he struck me on the head and partially stunned me. Before I got outside into the air I received a second blow, though I succeeded in lifting Robinson, by putting my arms round him, and wrenching the life-preserver from him. I continued to hug him till I found that he was very much weakened. I was blinded, however, from the blows I had received, and I forgot that there was a deep sunk fence about a dozen yards from the beerhouse door. I walked on, carrying Robinson, with my arms clasped round his body, pressing my chin as tightly as I could into his back, when his mother called out with an oath—

"Shoot them both, there are only two of them."

Just at that moment, however, we fell into the sunk fence, and Robinson was uppermost. His brother and sister began upon this to shout "Hurrah!" but I made a desperate effort, and turning Robinson over again, I succeeded in regaining my feet, and I then called out "Hurrah!"

Although I could feel faintness coming over me, from loss of blood, I was able to shout for the constable; and then, seeing a man looking through a bedroom window at what was going on, I shouted to him for help at the top of my voice. The Robinsons then turned the dog loose upon me, and the brute fastened its teeth in the calf of my left leg.

Owing to the exciting nature of the encounter all feeling

had temporarily left me, and the bite of the animal did not give me the slightest pain. My subordinate officer soon came up with his truncheon in his hand, but he had not taken the precaution of putting the strap attached to it properly round his wrist. He held it in front of Robinson, and threatened what he would do if the other did not surrender; but the prisoner's arms being loose, he at once grasped the officer's staff, and gave me a tremendous blow with it over his shoulder. I pretended to laugh at him, and shifted my head to the other side, just in time to receive another severe stroke on the same place from his other hand, to which he had shifted the staff. We fell down together, when I found that partial paralysis had set in, and when I put out my hand to again seize my man I had not the power to hold him, and he got up and ran away. As well as I could I told the constable to follow him, and if he did not want to attack, to hold him in sight and keep whistling until assistance came.

Afterwards I crawled to the house where I had seen a man at the window, which turned out to be that of James Naylor, and as soon as I got there I must have fainted. When I recovered, Naylor had a poker in his hand, and volunteered to go and follow the sound of the whistle, but his wife suggested that I should be carried into the house, and I remember her saying that I was dying. I replied, "While I hear the policeman's whistle I shall not be carried in." I again lost consciousness, and when I recovered the woman had fainted, and her husband was attending to her. I crawled away again, though with great difficulty, until I came to a cottage, where I fell against the door, as I had not the power to knock. The inmates spoke to me from the window, and, as well as I could, I told them what had taken place, and begged they would follow the sound of the constable's whistle, which they promised to do, while I was taken to a surgery, where my injuries were attended to. It afterwards transpired that the constable, being afraid of the man, had run to the right, while Robinson was running to the left, and had thus entirely lost the track. As soon as I was able to be spoken to, the following evening Mr. R. J. Walker, the magistrate's clerk, and the superintendent came up and took my depositions.

About a fortnight after this Robinson was captured in Sheffield by a number of the borough constables, who had surrounded the house where he was lodging, and found him very drunk in bed. His brother and sister were apprehended, and brought before the magistrates, but the case against the woman was dismissed. The escaped convict, and the brother who had struck me with the poker, were sent to Liverpool Assizes for trial, when "Lord Raglan" was condemned to transportation for life, while George Robinson, who was subject to epileptic fits, received a sentence of two years' imprisonment. The judge awarded me £20, and the constable was dismissed from the police service for cowardice. My head had been so pummelled that it was a long time before I was able to resume my duties, and even to this day I often feel the effects of the injuries I then received.

CHAPTER II.

RACECOURSE GAMING.

FROM the very commencement of my career in the police force I was constantly employed as a detective officer. In fact, I may say that I was the principal detective in the Manchester division, and in that capacity I attended nearly all races and other large gatherings of importance in the county. At first I paid much attention to gambling, and I remember the first case that I brought before Mr. Henry Leigh Trafford, then the stipendiary magistrate for the division of Manchester, and for Salford. I produced a box of dice, and Mr. Trafford began to measure them with a pair of callipers, and to feel and to balance them to see if they were loaded, when I very imprudently remarked—

"It is of no importance, sir, whether they are loaded or not."

Upon this he rebuked me in somewhat strong language for addressing him in such a strain, adding that others in authority over me had told him all about it. Not to be beaten, however, I thought I would make myself master of the trickery of all the gaming instruments that were used on the racecourse, so that I might perhaps induce Mr. Trafford someday to alter his opinion.

On such occasions as those I have alluded to, the police officers usually went on duty in pairs, dressed in plain clothes, with the object of detecting pick-pockets and gamblers, and at first I somewhat foolishly imparted my acquired knowledge of the gambling apparatus to my fellow-detective. This officer had been longer in the service than I had been, and I found that he was in the habit of making statements to the magistrate, showing how the instruments were used, and that he always took great care not to let the bench know that I was entitled to the credit of discovering the frauds. Feeling rather annoyed at this, and desirous of making my way to the front, I resolved upon stating my own cases, with the view of showing that I knew something about them. On one occasion I remember being on the Old Trafford raceground, watching three or four men with a board, upon which were painted four red and four white cocks and two crowns. The betting on this game was even on the cocks and three to one on the crowns. Now, as there were invariably on gambling instruments of this description four red cocks and four white ones, it will be seen that even if all was fair and transparent, one of the public making a bet would only have four chances against the gambler's six, or two chances against their eight, as the case might be.

After watching the operations at this board for a considerable time, I discovered that there was another mode of cheating in connection with it in addition to that which appeared on the surface, so after locking up its owners I took the instrument home and subjected it to a careful examination. As a result of this I found that there was a sort of cross-piece which came to the end of the board, which was covered with the canvas covering the table. In this cross-piece, which was hollow, there was a piece of cane or whalebone, of sufficient length to reach to the flange of the index protruding a little outside the board, thereby enabling the gambler to stop the index whenever he thought proper. I told my fellow-officer that the apparatus was "faked," meaning that it was designed to cheat those who made bets upon it, but declined to make any explanation. When the officer appeared in the witness-box Mr. Trafford asked him if there was anything about the instrument that was not transparent, and he replied in the affirmative, but when asked for a description he admitted that he did not know. I was called into the box, and at once informed the stipendiary, who had snubbed me on a previous occasion, that there was no gaming table used on the racecourse which I did not understand. I pointed out to him that every board whose fingers had a long flange was an instrument for cheating, and explained also that in each of these boards there was a brake which went to the finger. Then I broke the cross-piece from the one before the court, and a piece of cane flew out. Ever after that the stipendiary paid particular attention to what I had to say respecting every such instrument of gaming that was brought before him.

At another time I explained to the same magistrate in what way the roulette table was fraudulent, and instructed him how to work it so as either to win or lose as he thought proper. The fact is that there are a number of colours, and a person bets upon whichever he chooses, and as soon as the gambler ascertains which colour has the most money staked upon it he reverses the wheel, and then it is impossible to get into the one that would be adverse to him. This is done by the different wards into which the ball has to go being uneven, so that if you turn the roulette in one direction the ball cannot enter the ward, whereas if you turn it in the other direction it is almost impossible for the ball not to go into the ward.

This the stipendiary seemed to understand for a time; but one day, when the sessions happened to be on at the New Bailey, no doubt thinking to play a practical joke, he took one of these roulette tables into the consulting room, and there went along with him some of the young barristers then attending the court, whom he had invited to accompany him. He there proceeded to act as the owner of the apparatus, and at his solicitation the legal gentlemen, in illegal fashion, staked various coins on the turn of the wheel. Unfortunately for himself, the amateur croupier turned the wheel the wrong way, and lost fifteen shillings in a very short time. He afterwards came to me, as I chanced to be at hand, and asked me to conduct the gambling machine on his behalf. This I did, and soon managed to recover for him the money he was out of pocket, with the addition of five shillings for myself, which he allowed me to take away. This roulette table Mr. Trafford took home with him, and I never saw it again.

There is a game known amongst those who practice it by the name of "Titley Wink." It is something like a miniature "Aunt Sally," but on a very Lilliputian scale. The whole of the gambler's stock-in-trade consists of a peg about six inches long, and a bit of clay about the size of a halfpenny. The peg is cut at the top in a slanting position, and on it is placed a small button. The *modus operandi* is as follows: A piece of whalebone or cane is given to the player, for which he is charged a penny, and he has to stand about five yards from the peg. The rod is very light indeed, and nobody can throw it with any approach to accuracy, for the button can be so placed by the owner that it is almost certain to fall on the clay. If it does, the player gets nothing, but if he knocks the button off the peg, and it falls away from the clay, the gambler pays threepence for the penny.

I had seen considerable sums of money lost at this apparently simple game. People playing at it are accustomed to double their bets time after time, till sometimes the amount lost becomes rather serious, particularly for a working man. I mentioned the subject to Mr. Trafford on one occasion, and having explained the thoroughly fraudulent nature of the process, said I should be very glad if he would allow me to bring one or two of these gamblers before him, in order to have the process put to a legal test. At first he declined to give me permission, saying the game I had spoken of was only like "Aunt Sally." I told him that was so, so far as the stick on which the prizes were placed being cut in a slanting position, but that the chances of winning by playing "Titley Wink" were far more remote than by playing at "Aunt Sally," and that if he desired it, I would bring him a peg and show him how it was placed.

"Never mind, Bent," he answered. "Bring me one or two of the men before me, and I will see what I can do with them."

Accordingly I took two of the gamblers into custody, and they were convicted and sentenced to two months' imprisonment each under the Vagrant Act. The stipendiary, however, told me before leaving the court not to apprehend any more for the present. On my return to the racecourse, however, I perceived the same game again in progress, and lying down upon the grass and peering between the persons in the crowd, I saw a man, who appeared to be a warehouse porter, commence to play. I believe his first bet was sixpence, and his second a shilling, and he doubled the amount every time until he had lost all that he possessed, amounting to £16, when the gambler, who is still living, and walking about, gave him a shilling, and told him to go and play with someone else. This is usual when a man has lost all he has.

I felt sure from the nervous state in which the loser appeared to be that he had been speculating with another person's money. So I ran to the gambler, called him by name, and told him I wanted him.

"My God! Mr. Bent," he said, "this is a Derby day for me [meaning a good day]. Look what I have got."

"You will have to go to the station with me," I replied.

"You do not mean to lock me up?" was the query of the fellow, in a terrified tone.

"I do, Paddy, this time."

As a matter of fact I did not mean to do so after what the stipendiary had said to me, but I had a desire, if possible, to get the loser his money back, and, perhaps, to prevent him from ever doing anything of the sort again. I told the man to follow us, but when we had got a few yards the prisoner exclaimed—

"Oh, Mr. Bent, my wife is dying. Do not lock me up."

"It would have been a good job," I retorted, "if her husband had died a fortnight before—then this poor fellow would not have lost his money."

"I will halve it with you," he then declared, his cupidity still having the better of his fear.

"No, Paddy, £16, or you go into the cell. Put £16 into that man's hands and I will let you go," I said, decisively.

He still declined to come to terms, and we continued our course towards the police station, the individual who had lost the money still following us in a disconsolate mood. On reaching within sight of the station I determined to again test the fellow's determination, and said, "Now, Paddy, £16 to that man, or in you go head foremost." The grim portals of the station house, as his eyes fell upon them, proved too terrifying to my prisoner, and reluctantly forced to yield, he exclaimed, "Mr. Bent, I will give it," and at once handed the money to the man. Thereupon I released him, and sullenly he took his departure, no doubt bemoaning the ill-luck that had befallen him. Afterwards, turning to the gambler's victim, I said, "This money is not yours," and I noticed at the time that tears were flowing down his cheeks. He fell down on his knees, put his hands together, and sobbed—

"Oh, my God! you have saved my life. I am a widower with five children, and I have been out of work six months until last week, when I got a situation. I have been collecting a few debts for my master, and if I had not been able to give him the money I should have been in gaol to-morrow and my poor children in the workhouse."

He put his arms round my neck and wept like a child, and I experienced considerable difficulty in getting rid of him. About two years afterwards I met the same individual in Market Street, Manchester, and was happy to see that he had changed his corduroys for black cloth. From this I at once concluded that his adventure on the racecourse had been a lesson to him which had not been without beneficent results.

On one occasion, when performing duty at that popular carnival known as "The Eccles Wakes," as a detective, I noticed a man who had a wooden arm receiving a considerable sum of money from an individual in charge of one of the gaming tables, and I also saw him draw a good deal of cash himself when he took his turn as operator at the instrument. I apprehended the crippled man, but on making a search of his clothing could only find two or three pounds upon him, though I felt assured that he must have more. I searched his coat, collar, and clothing throughout very minutely, but without any good result. He was brought before the magistrates, and being an old offender was sent to prison for three months, while the money that I found upon him was ordered to be spent upon his maintenance while in gaol, the balance, if any, to be returned to him on his release.

I was still very much mystified concerning the amount of the money I had found upon him, and felt convinced that I had not discovered all. At first my impression was that he had swallowed it, but at last the happy idea struck me that it might be concealed somewhere in the piece of wood which did duty for his arm. Acting upon this inspiration I went and examined the aforesaid artificial limb, and found a screw just about the point where the elbow should have been. I unscrewed the arm, and in a socket which had been hollowed out on the inside I found no less a sum than £9 or £10, all of which, no doubt, was part of his ill-gotten gains. The extra money had, however, to be returned to the ingenious scamp at the expiration of his term of imprisonment.

There are many other methods practised by the gambling fraternity, by means of which they can at all times defraud the unwary frequenters of fairs and such like places who may be foolish enough to risk their money in the vain hope of increasing it by gambling.

Out of many which could be given, I may mention the following, often used by gamblers for catching "gudgeons":—

A table is set on the ground, and covered with two cloths, in the centre of which are holes, to allow the indicating finger of the machine to turn round. The hole in the centre of the under cloth is generally stitched like a button hole. In this case the gambler can, unseen by the player, by pulling the under cloth, stop the indicating finger whenever he thinks proper.

Then there is a gambling machine which, from the peculiarity of its shape, is called the "Potato Pie." In the bottom of the dish inside there is the usual indicating finger, with figures all round it. When the indicating finger is sent spinning round the gambler covers the "Potato Pie" dish with a lid, to convince bystanders that *his* game at least is all fair and square, and that no one can interfere with the instrument until the indicator has stopped and the lid has been lifted.

The gambler, however, forgets to mention that the finger of the "Potato Pie" is made of steel—that on the under side of the lid he puts on there is a small magnet, and outside, just over the magnet, a slight scratch or x to show him the exact spot where it is placed. By this means the gambler can very easily make the finger stop at any figure he pleases, and he always takes good care to place the magnet over a small number when others are turning, but when it comes to himself he places the magnet over a high number.

There is a similar gambling machine on which there are two colours—say red and black. On one colour all the high numbers are shown, and on the other colour all the low numbers. Round the inside of the machine there are a number of small holes for the small ball to go into. The gambler, before the operation commences, moves the dial slightly, and then whoever plays against him cannot make a higher number than 12, whereas by again slightly moving the dial before he himself plays, as can very easily be done without being observed, the gambler gets among the high numbers, and cannot possibly go lower than 13. This machine is also called the "Potatoe Pie."

"Pricking the Garter" is also a very old trick amongst gamblers. In this case the "garter," which is rolled up, is so cut round the edges that the gambler can in a moment tell whether you have pricked in the centre or not, and if you have happened to do this he can so easily manipulate the "garter" as to throw you out again by unwrapping the other end of the "garter," which is generally wrapped up unevenly to enable him to do this without detection.

CHAPTER III.

HOW TO DEAL WITH BRUTAL HUSBANDS.

DURING the time I was stationed at Newton Heath, information was brought to the police station that a man who dwelt in Factory Yard had been displaying the brutality of his nature by jumping upon his wife, after having first knocked her to the floor, and that it was feared the poor woman would die. I went to the place at once, and found some hundreds of the neighbours assembled round the door. The woman had been removed to an adjoining house, but the man was within brandishing a poker in one hand and a knife in the other, and swearing that he would kill the first person who crossed the threshold. I ran to the next door and asked an old lady there if she would kindly lend me a chair.

"What do you want the chair for, sergeant?" she asked.

"To sit down upon," I answered, "till the man is ready to be taken up."

"Oh," she returned, "that will be a good while. But you may take the chair."

I accordignly took possession of the substantial piece of

household furniture placed at my disposal, and put it down outside the man's door, then went across Pump Alley, and from there ran against the door with my shoulder, with the result that it at once flew open. I then picked up the chair, holding the back in my hands, ran the man's head into the bottom of the chair, and there held him until I took from him the knife and fire-poker he was then holding. This I had no difficulty in doing, so long as his head was fast in the chair.

He was committed for a term of six months' imprisonment, and at the expiration of his sentence he actually applied to the magistrates for a summons against me for putting his head in a chair, but he was only laughed at for his trouble.

On another occasion, a constable in my division—a big powerful fellow—informed me that a man on his beat, armed with a large carving knife, and in a state of nudity, who had severely beaten his wife, had the street in an uproar. This was about two o'clock in the morning. I told the constable he ought to have brought the offender to the station, instead of coming for help. He seemed incredulous, and asked me if I would take him, and I answered in the affirmative, much to my subordinate's astonishment.

I went to the place indicated, and found the neighbourhood in a state of great excitement, almost every occupant of the houses in the street being at their bedroom windows, shouting and calling for those representatives of the law who are said never to be found when wanted. On my arrival the man was on his doorstep defying anyone to come near him under the penalty of being stabbed. As soon as he saw me he ran into the house. I followed, and he went upstairs. Thereupon I picked up a chair, put it on my head, keeping the back to my face, and followed him. As soon as I got to the top of the stairs, he began to hammer on the chair, but without any effect. Ultimately I seized him by his feet, and threw him on the bedroom floor. The place was in darkness, and he broke loose from me and got into bed. I at once put my hand under the sheets, still holding the chair over my head to keep him from using the knife, and I felt for his large toe. Having obtained a firm hold of that portion of his pedal extremities, I dragged him off the bed and down to the bottom of the stairs. I then asked the man, who was still in the costume of Adam before the Fall, to put on his clothes, as I should certainly take him to the station. But he swore that he would do nothing of the sort, and that if I did take him I should have to do so in the condition in which he then was as regarded attire. His wife came in, and entreated him to dress himself and go with me quietly.

"I will do neither that nor walk," he said; and, turning to me, added, "If you take me you must carry me."

"Well, then, if you won't walk I shall have to drag you."

Thereupon he laid himself upon his back. The authorities had just finished cindering the road opposite his house, and when I got him as far as the path I tried to persuade him to walk.

"I will not," he replied with dogged determination.

"Well, as I shall have to take you," I said, "I shall have to draw you, if you won't use your feet."

"Do as you like," said he, with the same apparent resolve to give me all the trouble he could.

I then got hold of his legs as I might have used the two handles of a wheelbarrow, and drew him along the path for a distance of about three yards, when, finding the friction of the sharp edges of the cinders upon his skin to be far from pleasant, he swore a great oath, and expressed himself willing to walk. I allowed him to get upon his feet, but he still refused to have his nakedness covered.

After we had proceeded a considerable distance, and just as day was breaking, we reached the canal side, where the towing path had recently been repaired with broken stones. I took him that way purposely, thinking that when he got on the sharp metal he would consent to put his boots and clothes on, which I had brought with me, by the way; but he still declined to do so, and contented himself with some heavy swearing. Eventually, having covered him as well as I was able by means of a large handkerchief, I got him to the police station, where I found that by drawing him along the street I had been the means of causing his back to be scarred rather severely. I began to think that I might get into trouble through this; but was afraid, on the other hand, that if I let him go he might turn upon his wife again, and that I should probably be held officially responsible for any serious mischief that might befall her.

When I got to the station I put my prisoner in a cell, and again asked him to dress himself, but again he refused. On going to his apartment about ten minutes afterwards, I found that he had wrapped himself in one of the rugs which are usually allowed to the inmates of these abodes. I entered the cell and took the rugs from him, at the same time placing his clothing beside him, and when I next returned

I found that he was dressed. The following day when the man was brought before Mr. Trafford, addressing the magistrate he asked—

"Can a policeman pull a fellow out of bed?"

"Yes," said the stipendiary, "if he has done anything wrong before he got into it."

"Can he draw him on the floor?"

"Aye, if he won't walk."

"Can he take him two miles without clothes?"

"Aye, if he won't put them on."

The fellow got a fortnight's imprisonment, and it so happened that, about six months afterwards, I met him in Oldham Street, Manchester, when he shook hands with me, and said I had made a man of him, and told me he had never aken any drink since I had locked him up, adding, "I wish you had taken me a year before you did."

While at Newton Heath I was much troubled with a warehouseman, whose name need not be given, who occupied a position at a good salary, but was very much addicted to drink. He was married, and, so far as I remember, had six or seven little children, whom, along with their mother, he often turned out of doors when he returned home, sometimes as late as twelve o'clock at night, or as early as one o'clock in the morning. His wife was a very respectable woman, and did all that she possibly could to screen the faults of her husband. I threatened frequently to lock him up, but feeling that if I did so there would be nothing but the workhouse for his poor wife and children, refrained from putting my threat into execution. One night, however, I found him sitting on a rail drunk and asleep, and as I had a parcel of small tin tacks in my pocket, some of which I had been using that day to fasten the furniture print in my house, I thought I might as well play upon him a practical joke.

Accordingly, I got behind him with the view of nailing him fast to the rail. But I soon reflected that if I knocked in the tacks with a stone I should be sure to awaken him. I therefore took my staff out of my pocket, and by its means pushed about a dozen of the tacks into his clothing, and so fastened him to the fence. I then went on to visit my men, and returned in about an hour and found the man gone, but the rail had been thrown out of its place, and was lying across the footpath; and I also found a piece of cloth about the breadth of my hand sticking to the wood. I did not mention the matter to anyone; but next evening I met my liquor-loving friend, who was again in a state of inebriety. He began to abuse me in his usual style; so I told him that if he would only call at the police station he would find a piece of cloth very much of the same pattern as his trousers, which I had come across the night before fastened to a rail. This, as might have been expected, had the effect of quieting him for a time.

The practical joke had, therefore, served a good purpose, for it had checked the man in his evil courses, without causing him to undergo the degradation which his apprehension and appearance in a police court would have entailed upon a person in his position in life.

CHAPTER IV.

TROUBLES WITH THE COLLIERS.

IN 1881 a great colliers' strike occurred in Lancashire, and I well remember the day when I was attending the police court the idea occurred to me that some deviltry was in progress at the pits in Walkden. I engaged a cab and ordered out six men, who, by my instructions, brought with them a bag containing half a dozen cutlasses. We drove to Ordsal Lane Station, and there took the train for Walkden. On arriving at that great coal-winning centre I saw that some thousands of people had assembled near the Ellesmere Pit. They were all strangers to me, and most of them had come from other mines out of the district with a view of forcing the men employed at the colliery in question to join them in the strike.

First of all, I mixed amongst the colliers who were loitering outside the mob, the man who had the bag containing the cutlasses following close behind. Having a desire, if possible, to frighten the men in the crowd, I looked meaningly at the policeman and asked—

"Have you brought the caps?"

By this I meant percussion caps, as I had a desire that those who were in the crowd should believe we carried fire-arms. The constable did not seem at first to understand what I was hinting at, but afterwards the notion appeared slowly to dawn upon him, and he answered—

"Yes, sir."

"Come along, then," I said, in a loud voice, so that the stragglers might hear me, and then forced my way amongst the mob on the pit-brow, followed by the officers by whom I was accompanied. The man who had carried the cutlasses put them down at my feet and one of the crowd shouted—

"The —— has got some cold steel."

"Yes," I replied, "and I am going to warm it if you fellows do not get out of the way."

A cry was then raised of "Send him down the pit." Then they made a rush, and I was jostled right and left until I was carried to within about five yards of the pit-mouth, when I said loudly and distinctly—

"Now, men, remember, if I have to go down the pit, I am not going alone, but I shall take two or three with me."

This did not prevent them from again surging forward, thus bringing me still nearer the eye of the mine, while there were continued cries of—

"Shove him down! shove him down!" uttered in a hundred voices of fierce determination that was sufficient to appal the stoutest heart, and I believe to this day that I should have been thrown down that shaft had not a happy thought struck me. Acting under its inspiration, I called out to my men—

"Every one of you turn to the crowd, and see how many you can swear to to-morrow for murder."

The effect was electrical. All the men in the mob seemed to turn their faces any way in preference to looking at a policeman, and they soon began to move away in different directions. I consider that on the occasion referred to I had the narrowest escape from death that I ever had in the whole course of my life.

Long before this time, in 1867, there was a turn-out of colliers in my district similar to the one I have just alluded to, but on a much smaller scale. In those days I was a very great terror to the pitmen in the district who belonged to the class of evil-doers. They would at any time clear off the footpath, or do almost anything I asked them, in the daytime, though I must admit that after nightfall I was sometimes saluted with a shower of stones. At that time I had a horse found me, but as I was a very indifferent equestrian, I used only to proceed at a walk rather than run the risk of being thrown. Sometimes I dismounted and ran after offenders with what they called my switch, which was in reality a thick logwood stick which I always had about me. One morning, about two o'clock, I was making my way on horseback a little beyond the Seven Stars in Clifton. The night was very dark indeed, and my steed having made a shy, I pulled up to see what was the matter. Three men were crouching down under the hedge, and I heard one say to his fellows—

"Knock him off the horse with a brick."

Knowing that it was useless to do more than walk with the horse, I went close up and accosted them with—

"What are you three cowardly ruffians doing there? I shall get off my horse and bump your heads together;" and suiting the action to the word I took one foot out of the stirrup, but the cowards all ran away across a field, leaving, however, three bricks on the footpath to show that they had been ready for violence. Just at the moment a man named Jacob Barker, an owner of some carts and horses at Pendlebury, came along the road, shouting—

"Mr. Bent, where are you?"

"What is to do?" I asked.

"Eh, Mr. Bent," he responded, "I have just had such a dream. I dreamt that you were going by the Seven Stars, that three men went after you, and that one catched you on the head with a brick and killed you. Eh, master, let me walk with you all neet, because I cannot go to bed again. Please, Mr. Bent, do not go by yourself any more."

I could not persuade him to go home, and he persisted in walking with me till five o'clock in the morning. Whether he had really had such a dream or not of course I could not say. He is still living, and admitted a few days ago that it was not a dream, but that he had heard the men make it up to kill me.

In a week or two afterwards, at midnight, I was going up the road leading from the Seven Stars to the Clifton Hall pits, when a man ran out and met me, and, not knowing me, cried—

"Where are you going? Are you lost?"

"I think," I answered, "that I know my way," and on I went. When I got some distance along to a place where there was a good deal of mire, two or three men came out of the hedge. I pulled my horse up, and, turning quickly round, said—

"You ruffians, are you there again?"

Just at this moment the stirrup leather broke, and I slid under the horse, and no doubt the men believed that I was getting off to tackle them, for off they ran as fast as they could go. I found upon examination that there was a heap of stones piled up where they had been lying, which were no doubt intended for me, but I again escaped.

As a great number of Staffordshire men were working in the place of the Pendlebury colliers who were on strike, fights of more or less severity occurred between them almost every night, and I had very often to run and quell disturbances. On one occasion a very big young fellow, who had created many a row, had a man down on the ground, and was kicking him severely. I got my "switch," thinking of giving him a rather severe blow on the buttocks, but instead of doing that I caught him on the arm with such force that I was afraid I had broken the limb. The people cleared away, and the man having gone into a house in Knowles Square, I hovered about the dwelling for several hours to see if any doctor was sent for. About two in the morning I observed another man go into the same house, and I approached as near as possible to the dwelling to hear if anything was said. Immediately the man whose arm I had struck said to the person who had entered—

"Eh, Job, I have catched it to-neet. I were boxing one of them fellows, when Bent came up with his little switch and gave me a crack on th' arm which I shall never forget."

I was quite satisfied that the arm was not broken. I went away with a much lighter heart than I should otherwise have done.

Soon after my appointment to the rank of inspector I was directed to take a detachment of fifty men to the Rochdale Parliamentary election, at which the sitting member, Mr. T. B. Potter, was first returned. Superintendent Pickering was in charge of the county police who were employed to keep order during the election in the borough. I arrived in the town about eight o'clock on the morning of the nomination, and was kept patrolling the streets with my men until midnight, without relief; and at that time I asked a publican to allow my men to lie down on some straw in his stable. He consented, and I went to seek Mr. Superintendent Pickering. Having found that officer, I was engaged in conversation with him, when I saw two or three hundred men coming up the street armed with sticks and other weapons, marching in military order. I pointed this out to the superintendent, and asked him if I might call out my men. He replied, " No, there is no need of that : so well am I respected by the Rochdale people that I can by the move of my little finger do anything here I like. Come on with me." I acquiesced, and went on. We had not gone far, when I found out that the mob disregarded everything Mr. Pickering said to them. Seeing that the mob intended to sack a public-house, I ran in front and put my back against the door and tried to persuade them to disperse and go home, telling them that I believed many of them were married men with families, and very likely they might find themselves next morning in the police cell, with the prospect of six or twelve months' imprisonment before them if they committed any damage. Just at this time a little fellow, not much more than 5ft. high, struck me a most violent blow on my left jaw with a short thick cudgel, which he had been holding up his sleeve, knocking most of my teeth loose and causing me intense pain. Had I been in command, I certainly should have knocked him down on the instant, but, as it was, I contented myself with rubbing the injured part, and telling my assailant that I had done nothing to deserve such treatment, and that he had hurt me very much, but at the same time wishing I had an opportunity of serving him as he had served me. At that very moment Mr. Pickering was being struck at from behind, and I called out to him to get his back against the wall. He did so, but just at that moment someone made a blow at his head with a large poker, scarring his forehead; and at the same moment the little man, who had struck me on the left jaw, came up and paid me a similar compliment on the right jaw with the same weapon. I could stand this no longer, but with my fist I struck him under the jaw and knocked him down, and then used both fists and feet to any of the roughs who stood in the way. I soon made way for Mr. Pickering, and then, seizing a cudgel out of one of the men's hands, knocked everyone down within reach. Having got Mr. Pickering in a safe place I left two old women bathing his head. I then went to the stable where my men were, and as quickly as possible drew them across the street just when the mob were rallying from the effects of my cudgel, and I am sure I need not say how soon we had the street to ourselves.

In about an hour after the above occurrence, Captain Silvester, the chief constable of Rochdale, came to me and asked if I had not had a "brush" with the mob. I said I had, and that if he would go away for a short time I would so quieten the roughs that the police would be able to get some rest. I was still feeling the effects of the blows I had received a short time before. "Well," said the chief constable, "don't get into any trouble." I promised him I would not, and he left me. He had no sooner gone than I again drew the men across the street, and gave the word "double," and every man, with staff in hand, ran as quick as possible down the street after the mob, who yelled like madmen, and dispersed on the sight of the police. The result was that those of my men who could sleep did so when they again got into the straw, but my teeth prevented me having that luxury. Mr. John Henderson, then sergeant, now superintendent, in his eagerness to keep up with the rest in the darkness, ran against a lamp-post, and fell backwards, his head coming in contact with the flags with such force that he was laid up for several weeks.

THE COLLIERS' STRIKE.

SALFORD HUNDRED QUARTER SESSIONS.

THE Intermediate Sessions of the Peace for the hundred of Salford were opened yesterday, at the Assize Courts, Strangeways, in this city, before Mr. W. H. Higgin, Q.C., chairman, and other magistrates. The Chairman in charging the Grand Jury said, before he dismissed the Grand Jury to their duties there were two matters he desired to bring before them. In looking over the calendar he was very much gratified indeed to find that there was not a single collier sent for trial for creating disturbance or for rioting, and he thought, considering the deep misery, he was going to say almost starvation, through which the men had passed—whether it had been their own fault or the fault of others it was not for him to inquire or express any opinion—their behaviour was very creditable. That they had suffered great privation there could be no doubt whatever, and they knew that colliers were not amongst the most refined of men; they also knew that when thousands of rough men like colliers got together, generally speaking, there was a disturbance, and somebody was sent to prison, but whilst he said he was glad no colliers had been sent to the sessions for trial, he must also say that the greatest commendation was due to Mr. Superintendent Bent, who had been at the head of a large body of constables engaged in watching the colliers and putting down disturbances. When he mentioned that officer's name he desired also to refer to the officers under him, as well as the constables. He thought one and all had behaved during this crisis with unexampled good temper, judgment, and discretion, and he had not the least doubt that if that good temper, judgment, and discretion had not been exercised in a remarkable manner the fact to which he had drawn their attention of the absence of colliers from the calendar would not have existed. He therefore thought the thanks of the hundred of Salford were eminently due to the police force Mr. Bent had under his control for keeping those rough persons quiet. He need not, of course, tell them that he had been consulted, amongst other magistrates, with reference to what ought to be done or not to be done. What had been done had been done, no doubt, on the recommendation of himself and other magistrates that the police ought to commend themselves as the protectors and defenders of those men who were willing, nay anxious, to go to work and to earn an honest livelihood for the maintenance of their wives and families, the police ought to be their protectors from the violence of those who desired to interfere with their work, and he had very good reason to suppose that there were a great number of men who had been compelled to join the strike, not of their own free will, but under compulsion, who did look upon the police, not as their enemies, but as their protectors.—*Manchester Courier*, 1st March, 1881.

CHAPTER V.

LARCENY INCIDENTS.

ON one occasion a gentleman residing at Old Trafford came to my office and made a statement to the effect that a lady had been staying at his house for a few days, and a gold watch and chain belonging to her had been stolen. I at once sent one of the sergeants to inquire into the case and report the result to me, which he did in course of the day. Not being satisfied with his report, I went to the house and put several questions to the servant. Her replies being of a conflicting character, I told her I should take her into custody on the charge of stealing the watch and guard. She at once began to scream, and her sister, who had just entered the house, came into the room, and threatened an action against both the master of the house and myself for making such a serious charge against her sister. Feeling anxious that the lady should, if possible, recover her property, I thought I would try another way. I therefore asked the sister to come with me into one of the rooms below. She did so, and I then told her that I did not care much about the master of the house or the lady who had lost her watch, at the same time I should be compelled to take her sister into custody unless the watch and chain were forthcoming, and I made a suggestion that her sister should, after I left the house, put the watch and chain into the firegrate, behind a fire screen in the room where I was standing, and that I would come into the room the following morning and find the watch and chain, and then I would give the master of the house a good blow-up, and tell him either he or the lady had placed the articles in the firegrate, just to make a thief of her sister. All this time the girl was unaware that the master was in the yard looking at us through the window. I further told her that if the watch and chain were turned up as I had suggested I might possibly give them a treat to some place of amusement, which seemed to please her very much. I then asked her to call her sister, the servant, out of the nursery, and tell her what to do.

"Oh, well," said the girl, "I will tell you the truth. My sister has the watch. I will call her."

She did so, and the girl came into the room. Her sister told her all that had passed between us, and she seemed highly delighted, and promised me that I should find the watch and chain, and hoped we should enjoy ourselves the following day. I bade them good night, and went home and told Mrs. Bent I was engaged for the following day. However, I paid somewhat dearly for my little joke, as, having leaned my chair against the wall, the feet slipped and I fell, my head coming in contact with the flags with such force that it ached for several days. The next morning at eight o'clock, according to promise, I again went to the house. The servant, her face radiant with smiles, and giving me a knowing wink, let me in. I called for the master, and pretending to be angry, asked him if he had thoroughly searched the house, had he looked in the firegrate. He replied he had. While I was talking to the master the two girls were pulling faces and winking at me behind his back. I took the screen out of the firegrate, and there found both watch and chain, and handed them to the master, and left the room.

Of course I need not say that having made promises to the girls I could not produce what they had said in evidence against them, and even if I could, the owner of the watch was not willing to prosecute, and therefore the matter dropped.

About two o'clock one winter's morning, when on duty at Newton Heath, I heard the footsteps of someone who was apparently wearing clogs shod with irons. I could hear the sound for a considerable distance, and making my way towards the spot from whence it proceeded, met one of my officers, and asked him if he had seen anyone passing who was wearing clogs.

"Oh, aye," said he, "it is the baker living at so and so."

"Had he anything with him?" I asked.

"Yes," replied the constable, "he had a bag on his shoulder."

"Do you know," I next inquired, "what its contents were?"

"No," was his answer.

I sent the constable up the back streets to look for the man, and took another direction myself. Shortly afterwards

I met a second officer, from whom I ascertained that he had seen a man with a bag on his back, but he had not taken any particular notice of him. While we were talking, the baker made his appearance, having come out of a short street towards me, apparently on his way to his work.

"Where," I said to him, "is that bag you had on your shoulder just now?"

"Eh, I have left it at home."

"Very well," I returned, "we will go to your home and see what it contains."

"I do not live about here now," was his evasive reply.

"Then," I returned, "we will go to the house I saw you come out of."

I had not seen him come out of any house, but I supposed he had seen me when he made his exit. He then turned and walked in front of me, and went into a cottage a short distance from where I had met him. As soon as he had opened the door he rushed to the fireplace, seized the poker, and was about to strike me with it, when I picked up a chair and knocked him down. I took the weapon from him, went upstairs, and found a half-load sack containing about 20lb. of mould candles, sugar, and other articles, which he had stolen from his master's shop. He was convicted of the offence. His master had for a long time previously missed a very large quantity of groceries and other articles, which, there is no doubt, had been taken by his servant and disposed of.

On another occasion, when employed as a detective officer at Old Trafford raceground, I saw a man going into the scullery at the Trafford Arms Hotel. I followed, but he turned back and met me. I went into the scullery and pretended to wash my hands, when the fellow came in again and took a half leg of mutton, which he put in his coat pocket. At this time the cook came and looked in the scullery, saw me, and went away. When she had gone, the man said to me—

"Mate, have you a knife?"

"What for?" I said.

"There is a piece of beef there," he replied. "I will cut it in two and divide it."

Looking round, I saw there was a piece of beef at the place he indicated, weighing over 20lb. At the same time I noticed that he had several pies in his pocket.

"I will just go and inquire for a knife," I said, intending to see the landlady and ascertain who he was, but just at that moment he bolted. I followed and caught him after a smart chase, and then we had a tremendous struggle. No one seemed to know either him or me. However, after a severe tussle, some policemen came running up and secured my generous and pugnacious friend, and next day he was sentenced to two months' imprisonment. He told me on the road to the court that he thought I was an old cabby, or else he would not have gone back into the place a second time. I have no doubt my dress deceived him.

One Sunday, having been on "plain clothes duty" all day, I was returning home very late and very tired, and just as I was passing Barton Church, where it was very dark indeed, I saw a tall man in the hedge. I went past him, and when I got a few yards away, I could hear a rustling as of paper. The idea occurred to me that the man might have stolen the communion plate from the church, and was engaged in packing it up in paper. I got quietly through the hedge, rushed in the direction where he was standing, and catching him from behind, ran him into a public-house, which has since been pulled down, but was then kept by a Mr. Oldfield. Seeing that he had a large brown paper parcel nicely tied up under his arm, I felt certain that he had succeeded, as I said before, in getting hold of the church silver. When I got him into the public-house I asked him what he had in the parcel.

"You may look," he responded.

The coachman from Trafford Hall, who happened to be in the same room, observed that I had got a good catch that time. I at once got a knife, cut the string that bound the parcel, and found to my intense astonishment that it contained four large, heavy bricks. I was dumbfounded for some time as to what he could want with them.

"What on earth," I inquired, "did you want these for? Were you going to tie them round your neck and drown yourself?"

"Well, no," he answered. "I only thought I would take them home."

Feeling some grave doubts as to what the fellow's intention really was, I went to his house, where I found in one of the rooms about five hundred bricks of a similar kind. In addition to that I also discovered a number of gateposts which had been missed from the neighbourhood. I asked him what he meant by having all these building materials in his house?

"Well," he responded, "I thought I might some day build a little cot of my own, and then keep pigs."

The brick-stealer was taken to Eccles Police Station and locked up; but as I had to take the bricks to the court next day, I asked him to carry them.

"You will have to carry them yourself," he said.

And so I had the pleasure of carrying the four bricks to the New Bailey, where the stipendiary sentenced the prisoner to fourteen days' imprisonment.

The owner of the wall from which the bricks had been taken had supplied fresh bricks more than a dozen times during the six months prior to my catching the thief; and there was no doubt that nearly all that were found in his house had been taken at different times from the wall. It was allowed to stand erect for years afterwards, however, without any more being taken away.

Once, on returning home from the Salford Sessions, in company with two other constables, when within about three-quarters of a mile of Eccles a man passed us, apparently very respectably dressed. It was rather dark, but I could see that he was carrying something on his head.

"By jingo," I remarked to the others, "I believe that fellow has got some stolen property."

"Oh, no, he has not," they both joined in saying; "the man is all right;" and ridiculed my suspicions.

I determined, however, to see whether he had or not, so I turned back and ran after him as fast as I could. The moment he heard me he threw away his load and started to run at his utmost speed. I continued the chase for some distance, till he suddenly stopped, and putting one arm round a lamp-post, aimed a tremendous blow at my head with the other; but I at once clenched my fist, and in place of receiving his stroke he received a blow from me which felled him to the ground. I took him back to see what he had thrown down, and found that it was nearly three-quarters of a hundredweight of lead. On searching his pockets I found part of an onion and a knife.

I made inquiries up and down, but could hear nothing of any lead being missing; but as it appeared to be very old lead, it occurred to me to go to Eccles Church and examine the roof. I went there, and in the course of inquiries the sexton told me he had made an examination, but that there was not a bit of lead missing. Not being satisfied with this statement, I got upon the roof of the church myself, and not only discovered that a large quantity of lead had been stolen, but I also picked up part of an onion, corresponding with the piece I had found in the prisoner's pocket.

After several remands it was ascertained that the prisoner had attempted to perpetrate a similar robbery at Bury a short time previously, and had been shot in the leg by the watchman. At the sessions he was sentenced to seven years' penal servitude.

Whilst stationed at Croft's Bank I received instructions from my superintendent to look after a young man, the son of a farmer, who had committed several robberies in the district. I had spent a good deal of time looking for him, but was unable to catch him till one afternoon I saw a man come up the road with his arm in a sling, going from house to house begging. I was in plain clothes at the time, and, walking up to the man, I asked him what was wrong with his arm.

"It is broken," he said, in reply to my question, "and I have nothing to live upon. I am starving, in fact," he added, "and I do not think the arm was properly set."

"I am a bit of a doctor," I remarked, "and I have a great desire to see if that is the case."

He declined to allow me to look until I told him I was a policeman, and then, with his permission, which, in the circumstances, could not well be withheld, I began to unwrap about a dozen yards of bandage, consisting of strips of sacking and cotton rags. Having taken these from him, I ordered him to put his coat on, as there was nothing the matter with his arm, and that I should have to lock him up as an impostor. After we had proceeded on the road a little he took my advice, and experienced no difficulty in putting that which he had called a broken arm through his coat, and then he accompanied me quietly.

On the same day I had in custody a notorious fowl-stealer from Flixton, on a charge of attempting to break into a poultry house, for which he was liable to a sentence of three months' imprisonment. These two men were both locked up at Stretford Police Station. I do not believe in dreams, but strange to say, the night after these apprehensions had taken place, I dreamt that I saw the farmer's son, of whom I was in search, near to the then toll-bar on Chester Road, beside Longford Bridge. The next morning I handcuffed my men, and was taking them to the New Bailey, when, near to the toll-bar, I saw the farmer's son behind a cart on the road. I left my two prisoners, ran to him, and apprehended him. The man in charge of the horse and cart then called out—

"What must I do with this lead?" alluding to some lead which my new prisoner had left in the cart.

"Oh," I said, "let me have it." It was accordingly handed over, and I found it to be about 60lb. in weight.

It had been stolen during the night. I scarcely knew what to do with the heavy piece of metal, especially as I was without handcuffs to secure the third prisoner. Addressing the old fowl-stealer, I said—

"Well, Jack, for as many crimes as you have committed, you have never stolen lead. You might help me to carry this."

"I will that," he answered. "He's a bad fellow as'll steal lead."

Thereupon I took the farmer's son's handkerchief from his neck and tied one of his hands to the impostor.

"You will do what you can for me at the other end," said the fowl-stealer, "and I will carry this lead."

"All right, Jack," I returned, and assisted him in getting the metal on his head. His wife, who was with him, remarked—

"Eh, Jack, thou art a fool! He will do nothing for thee." But Jack swore that if he were not fast he would knock her down for saying such a thing. He believed that I could get him off if I told the magistrate that he had carried the lead. We had to walk to Cornbrook before we could get a cab, and though my other two prisoners offered to help to carry the lead Jack would not allow them. He carried it himself until he was perspiring from every pore.

When we got to the court the stipendiary had taken his place, and the cases that I had were at once proceeded with. After I had given my evidence against him, Jack put his hand to his mouth and whispered—

"Now, Bent, tell Mr. Trafford what I have done," but I dared not look towards the bench.

"Well, my old friend," Mr. Trafford then said to the

prisoner, "this time you go for the term of three calendar months. Hens will be quiet about Flixton for a bit."

A few minutes after, I had occasion to go into the dock where this man was, and he whispered—

"Bent, I want thee. If ever tha gets any more lead, by George, tha will ha' to carry it thysel'. Tha's done a lot for me this time, hastna?"

On another occasion a warrant was issued against this same man, who was charged with having done a good deal of damage to a gentleman's fence, and I took him into custody. When at the court, I noticed his shirt, and said to him—

"Jack, that shirt you are wearing belongs to Mr. Derbyshire."

His wife, who was standing beside him, exclaimed, "Nay; I made that."

The stipendiary, who had been listening, remarked that if I suspected that the shirt was stolen, I must arrest him. Jack then asked that he might not be handcuffed, but Mr. Trafford declined to interfere, observing that the prisoner was in my custody, and that I must do what I considered right. I took him without handcuffs down the river side, to Cordi Bank, Davyhulme, and showed Mrs. Derbyshire the shirt, which she at once identified as one which had been made by herself. The next day Jack was sent for trial at the sessions, and was sentenced to four months' imprisonment.

At another time the same man met a farmer named Fogg, who kept some very nice turkeys at Davyhulme, and asked him if the birds were fat.

"Not yet," he replied.

"Get them fat," said Jack. "I shall fetch them some night."

Shortly afterwards the turkeys were stolen, and although I could find traces from the farmhouse to where Jack lived, I was not able to find the turkeys. No doubt they had been sent to Manchester by boat. I visited the suspected man's house, however, in company with a constable named Blythe, and whilst making a search I found a sack, half of which was wet and the other half dry. While I was examining it Jack came into the house, and asked me what I wanted there. I told him I was looking for some ducks that had been stolen from Boysnip Farm, and I added the question—

"To whom does this sack belong?"

"It is mine," he made answer.

"How comes it," I asked, "to be one half wet and the other half dry, and also to have feathers in it?"

"I had it over my shoulders," he responded, "while working in a drain, and it got wet that way."

"Well, we will go upstairs and see what you have there."

I found some feathers, but no ducks or turkeys, and my fellow-officer seemed to be a bit afraid of the matter, as this Jack had threatened an action against us for illegally searching his house. However, I stuck by the bag, and after some inquiry took it to Boysnip Farm, where I saw the tenant and two of the workmen, when the latter at once identified it as their master's property, and the same sack which had been taken away when the eight ducks were stolen a few nights before. I then went in search of Jack, and found him between ten and eleven o'clock on Barton Bridge, when I at once apprehended him. When 1 got to the police station I learned with surprise that my prisoner, accompanied by a gentleman of some standing in Flixton, had been to Mr.

Trafford, and complained that I had searched the fowl-stealer's house without authority that day, and that I must give some account of my conduct before the magistrates and the superintendent. As, however, I had captured my man, and the bag was identified as stolen property, Jack was committed for trial, and sent to gaol for nine months. He was afterwards apprehended for stealing wearing apparel, and received a sentence of fifteen months. I may add that he was considered one of the greatest thieves that ever troubled Flixton and neighbourhood.

When I was stationed at Pendleton, in the early days of my service, a coal dealer, named Whitehead, who was also an inspector of weights and measures, made a complaint that a great deal of coal was stolen from his carts during the night. I was sent to watch. It was not long before I caught a man with a very large piece of coal, and I took him to the New Bailey, whence he was sent to prison for a month.

In another coal-stealing case with which I had to do, I was led to think that there was something wrong somewhere, either with law or justice. I was sent to watch Pendleton Church, as it was believed that a man who cleaned it was in the habit of going there every morning and bringing away a basket of coal, which he called "blue chips"; and it was said that his neighbours could get a supply of black diamonds cheaper from him than they could at the coal-yards. Be that as it may, down I went at six o'clock the following morning to watch the church. It was winter at the time, but about seven o'clock the church-cleaner came out with his basket, and I saw a few shavings at the top. On examining the contents of the basket I discovered about 50lb. of coal.

"My superintendent wants you," I said, accosting him.

"Well," he said, "I will take these chips home, and come and see him."

"No," I answered, "you must come now."

"If your superintendent wants this coal," he retorted, "you must carry it."

"I won't," I replied on the impulse of the moment; but although I felt my dignity wounded at the idea of having to carry 50lb. of coal for about 500 yards, I had to do it. When I got to the police station a county magistrate was sent for, who happened to be one of the churchwardens, and to my surprise and indignation he discharged the prisoner, who had actually the audacious effrontery to come to me wanting me to carry the coals to where I had found him; but this, of course, I declined to do. Is it surprising that I thought, as this man was not sent to gaol, that there was something wrong either with the law or its administration?

I remember one old man who was a notorious fruit stealer, but was of rather weak intellect. One Sunday afternoon I saw him stealing apples, and I also saw him go into an orchard and sit down under a tree. I followed, and got behind him, when I overheard him talking to himself. Looking at one of the apples, he thus addressed it—

"You are a nice one; but, by gum, Bent would have liked to have seen me when I were pulling thee off the tree. Thou art a good one, and thou smells well, but I will not eat thee yet. Thou wilt not be long in this country in the same shape thou art in." Then turning to another, he continued, "Thou isn't as good-looking as t' other, but thou may be as good. I will bite a bit off thee."

Getting hold of him, I observed, "What do you say, Bobby?"

"What I do not mean to do now, James," he replied.

"Come out, Bobby," I went on. "I must try to get you transported this time."

"Well, James," he replied, "I have deserved it a good while."

I took him to my house, and not having any other room, I put him under the stairs, where we kept our preserves, and locked him up for an hour; but to my surprise, when I let him out I found that he had emptied two jars. I gave him clearly to understand that I should not lock him up in the same place again. Although he had an income, this man used to steal anything he could lay his hands on—not for his own use altogether, for he could not possibly have eaten or used what he stole—and I had every reason to suspect that the people with whom he lodged got the benefit of his wrong-doing. I remember stopping him one day, and asking him when he was going to give over this contemptible work of pilfering and stealing what he could get hold of.

"Well, James," he answered, "I am very sorry to tell you that there is another man who has started the same game as me, and he does not live very far off me neither. I wish you could catch him, for it gives me no chance when there are so many on the same ground."

There could be no doubt that this statement was true, for another man, who had seen better days, but who had become thoroughly depraved and reduced to poverty through drink, and had also been in the Union Workhouse, had been guilty of the very same practices.

When a constable at Davyhulme, and attending the court at Worsley, I one day saw a man whom I strongly suspected of having stolen property in his possession, and upon searching him I found a suit of clothes in his bundle. He told me they were his Sunday clothes, but I did not believe him, and after a little while I found that he had stolen them at Bolton, from people who had kindly taken him into their house and given him food.

A Mr. Brown, who then kept a public-house at Newton Heath, came to me one morning with the information that the night before his wife had been unwell, and as no one was in the taproom, she had gone there to put a mustard poultice on her side, and had unfortunately left a bag containing about £40 on what is called the hob of the fireplace. She had never thought anything more about the matter until the morning, but on going into the taproom to look for it she found that it was gone. My suspicions were fixed on some women who were in the habit of calling at the house, and who must have found it on the hob and taken it away. Thereupon I called at a small cellar, kept by one of the women who was known as "Polka Sall," and asked her to get ready, as I intended to take her into custody on a charge of stealing £40 from the Woodman Inn. She denied all knowledge of it, and declared that she had never been in the house at all on the previous night.

"That is not true," I said in return. "I saw you go in myself."

"Oh, sergeant," she observed when I got her outside, "I am not going to be taken alone. I will tell you all about it. I went into the Woodman with Mary Ann Brown and

Kate, who lives at Donty Prestwich's. I found the money on the hob, and we took it away. Donty Prestwich said that as I had found it, the money was mine, and that he would go and get two £10 notes, which formed part of it, changed, and then no one could swear to it."

I took the prisoner to the station, and then went for the woman Brown, and told her that she was charged with stealing about £40 from the Woodman the previous night. She at first denied all knowledge of it, but when confronted with "Polka Sall" she admitted having been with her when the money was taken, and added that they had been on the spree with some of the money that morning. Then I went to a beerhouse which was kept by Prestwich, who was not in. I went upstairs and found £15, which Mrs. Prestwich admitted was part of some money which had been brought there the previous night by "Polka Sall" and others. I therefore took charge of it as part of the money stolen from the Woodman Inn. I left "Polka Sall" sitting in Prestwich's house, and told her to remain sitting at her ease there as if she was not a prisoner. I then left, but watched the place carefully from the outside until Prestwich returned, which he did in about an hour afterwards, and on going inside Prestwich said—

"Sergeant, you have been here, have you, asking for me? I will let you know that I am a cursed sight honester than you are, and if you come again I will put you out."

"Polka Sall," then handed me six sovereigns, saying—

"Here, sergeant, this is all that Donty will give me. He has kept the other for himself."

I then took the man into custody, and having made

inquiry at several shops in Manchester, I found one place, a tobacconist's, where he had endeavoured to change a £10 note for gold. Afterwards I discovered that he had been more successful at a public-house hard by, and had obtained the change.

"Polka Sall" was accepted as a witness for the prosecution, and the beerhouse keeper, Prestwich, and Mary Ann Brown were convicted, the other being acquitted. I succeeded in recovering about £36 of the stolen money, and Prestwich afterwards lost his licence in consequence of this conviction.

As a detective I was sent at one time to make some inquiry respecting several bales of rags, which had been stolen from Bradley Wharf, Prestwich. I soon satisfied myself that the thief was a man who went with a barrow hawking sand, but it was some time before I could get to know where he resided. However, after a good deal of search and investigation, I found that his mother lived in a small street off Oldham Road. Having watched the house for a considerable time without meeting the man I wanted, and being quite tired of the delay, I thought I would try another method. Therefore, I obtained a white "choker," an old shabby coat, and an old hat, which no doubt caused me, as I thought myself, to look very queer indeed. I then obtained some religious tracts, and when I arrived at the house where the sand-hawker's mother resided I got into conversation with her, asked her what family she had, whether or not they were married and doing well, or if she had any younger children whom I might call upon and try to put in the right way.

After a little time she told me she had one son a scapegrace, who had given her a great deal of trouble, and that he was living with an unfortunate two or three streets further down. Having obtained this information, I exchanged tracts with the old woman, and after calling at a few more houses for appearance sake, I slipped away with the determination to visit the house she had indicated the very same night.

Having obtained the services of the policeman on the beat, I asked him to go and knock at the front door while I concealed myself in the back yard. Ere long, I heard a feminine voice answering the officer, and evidently talking loud to prevent him from hearing that someone was leaving the house at the back door. It was immediately opened stealthily, and the man I was seeking came out with a life preserver in his hand, but I at once threw him on his back, caught him by the legs, and secured him, and then walked round to the front, the other constable not being aware of what had taken place in the yard. The next day the prisoner was brought up at the New Bailey, and his mother was present in the court, but did not seem to recognise me at first. Ultimately, however, she came up to me, and shook her fist in my face, exclaiming—

"You red d———l, if ever you bring any more tracts to my house, I'll burn both them and you!"

The son was sent for trial at the sessions, where he received a sentence of six months' imprisonment; but I believe that, for a subsequent offence, he was sentenced to penal servitude.

About the year 1864, when residing at Prestwich, it was reported to me that a certain vinery belonging to Mr. C.

had been broken into during the night, and not only had the unripe grapes been thrown on the floor, but the offender had cut the vines down almost to the ground, doing a great amount of damage.

Having satisfied myself that the perpetrator of the outrage was a man named Batty, living in Rooden Lane, I told a constable to look out for and apprehend him. In a day or two he was taken into custody, and when I charged him with the offence he pleaded guilty, and said he had cut down the vines with a pair of shears that he had stolen from another place. In fact, before I had done with him he confessed to having committed about twenty such robberies, and he seemed to pride himself in explaining to me how he had accomplished them.

This man was sent to the sessions, where he received a long term of imprisonment, after which, for subsequent offences, he was sentenced to penal servitude; and, like a great many more of that class, when he came out he was constantly complaining that he was watched by the police and could not get an honest livelihood. This was not the case. He was a lazy, drunken fellow, and would not work.

Whilst I was at Newton Heath, a young man, who had been working for a small manufacturer named Johnson, was sent to get change for £14, with which his master was to pay wages, but he went away and did not return; and though we searched for him a good deal, it was for a time of no avail. One night I happened to be seated in the Detective Office at Manchester, with Mr. Superintendent Maybury, when he addressed me with—

"Bent, we have three silk-stealers here, and I am going to

turn them out, as I can get no evidence. You had better have a look at them."

I agreed to do so, and shortly after three policemen entered, each bringing a prisoner with him. On occasions of this sort it is usual to ask the persons in custody their names, and where they live, and in reply to Mr. Maybury I heard one of them say that his name was Birtles, and that he was a loom jobber. At that moment it struck me that he was the man I wanted for stealing the £14, so I went up to the superintendent and said—

"I want this man for stealing £14 from Newton Heath."

"No, it's not me," Birtles replied. "It is a cousin of mine you want for that."

"I care nothing about your cousin. I shall have you."

Mr. Maybury asked me privately if it was a fact, and I answered that it was, and walked out of the office with my prisoner. On the way to Newton Heath, Birtles observed—

"Sergeant, it is right. I am the man you are looking for."

On getting him to the police station I told him that I was afraid that he would have to be tried for stealing the silk as well as the £14, as I had seen one of the other two men who had been brought in with him speaking to the superintendent, and I believed he would "spring" the silk before twelve o'clock that night—meaning that he would tell Mr. Maybury where it was. I pressed the prisoner to tell me all he knew, and promised that he would not be tried for stealing it, a promise which was afterwards faithfully carried out.

"You don't know me," I said to him. "You need not be afraid to tell me where it is. You may at least tell me this much. If you were a policeman here, where would you go to look for that silk?"

He gave me a number in London Road; and after I had put him in a cell I went down to the detective office in Manchester and told them that I believed the silk was somewhere in London Road; but was informed that they had been to the place and could not find it. Upon this I went back to the prisoner, and got hold of him in rather a savage way, asking him what he meant by telling me such a deliberate lie, and causing me to go so far for nothing.

"Well sergeant," he said, "put the handcuffs on me, and I will take you to the house where it is." Accordingly I put the handcuffs on, and took two of my constables with me, and the prisoner conducted us to Birtles Court, Salford, the name of the square being oddly enough the same as his own. But before we got there he asked me to go with him to where his wife resided, and he could get the key of the house where the silk was concealed, and unlock the door properly. Fearing that if we went to his wife we should learn nothing, I asked him first to show me the place, and then I could talk to him about the key. When we got into Birtles Square he pointed out a house to me, and as soon as he did so I went across to the other side, and then ran full force against the door and burst it open. On reaching the interior the whole of the missing silk was disclosed to my view. It appeared to me that the thieves had wound it on a reel from the bobbins and then made it into skeins. It was not the work of many minutes to get the silk, except that on the reel, into bags and baskets, obtain a cab, and take the whole to Newton Heath, and I handed it over to Mr. Maybury in a few days afterwards.

The next day, as I was going to the New Bailey Court, the other two men whom I had seen brought into the Manchester detective office came to me and asked if I had got anything out of Birtles about the silk.

"Oh," I said, "I care nothing about that. It is a Manchester case, and I care only about my own. I am not going to ask him anything about it"—which was then true enough.

"See his wife, and she will tell you all about it," one of them remarked.

"No, I shall not."

Of course I knew well enough that as soon as I had turned my back these two men would make their way as speedily as possible to the house in Birtles Square, where they expected to find the silk. I saw two Manchester detectives who had the case in hand before me, and gave them the key, telling them to get to the place as quickly as possible, for as sure as fate the two men would go there for the proceeds of their robbery. The officers acted promptly upon this advice, got into the house, and locked the door; and about ten minutes afterwards the two men entered and went upstairs for the plunder, when they were immediately apprehended. They were tried at the sessions, and convicted, and it was found that the value of the silk, which had been stolen from a carrier's cart, amounted to several hundred pounds. Birtles, who had run away with the £14, was tried for that case alone, and received a sentence of four months' imprisonment.

About the year 1864 there were a great number of watches stolen from the different cricket fields about Manchester, chiefly from the Old Trafford and Rusholme grounds—in fact, to the value of more than £100. On making inquiry, I found that the robberies were committed in this way: A man dressed as a cricketer would go to the ground along with the cricketers, who were invariably so numerous that they did not know every member. Just before they commenced playing this man would return to the tent, feigning sickness to the keeper of the tent, and say that he had been taken so bad that he should have to dress and go home. Unsuspectingly, the keeper would allow the man to go into the tent, where he took the opportunity of stealing not only watches but all the money he could find in the pockets of the players.

This had been going on for some time, when one morning, at the New Bailey Police Court, I saw a man brought up on the charge of stealing a watch and about 15s. from some man who was in a state of intoxication at the time. Having made a good deal of inquiry about the stealing of the watches from the cricket grounds, I at once suspected this man to be the thief, and intimated to my predecessor (Mr. Superintendent Chadwick) that it was my intention to interrogate the prisoner. Shortly afterwards, Inspector Striem, of the Manchester police force, came into the court, and said to me—

"Oh, Bent, you have a fellow here for stealing a watch."

"Yes I have, and I am going to interview him shortly."

"I wish you would let me see him for a short time in a private room."

"Mr. Striem, this is not fair," I said. "This is one of our prisoners, the watches that I suspect he has stolen have been taken in our district, and consequently I think it is hardly right."

"I only want to get a watch for a friend."

"Well, if it is for a friend I will bring him out of the dock into the consulting room, where I can talk to him," and I at once did so. But when I got into the consulting room, Striem pushed me with his umbrella, as good as for me to leave the room. I felt rather annoyed at this. However, I left the room, went to the dock, and waited until Striem came to me with the prisoner.

"Well, Striem, how have you gone on?" I asked.

"He won't tell me a word," he replied.

Now, I did not believe this statement of Striem, and as good as told him so. However, as soon as he had left the court, which he did immediately afterwards, I took my book out of my pocket, went to the prisoner, and said to him—

"Here, take this book. Striem has forgot the name and number of the pawnshop where that watch is."

The man, without hesitation, put down the name and number of the shop, and when the watch was pledged, and the description of it.

As soon as I got that information I directed Sergeant Duncan to go at once to the pawnshop as quickly as possible; and although he took a very fast cab, he only got to the shop just as Striem entered it. A struggle then took place between Sergeant Duncan and Striem as to which should have the watch, but ultimately the pawnbroker decided to give it to neither without more information. In the meantime, I had obtained full particulars from the prisoner, and having supplied Sergeant Duncan with these he went back to the pawnbroker's and obtained the watch.

Now, knowing that there were two clear cases against this man for watch stealing, I knew very well no other cases would be taken against him; but still I thought I would do my best to find out where the other watches were. I therefore went into the dock and said to the prisoner—

"I have every reason to believe that you have pledged every one of these watches," showing him a list of watches stolen.

"I know nothing at all about them," he replied.

"Well," I said, "I do not say you have stolen them; possibly somebody else has made a cats-paw of you. But I may as well tell you the truth—it is known that you have pledged them."

The man hesitated, and I said, "Look here. I know perfectly well that you have pledged these watches. Nevertheless, I have a great desire to restore to the owners their property, and if you will do what you can to assist me I will do what I possibly can to assist you. I promise you one thing—viz., that you shall not be tried for stealing the watches not recovered if you will give me the information I am asking for."

"Shall I be tried for them?" the prisoner asked.

"No," I said, "if you will tell me where they are; but if you do not, and I find them, it is just possible that at the expiration of your imprisonment for the stealing of the two present watches I shall look out for you. Take this book, and put down where you have pledged them."

He, without hesitation, took the book from me and filled in, I should think, two or three columns in my pocket-book,

LARCENY INCIDENTS.

giving me particulars of every watch except one that had been stolen from the cricket grounds, and one gold watch about which I had no information.

I went that afternoon and reported to the superintendent what I had done. He was so elated with my good luck that, for the first time, he asked me to have a glass of beer with him, and he then went with me to many of the pawnbrokers' from whom I received the watches.

On the following Saturday morning, the day to which the prisoner had been remanded, I went down to the police court and into the dock where the prisoner sat awaiting the commencement of business. Knowing other prisoners in the dock I spoke to them in a friendly way, but as to the above prisoner I took no notice of him for some time. He then pulled me by the coat and said—

"Mr. Bent, what is to do with you this morning?"

"Nothing," I replied.

"I am afraid I have told you more than I should have done."

"By no means. You have told me less," I answered.

"Oh, Mr. Bent, you said you would do the best you could for me if I would do my best for you."

"So I will," I replied; "but do you think I am foolish enough to tell the magistrates you have made a clean breast of everything. There is still one gold watch missing, and I know very well you know where it is."

The prisoner said, "It is not in England."

"Well," I said, "I am afraid you won't be in England long; but, however, look here, if you will tell me where that gold watch is I will be as good as my word, and tell the magistrates what you have done, and if the watch is with your father, mother, or friend, I promise you that you shall not be tried for it."

"Oh," said the man. "Sit down, and I will tell you all about it. You have a gold watch and chain for which you have no owner, at the end of which is an appendage. I exchanged the gold watch and chain you are looking after for that watch and chain, and I gave £2 for that appendage. The watch you are looking after is a very old one and a good one, too. I exchanged with Mr. R., of —— Street."

I said, "All right," went out of the court, met Mr. Chadwick near Albert Bridge, and told him I thought I should get the last watch, but that it would be necessary for me to be very careful indeed, as the person who had the watch knew me, and I was afraid he would not turn it up without a deal of trouble.

I went to the shop, with my handkerchief covering two-thirds of my face, pretending to have the tic.

"Good morning," said the shopkeeper. "What can I do for you?"

"You have a gold watch here that you exchanged with a young man, a friend of mine, for this," I replied, showing the jeweller the watch which the prisoner said he had exchanged, "and I should like to have that watch if it is not too dear." I was still holding the handkerchief over my face and pretending to be in pain.

"Oh," said the jeweller, "I remember the transaction perfectly well. I have the watch in stock, and it is really a downright good one."

"Are you quite sure you have it? Will you kindly look in the stock and let me see what it is like?"

He went to a case, brought out a watch, and said, "This is it," but held it in his hand.

I felt a bit ashamed to remove the handkerchief from my face all at once, but did so partially, when the jeweller at once recognised me and said—

"Bent, is that you?"

"Yes," I replied. "That watch has been stolen, and I want to take it to the court at once, as the magistrates are waiting."

"But I will not let you take it. Give me the name of the maker and the number of the watch."

I said to him, "Oh, yes, I will soon do that," and, putting my hand in my pocket, I took out some bills relating to stolen watches, but at once put them back, saying—

"Oh, you told me that was the watch, and that you knew it to be the watch, and now you refuse to turn it up. Now," I said, "I will give you one more chance—that is, if you will not give me the watch, will you carry it down to the court? If not, there will be a bother."

"Yes," he replied, "I will do that," and we started off for the police court together. When we got to Albert Bridge the jeweller said—

"Mr. Bent, I want to speak to you. This watch is a very good one indeed, and is one of the very best I ever saw. We sent it to Liverpool, and had it done up a bit, and put our name on it, and little alterations, &c."

"That is quite right," I replied.

As soon as I got into the court the prisoner was put up, and I went into the witness box, and began to take a number of watches out of my pocket and place them in front of me, when Mr. Trafford at once said, "That will do. We only want the two watches," meaning the two above-mentioned.

The jeweller stood close to the witness-box, with the gold watch in his possession.

"There is another watch which this man holds, and which I want producing," I remarked to Mr. Trafford.

"Very well. Produce that watch," said Mr. Trafford to the jeweller.

The man did so, and as soon as he laid it on the witness box I got hold of it.

The jeweller called out, "Stop, stop! You requested me to carry the watch here."

"But I did not say you must take it back," I answered.

Just at that moment another member of the firm came into the court, and I heard him asking for me. I turned and exclaimed, "I am here."

He replied, "I shall have that watch or the value of it."

"I am sure you will not," I retorted, whereupon he said—

"Mine was an honest transaction."

I turned round and whispered in his ear, "Is it honest of you or any other person to christen watches?" (meaning to put their names in a watch as makers, when they were not.) These words took him aback, and he went as quiet as anybody else in the court, and at the finish privately asked me to do the best I could for him, which I did, and he received back the watch which he had given in exchange for the stolen one.

The man was only tried for stealing the two watches, and he got off with about eighteen months' imprisonment. The other watches were restored to their owners.

Some years ago I was on detective duty at Manchester Races, in company with Sergeant Barlow. I saw two "swells," who I thought were looking out for watches. We lay down on the ground near the rails which surround the racecourse, and while there saw a gentleman come up to the rails. He was wearing a heavy gold guard, which no doubt attracted the attention of the two "swells," who immediately took up a position, one on each side of him. The one on his right-hand side pretended to be looking down the course, and gave the gentleman a push in the ribs, which he did not appear to like, and expostulated with his assailant. While this was going on the "swell" on the left wrenched the gentleman's gold watch from the chain. I immediately seized the thief by the hand, and held it to prevent him from dropping the watch. I called out, "You have been robbed." This caused a commotion amongst the crowd, and the thief and I were roughly handled. My hands were fully employed in holding the hand of the thief to prevent him from dropping the watch. I called for my companion, who had seized the other "swell," but found that he was faring no better than myself, and therefore could not assist me. A cry was raised, "Throw them into the river." It occurred to me that as the thief was well dressed, and I was not, the crowd were taking me for the thief and the thief for the policeman, so I shouted, "If you will make a ring I will show you who has the watch." A ring was formed, and I opened the man's hand, out of which the stolen watch fell. There was then no difficulty in securing the thieves, for the crowd gave assistance to both Barlow and myself.

Next day they were brought before Mr. Trafford, the

stipendiary magistrate. A man in the court called out to one of the prisoners—

"Joe, I have got you a mouthpiece" (solicitor).

The solicitor made what the people thought a powerful case for the defence, when Mr. Trafford remarked—

"Bent, were you at the races yesterday?"

"Yes, sir."

"Did you see a hand there?"

"Yes."

"Did you see that hand do something?"

"Yes," I replied.

"Did you get hold of that hand?"

"Yes."

"What was in the hand?"

"That watch."

"Did you take the watch out of that hand?"

"Yes."

"What did you do with that hand?"

"Locked it up," I replied.

"Who did that hand belong to?"

"To that man," pointing to one of the prisoners.

Mr. Trafford, turning to the solicitor, remarked, "Have you any further questions to ask Bent?" and receiving a negative reply committed both prisoners for trial. It was found they had only come out of prison a few days before, and for this offence they were each sentenced to seven years' penal servitude.

A few years ago I was in Belle Vue Gardens, when I saw an old man making a complaint to Mr. C. Jennison, the senior proprietor of that popular pleasure resort. I went to them, when Mr. Jennison explained to me that the old gentleman had had his watch stolen out of his pocket. Mr. Jennison and I had a few words together, and it was arranged that he (Mr. Jennison) should go to the entrance of the monkey-house, and I would go in and see if any of the light-fingered gentry were about. I had not been there long before I saw a young man try two or three gentlemen's pockets. His eye caught mine, and although I did not know him, he bolted, and I ran after him. I caught him, and at once ran my hand from his pockets down to his ankles, and found the old man's watch pinned in the tail of his shirt, which was torn so that the watch would hang near his ankles. As soon as I found the watch, the thief called out, "This is a clear cop, Mr. Bent." We then went and reported progress to the old man, who was delighted that his old timekeeper had turned up again. The prisoner was sentenced to six months' imprisonment.

While stationed at Newton Heath as sergeant I one day left the station in a great hurry to catch the post. On my way I saw one of my men pass a man who was carrying a very large bundle. Suspecting him, I directed the constable to take the man to the station and keep him there for a few minutes. When I returned, the constable told me the man was all right. He was hawking dress-pieces. Not feeling satisfied, I asked the man for his licence, when he replied that he had not got one.

"Let me see your measure, then."

"I have none," he replied.

"Well, now," I interrogated, "how much per yard do you want for this cloth?"

Suiting the action to the word, I picked up one piece after

another, pinned the price he gave me in every case to each piece, and sent them to a draper in the district for his opinion as to the prices of the different materials. The draper's prices soon convinced me that the whole of the property had been dishonestly come by. I therefore locked the man up on suspicion of stealing the cloth, and the following morning I read in the *Police Gazette*, "Stolen from Guide Bridge Railway Station, a large bundle of dress-pieces to the value of £15." Now, I thought the constable deserved but little credit for what he had done in the matter, but, nevertheless, I told him he might take the case to the court himself. He did so, and told the bench that he was on duty in Oldham Road, Newton, at about three o'clock the previous day, when he saw the prisoner, and, suspecting him, took him into custody; that he had had the cloth valued; also that he had now got an owner at Guide Bridge. So well did he tell his own story that the stipendiary magistrate hinted that the constable had done very well, and deserved a little promotion. The superintendent took the constable into the clerk's office, where an officer who knew all about the case happened to be, and who clearly explained to the superintendent the real facts of the case.

After this, the superintendent explained to the magistrate that the credit, if any, was due to me, and not to the constable who stated the case. The prisoner was taken to Guide Bridge, and committed for trial at the sessions, where he received a long term of imprisonment for this offence.

CHAPTER VI.

CAPTURE OF ESCAPED PRISONERS.

ABOUT the time last mentioned in the preceding chapter a young man, who was a professional gambler, had been apprehended for housebreaking, and was placed in the cells at Leigh, out of which he managed to escape in a rather mysterious manner. Inquiries were made in the country round about regarding the runaway, but without effect. The case reverted to me, and I was requested to find the escaped gamester if possible. I went that night to the house of the young man's father, and there found a photograph, which I supposed to be that of the person I wanted, and my suspicion proved afterwards to be correct.

After thinking over the matter I resolved to proceed to Warrington, and then, if necessary, go on to Liverpool. At the former place I ascertained that a young man answering the description I had with me had been seen in the town on the previous Sunday, and had then gone on, it was believed, to Liverpool. I thereupon proceeded to the city on the Mersey, and sought the assistance of the Liverpool police, when one of their number was directed to give me what help he could. Before we commenced business he expressed a desire to go and have a smoke in a public-house known as the Three Jolly Tars, and while he was enjoying his pipe I looked through the window. I had not been long there when I saw a Manchester thief whom I knew by sight, and in his company a young man whom I at once recognised as the original of the photograph in my possession. I mentioned my suspicions to the Liverpool officer, but he proved of a contrary opinion, and although he went with me, he did so very reluctantly, believing that the man I pointed out was not the one wanted.

In order to make sure, I ran out and caught hold of the two men, and handing the one I wanted over to my friend, requested him to retain him in custody, whilst I dealt with the other. When beyond earshot of each other, I told my prisoner that I believed he had assisted his companion to get out of the cells, but he very soon told me to "shut up." However, we conveyed them both to the bridewell, where they were placed in separate cells. I left them there for an hour or two, and then went back again. I went into the cell where the young fellow whom I suspected to be the man I wanted for breaking from gaol was confined, and said to him—

"Now, tell me the truth. Has Jack Raglan, the man who was with you, had anything to do with getting you out of the gaol?"

His reply was, "I did it myself," and I was then satisfied I had the right man.

Afterwards I took him away and handed him over to the superintendent of police the same night at Leigh, where he was identified as the person who had escaped.

About 1857 or 1858 a person named Braithwaite, who was better known by the sobriquet of "Sir Robert Peel," had been committed to gaol for nine months for stealing slates. This man had, it was said, a head that was as hard as iron, and would, for a quart of ale, undertake to break with it any mantelpiece before which he was placed. He was a complete terror to the police in Salford, but in addition to that he had assaulted several officers in Ashton-under-Lyne, and it was well-known that it was unsafe to tackle "Sir Robert" without the assistance of three or four constables, no matter what offence he had committed.

During his incarceration in the New Bailey Prison, in Salford, at the period I am referring to, he made one of the most wonderful escapes ever known. To do so, he had to stand with his bare feet upon some iron spikes, which acted as a guard to the windows from the courtroom, and then his body would have to be erect before he could reach the top of an adjacent wall with his fingers. Nevertheless, not only did he succeed in doing this, but he also contrived to mount the wall, and walking along, when opposite the Bolton Arms, on the other side of New Bailey Street, he dropped to the ground outside the gaol.

This escape having taken place in Salford, it was the duty of the borough police to make search for the fugitive, but for some reason or other they did not succeed in finding him. The county police, at Eccles, had the matter deputed to them, and on explaining to my superintendent that I was acquainted with Braithwaite he said—

"Well done, Bent. You can go and find him, and you can have all the assistance you require."

The chief constable of Salford, who was present, added, "There is £5 reward if you get him. I am told he is in Clayton."

Having attired myself in rough clothing, and put a life-preserver in my pocket, I started off. I called upon Police-Constable Stafford, who is now Mr. Superintendent Stafford, and telling him that I was going to Clayton, in search of "Sir Robert Peel," I asked if he would go with me. He said he would, and we went to Clayton. Thinking that the officer stationed there might know the man better than we did, I asked him to assist us, to which he agreed, but the individual we wanted was not to be found.

About three o'clock the next morning we happened to be passing Johnson's Wireworks. Prior to that, I had blackened my face. Looking through the bars of the gate, the watchman came up, and I asked him if he knew So-and-So, meaning an uncle of Braithwaite's.

"I do not know him, boys," replied the man. "I only came here last night. But I will go and see Michael, who is working in the shop."

He closed the door while he went to make the inquiry. I at once jumped up to the bars, and could see the watchman talking to a young man. Shortly afterwards he came out and said—

"Well, boys, I do not know who you are, but Michael says he knows that you are policemen, and that the man you want was at their house last week."

Pretending to be under the influence of drink, I said, "It is not true. If Bill Howarth knew where I am he would very soon find me."

"Then, lads," resumed the watchman, "I will show you where he lives," and he pointed out the door of a house about a hundred and fifty yards from where we were. We then went round, and I noticed a light in another house and a bill in a window, on which were the words, "Knocking-up from 4 to 6." I went inside the house, and inquired of a man whom I saw if he was a "knocker-up." He replied in the affirmative.

"Then," I said, "do you knock Bill Howarth up?"

"Yes," was his response.

"What time?"

"5-30 o'clock."

"Now," I said, "look here. We are policemen, and if you make any signs to Bill Howarth when you are knocking, as sure as you are born you will be locked up. We shall be watching you."

The man seemed very much frightened, and promised not to do anything. However, Stafford and myself watched him go to the door of the house, and, after a delay of a few minutes, it was opened. I immediately rushed in the house, followed by Stafford, who I told to run through into the back yard and watch there, while I requested the Bradford constable to remain at the front of the house outside. I then heard something tumble on the floor above, and rushed up stairs, where I noticed a woman in the bedroom on my right. Then I went into the bedroom on my left, and saw five of, I think, the worst-looking men I ever gazed upon in my life, occupying five different beds in that room. I also observed a man's foot protruding from under one of the beds. I at once caught hold of the big toe of the foot, and getting my life preserver in my hand, I called out—

"I am a policeman, and if either man, woman, or child interferes, I shall knock their brains out," and then in a loud voice I shouted, "Stafford." I drew the man by his big toe from under the bed, and placed my knee in the small of his back. I now knew I had got the man I was so anxious to capture, and said—

"Bobby, are you going to have it rough or smooth this time?"

"Smooth, by Jove!" he said; and he added, "Look here. 'Sir Robert' has left me," meaning his strength.

We took him downstairs very quietly, and conveyed him to the New Bailey, where we arrived about a quarter-past six in the morning.

I was afterwards very much amused to hear people talk about "Sir Robert" having been again apprehended, and that the man who went up the stairs first carried a blunderbuss, while others said that he had a revolver in each hand.

The prisoner was ordered to received three dozen lashes, which he endured without a murmur, and when his punishment was finished he told the doctor and the others around that he could stand three dozen more. The last I heard of this man was that he had enlisted, had shot at his officer, and had received a sentence of fifteen years' imprisonment.

CHAPTER VII.

HORRIBLE BURNING WITH RED-HOT IRONS.

DURING the time I was stationed at Newton Heath I had frequent complaints from my men of being assaulted whenever they had to serve a process upon any of the workpeople employed at Messrs. Norton and Co.'s Steelworks, Miles Platting. On one occasion, which I shall never forget, I had been making inquiries respecting the murder of Police Constable Jump, and was walking down Oldham Road in the direction of Newton Heath, in company with then Inspector Richmond, when Constable Shaw, who was afterwards a sergeant, came to me and said that the Court of Record officers had been to serve a process on, or had seized furniture belonging to—I do not recollect which—a man named Whelan, and that the men working under this person at the steelworks had not only beaten the bailiffs but had also attacked the police who went to protect them. Addressing the inspector, I said I thought it was time that something was done in the way of securing for the police, who had to serve processes or execute warrants at the works in question, reasonable protection from personal attack, and suggested that we should go there at once and see why our officers had been assaulted.

Accordingly I directed one of the constables to concentrate as many men near the steelworks as were available, and after some persuasion Inspector Richmond agreed to accompany me. I asked Shaw to go into the shop and point out the man or men who had assaulted him, and he did so. He went first, I followed him, and Richmond was behind me. Almost as soon as we entered the yard Shaw pointed out two men who were working at a furnace on the right-hand side, and, indicating one of them in particular, said, "That is one of the men who assaulted me."

Thereupon I went up to the fellow pointed out, but being in plain clothes, I informed him that I was a sergeant of police, and further said, alluding to Shaw—

"This man tells me that he and others of our men have been attacked here this afternoon. Come outside and let me hear what it was all about."

The steelworker had a hammer with an iron shaft in his hand, and without saying a word he swung the heavy implement round and tried to hit me with it on my head. Had he succeeded there is no doubt that I should have been killed in an instant. However, I avoided the blow, and he lifted up his hand again and held the hammer over his head as though preparing to strike me. With a view to get his hand lower, so that he might not have the same force, I began to talk to him, saying—

"What did you do that for? I said nothing harsh to you, and had you caught me on the head you would certainly have killed me, and in all probability you would soon have been standing your trial for murder."

Although the man's hand dropped by degrees, as he was

not able to hold the hammer perpendicularly, I could see by his gestures that he really intended to aim another blow at me. When his arm got on a level with his shoulder I jumped at him, wrenched the murderous weapon out of his hand, and said, "Now I will make you go." The only garment that covered the upper part of his body at that time was a guernsey. I clasped my arms round this, and he slipped it over his head and broke away from me. I got hold of him again round his body, and he struggled violently, and began to shout at the full pitch of his voice. Upon this about thirty men came running down the yard, all armed with red-hot bars, which they had drawn from the various furnaces. I was struck by them several times, and my grasp of the prisoner was again broken, and I fell.

At that moment I noticed two men, with red-hot bars, running Constable Shaw backwards, with the irons against his stomach, while at the same time his trousers were on fire. About half-a-dozen men then got hold of me and pitched me on an iron wheelbarrow. I jumped off, and again got hold of "Black Joe," as they called him, when all the men who had red-hot bars in their hands yelled and shouted, "Hit him on the head," and actually some of the bars were so pliable with heat that they got entangled with each other.

A fellow caught me a blow on the head, inflicting a severe wound, which penetrated to the bone, and I fell down, bleeding frightfully. Whilst on the ground, as many of the men as could possibly get upon me with their feet did so, beating me with red-hot irons and nearly burning the clothes off my back. One man called out, "Fetch another heated bar, and shove it down his throat."

Another man, whom I believe they called Kennedy, put an iron bar into a furnace, and came back with it when it was red hot. Placing a foot at either side of my head, and grinning like a fiend, he put the bar to my mouth. On the instant I grasped the bar with my left hand, which it fearfully burned, and I swooned, and for a time was unconscious. When I came to my senses it seemed very much like a dream. No one was near me, but there was a large pool of blood where my head had lain, and it was some time before I could realise my position. When I did so, I went towards the gates, and as soon as I arrived there a number of the men came with red-hot irons and pushed me against the office door. I got out, bleeding profusely from my wounds—in fact, the blood was almost like a shower of rain.

I had not seen the inspector, nor any policeman, excepting Shaw, from the time that I first spoke to "Black Joe" inside the works; but when I got outside after the struggle I found two or three of our men there, and some hundreds of other people. The constables wished to assist me to a doctor's, but I declined their services, saying that if I fell someone would pick me up, and that they must stop the men from escaping from the yard until assistance came.

On I went, but I fell when I was between fifty and sixty yards from Dr. Steel's surgery, to whose house I was afterwards conveyed. There I was attended to by the doctor, who sent me home in a cab in an exhausted and painful condition. The same night two men were brought to my bedside, both of whom I was able to identify. I could not be so sure of a third, but he was recognised by other witnesses. Afterwards the three were committed to take their trial at Liverpool Assizes for the assault upon me. I subsequently learned that about a dozen others who had taken part in the ferocious attack had made their way to America, but no proceedings were taken against them.

The Assizes at Liverpool came on within a short period from the time I was assaulted. I was still in a very low condition, my hand was bad, and the wounds on my head had not yet thoroughly healed. When I got to Liverpool, I should think thousands came into the room, where I was allowed to sit until I was required in the court, just to have a look at me, no doubt in consequence of the numerous large placards put out by different newspaper publishers having the line, "Horrible Burning with Red-hot Irons," the most conspicuous in their lists. The three prisoners were put on their trial. Mr. W. H. Higgin, Q.C., now Chairman of Quarter Sessions, assisted by Mr. Hopwood, now Q.C., and Recorder of Liverpool, and Mr. Grimshaw, conducted the prosecution; while the late Mr. J. B. Torr, afterwards Q.C., and Mr. E. Jones, defended the accused. The case lasted a whole day, and at the end of the trial the two men whom I had identified were each sentenced to twenty years' penal servitude, while the one I could not recognise was acquitted. The Judge remarked that he sincerely hoped the authorities would reward Sergeant Bent, not only for his courage and determination, but also for his other good qualities. The full reward that I could receive was £3, but a short time afterwards I was promoted to the rank of Inspector, though it was a considerable time before I could perform duty, and I do not think I have passed a week since that time without experiencing very severe pains in the head, and occasional attacks of dizziness, things which were quite unknown to me before the assault.

After the trial, a boy who was present in the works when I was assaulted, and who had been sent to Sheffield out of the way, made a statement in the presence of the inspector and myself, which corroborated the story I had given of the occurrence in every particular. His account of how it came about that my comrades failed to render me any assistance in my perilous situation I need not describe. I may, however, add that the lad stated that as soon as I had seized the red-hot bar intended to be forced down my throat, and swooned, the men all ran away; but four of them returned, one of whom said, "Put him in the furnace, and nobody will know anything about him." Fortunately for me, the men, thinking I was already dead, failed to carry out this diabolical suggestion.

CHAPTER VIII.

OFFENCES AGAINST INFANTS.

A BABY was on one occasion found by a cabman lying deserted on the footpath, on the Lancashire side of Cheadle Bridge, and taken, I believe, to the workhouse. On inquiry, it was discovered that a young woman, a servant with a gentleman whom I shall name Brown, at Cheadle (or at least one answering to her description), had taken a child to Runcorn some two or three months before, to nurse, and had been to fetch it on the day the child referred to was found at Cheadle, and hence suspicion fell upon her as having deserted her offspring. My superintendent had, however, got the wrong name, and was not quite sure of the house where the woman lived. In the course of my investigation I got to Mr. Brown's, and there was the servant. I asked her if her name was Johnson, and she answered, "No." I then asked, "Have you had a baby?" and again she answered, "No."

The old gentleman, who sat in a corner, wanted to know all about it, and I told him that a child had been found deserted, and I was trying to trace the mother. He got up in a temper, and ordered me out of the house, saying that his servant was a respectable woman, and that I had no right to go there and ask such questions. I told him that I was very sorry if I had offended him, but that I should feel much obliged if he would furnish me with his servant's name. Just then his daughter-in-law came into the room, and she incidentally called the servant by the name of Hamilton. I then left and went to my superintendent, and informed him that, although I felt sure the servant in question was the mother, I had got the wrong name. I asked him if it was possible that the girl's name was Hamilton, and he at once remembered that it was. I returned to the house, and told the girl that she would have to go with me, as I had every reason to suppose that she had left the baby on the footpath. She strongly denied the charge, and ultimately her master's son came in, and I was very soon convinced from his manner that he knew more about it than he chose to tell, and his wife and the old gentleman persisted in saying that Hamilton had never left the house a day for a long, long time.

"Well, now, listen," I remarked, "to what I have to say. Did not this girl go away about eleven months ago, in consequence of being unfit for work?"

"Yes," answered the old gentleman; "she was away for a month with a bad knee."

"Was she not away on such and such a day?"—namely, the day upon which the child was found.

"Yes," was the reply.

"On the first occasion," I continued, "she went away from you to be confined at Runcorn, and when she had that last day out she placed the child on the footpath at Cheadle Bridge, and so I shall be compelled to take her into custody."

The girl then began to cry, and admitted that it was her baby. She was committed for trial at the sessions on a charge of assault upon her own child, by exposing it on the highway.

The case was well argued at the trial, but inasmuch as the little one had been found very soon after it was deserted, and had suffered no harm, the jury, by the direction of the chairman, acquitted the prisoner. This acquittal was, I believe, the means of bringing about an alteration in the law, for in a very short time after it was made a criminal offence to leave a baby in such a state as to be calculated to injure it, and several accused persons have to my knowledge been convicted under that Act, whereas they would have escaped under the old law.

When I was at Newton Heath my superintendent on one occasion informed me that the body of a child had been found in the canal at Stretford, and that on the following day a woman called at the Talbot Hotel there, where the body was lying awaiting the inquest, in a very excited state, and asked to see it. She said she was a boatwoman, but was so agitated that she hardly knew what she was doing. It was also observed that she had a black eye. Putting all these things together, it was thought necessary that whoever the woman was she should be found.

I had been on duty all the previous night, but seeing that my superintendent was very anxious in the matter, I determined to try and find the woman whose disfigured face, one would suppose, would render my task of identifying her comparatively easy. My superintendent suggested that I should go to Worsley, and if I met any boatwoman with a black eye I should take her to the station in order that he might see her, but I told him that black eyes amongst the wives of canal boatmen were exceedingly common, and that I thought it better that I should go to Northwich in the first instance, and come back from there to Worsley, searching the different boats as I came along.

It was a wet, cold day in November when I went off to Northwich, which appeared to me a very dark and dismal place. I went into a public-house amongst a lot of company, principally composed of the canal boatmen. I got into conversation with them as well as I could. I attempted to work myself into their good graces to begin with by telling them that I had a brother-in-law who was a boatman, and that I thought he carried salt. One after another they began to question me, but I found that I did not get on very well, as I could give practically no description of the woman I wanted, except that she had a black eye. That was all the information I had received upon which to base my investigation, but while I was in the public-house the landlady began to talk about a boatman who had recently had a row with his wife, and had discoloured one of her organs of vision, and that for some reason or other they had sold up their furniture and left the district two or three days before I arrived. She added that they had a child who had died a week prior to that. This I thought was a clue to the woman I wanted.

I experienced little difficulty in ascertaining that the boat this couple navigated belonged to the Bridgewater Navigation Company, and I at once sought out the individual who represented them. He was a Scotchman, and I shall never forget his kindness. I was wet to the skin when I knocked at his door, and informed him that I was a police-officer in search of a boatwoman with a black eye, who had passed through Stretford the previous Sunday, and had there stated that she had recently buried a child. The gentleman at once looked at his book, and gave me the name of the boat which he said had left Northwich, and was on its way to Liverpool. Thereupon I sought the sergeant of the district, who very kindly gave me something to eat, and then I started the best way I could go to Stockton Quay, where I saw the chief official at the navigation offices. I told him who I was, and what was my business, and asked him to render me what assistance he could. Having acquainted him with what I had learned from the gentleman at Northwich to the effect that the husband of the woman with the black eye of whom I was in search had charge of the boat Alma, he gave me a seat in the general office without telling the clerks who I was, and we arranged beforehand that he should then go and ask some questions about the boat. In a few minutes afterwards the chief came into the room pretending not to notice me, and accosting one of the clerks, said:—

"I see the boat Alma passed yesterday?"

"It did, sir," returned the clerk.

"I see you have lent them some money, too," added the gentleman, continuing to examine the book.

"Yes," replied the clerk, "the woman borrowed fifteen shillings from me, as one of her children had died last week."

"Had she a black eye?" queried the official.

"Yes, she had," was the clerk's response.

"Where is she now? Do you think the Alma will have got through the Gap?"

"I do not think she will."

"You should not lend these people money," commented the chief, and then he walked away.

Upon thinking the matter over I found that it was possible I could get to Runcorn Gap before the arrival of the boat Alma, if I were to proceed along the towing path of the canal, and I ran along as fast as my pedestrian powers, which had now become somewhat enfeebled for want of rest, would allow, sometimes kneeling down to dash water out of the canal upon my face to refresh me.

When I got to Runcorn Gap I saw the chief officer there but found him to be exceedingly reticent, until I informed him that I wanted a person on a charge of murder. This secured an alteration in the official's demeanour, and he then said, "I will make inquiry, sir." Shortly after he came to me with the information that the boat I wanted had not passed the Gap, and just while I was talking to him, I saw at a considerable distance a boat, and could read very distinctly the name Alma painted on it. Leaving him, I proceeded to the police station, which was only a short distance off, and there saw the inspector on duty. I acquainted him with my errand, and requested him to render me every assistance that lay in his power. He came out of the office as quickly as possible, and we went together to the Gap, the inspector evidently believing, as I did, that the case was a serious one. All at once he left me and ran round the Gap, with a view as I thought, of forestalling me. However, the boat happened to turn a little in the direction where I was standing, and although I was greatly fatigued—quite "done up," in fact—I jumped from one boat to another, until I got upon the deck of the Alma before the inspector could do so, and I could see that this part of the business did not please him.

As soon as I got on the deck, the woman with the black eye made her appearance, and asked me what I wanted. I informed her that I wished to make some inquiries, and asked her if she had not recently lost a child. She said she had.

"By what means?" I asked.

"It was scalded to death" was the reply.

In answer to a question as to where it was interred, I believe she said Birkenhead. I asked her if she could show me the certificate of its death, and she said she could, and at once produced it. This, of course, cooled my excitement a very great deal, and the woman furnished me with satisfactory proof that the body found in the canal at Stretford was not that of her child. She admitted that she was at the Talbot Hotel in Stretford the Sunday before, and that when she saw the child which was awaiting the coroner's inquest, she was so excited that she did not know what she was doing. It was therefore quite clear that she was the same woman the people of Stretford supposed to be the mother of the child which was found in the canal. My superintendent was satisfied with the information I had gained, and it allayed the feelings of the people in the district.

I arrived home after having been three nights out of

bed, drenched to the skin with rain during the greatest portion of the time, and living as I could without getting a proper meal. About four o'clock in the morning of the fourth night during which I had been without bed, I reached Newton Heath, but the exertion had been too much for me, and I was laid up with a fever for two or three weeks.

CHAPTER IX.

ROBBERIES BY DOMESTIC SERVANTS.

A FEW years ago, one of the justices of the peace came to me with the information that for some time a good deal of pilfering had been going on at the hall where he resided, and expressed a desire that I should proceed myself on the following morning to investigate the matter, and I went accordingly.

First of all I assembled the servants, and told them that I had every reason to believe that there was a dishonest person amongst them, that a number of articles had been missed from the hall, that I had examined the windows and doors, and found that there had been no breaking from the outside, and that, therefore, I had come to the conclusion that it must be one of those present who was guilty of the thieving. Amongst the rest there was a lady's maid, a fine, portly woman of about forty years of age, who seemed to some extent disgusted that she should have to stand there with the other servants; and, somehow, the moment I set my eyes on this person I felt convinced that if the thief was in the hall at all she was the one. In order to throw her off her guard, I said to a girl, whom I took to be a kitchen maid :—

"Now, I want you to show me which is your bedroom."

The girl did so at once, and I just looked round and was quite satisfied that she was not the individual I wanted. As the lady's maid had said her time was of importance, I then remarked that I would go to her bedroom next, if she would kindly show it me. She did so, though with no very evident willingness, and the first thing that met my gaze when I entered the department was a very large wardrobe.

"To whom does this belong?" I asked.

"It belongs," she answered, "to one of the servants."

"Very well," I said, "I must have her up here, as she must be present when I search it."

Then she sobbed, "Oh! oh! it is mine."

I ordered her to unlock it, which she did, and I soon discovered a great many articles which had no right to be there a great many more, in fact, than had been named to me as missing by the owner. They consisted of jewellery, table-cloths, bed quilts, blankets, skirts, and so forth; and I should think, without exaggeration, that the wardrobe contained at least £100 worth of property.

The gentleman to whom I have been referring had told me before I began my search, that a short time previously a young country girl came to his service, from Knutsford I think he said; that the very first night she was there his umbrella had gone, and that the lady's maid had so satisfied him that the new-comer had stolen it, that he discharged her the next morning. Now, amongst other things which I found in the wardrobe was this same umbrella. I had all the articles laid out on the floor of the chamber, and called the gentleman up, and those which had been stolen were mostly identified by himself and his sister. As, however, many of the things could only be spoken to by their mother, who was over ninety years of age, and not fit to be removed from the hall to give evidence, I was requested not to take the thief into custody, but to see her from the place. Having heard this she began to bounce amongst the servants, but I very soon put a stop to this by telling her that whether her master prosecuted or not I myself should do so if she made any noise in the hall.

I did not believe that this was the first time this lady's maid had been guilty of offences of that kind, for she had three immense boxes which contained a very large quantity of property, and which, I do not think, could have been all her own. The girl from Knutsford was, I understood, fully compensated for having been wrongfully discharged.

Two other magistrates, one of them being Mr. Taylor, of Booth Hall, Blackley, called upon me, I remember, one evening, when one of them stated that he had good reason to believe that a servant who had been in the employment of his mother, who had recently died, had carried away some things that belonged either to him or to her late mistress. One of my sergeants having ascertained that a person named—shall I say Bolton?—and answering to the description of the woman wanted, lived in a street off Stretford Road. I went to the house about midnight, knocked at the door, and was answered from an upstairs window by a man. I asked if Mr. Bolton lived there, and he replied in the affirmative. Then I told him that I desired to see him, and would be glad if he would come downstairs. He then unhesitatingly complied. When he had opened the door I informed him that I was a police-officer, and that I wanted to see Miss Bolton, who had lately been a servant at Booth Hall. The man declared he knew nothing at all about her.

"Is not your name Mr. Bolton?" I naturally inquired, in unfeigned surprise.

"No," said he.

"Why did you tell me it was just now?"

"Well, really," he returned, "I must have been dreaming. I do not know what I said."

"Do you know any person of that name living in this street?"

"Yes," he replied, "there is, I think, a man of that name living three or four doors lower down. He is a single man, and lives alone."

Thereupon I went to the door indicated, and, when I had knocked, a man got up to the bedroom window, but declined for some time to come down. He persisted in his refusal until I informed him who I was, and brought the constable on the beat to assure him that I did belong to the police force. He then came downstairs, and I asked him if a Miss Bolton lived there, a person who previously had been a servant at Booth Hall.

"No," he said, "she does not live here."

Then I changed my tactics, and exclaimed, "Ah, but I saw you come out of the house where she is living, this very evening."

"Do you mean her," he then said, "that lives at No. 4, D— Street?"

"Yes," I responded, "and" I added, "you have got some

new mattresses and bedding, and I hear you are going to be married to her."

"Yes," he replied, "we are going to be married."

Then I left the house and ran as fast as I could to No. 4, D— Street, placed a constable at the back door and knocked myself at the front. The occupants of the premises refused to open the door of the house unless I could show that I was a policeman. Again I had to go to the end of the street to find a man in uniform, who went with me and stated that I was an officer. The door was then opened, and I went upstairs, and then asked who was the occupant of the first bedroom I came to.

"She is a servant," was the answer. "I do not know much about her, but I believe she did live in service somewhere at Blackley."

"Well, go in, and tell her to dress herself," I resumed, "as I want to search her bedroom."

The girl got out of bed readily enough, but protested that she had never taken a farthing's worth from anyone in her life. At the same time she admitted that she had been a servant at the residence in question. Seeing a satin dress hanging up behind the bedroom door, I said—

"I believe this to be one of the articles belonging to your late mistress, and I shall take it with me."

When I got the girl to the police station—for I had taken her into custody—I gave her to understand that I had reason to know that she had sent away a large quantity of jewellery, when she at once observed—

"Well, I will tell you where it is. It is at the house of a gentleman residing at Rusholme. His servant has it. I have asked her to keep it for me."

Next I proceeded to the house indicated in Rusholme, and threw some pebbles at the top bedroom windows, and presently two servants came down, and from their manner no doubt expected to encounter a sweetheart instead of a police officer. When they had opened the door I informed one of them that I was a policeman, and I had reason to believe she had a very large quantity of stolen property concealed in her master's house, and that I must search it. Upon this she proceeded within, and on returning handed me several articles of very valuable jewellery, and told me that Miss Bolton had asked her to take care of them.

"But there is a lot more stuff here," I remarked, "besides the jewellery."

"Well, there are some plates and other articles," she answered. "I will bring them to you."

She took me to the cellar, and pointed out a large quantity of costly plates—in fact, Mr. Taylor was afterwards made an offer in my presence of £5 for each plate, which he refused.

Next morning this girl came to me with some blankets, and said these had also been left in her care by Miss Bolton. It was abundantly evident that she could not have received from another domestic such a large quantity of articles, amounting altogether in value to about £700, without knowing that the person from whom she received them had obtained them by dishonest means, and therefore I made her my prisoner. She was tried at the sessions along with the actual thief, but was acquitted, while Miss Bolton was sentenced to either twelve or fifteen months' imprisonment, the whole of the stolen property being handed over to Mr. Taylor.

The incident is not without its romantic side, for at the expiration of the girl's sentence the young man to whom she was to have been married came with her to the station and informed me that he still intended to marry her. He did so within two or three weeks after she had been discharged from the gaol, but I have never seen or heard anything of them since.

A Prestwich gentleman sent for me on another occasion and stated that within the space of a fortnight or three weeks between £30 and £40 had been abstracted from a drawer in the bedroom occupied by himself and his wife. I inquired if any fresh servants had come to him lately, and the complainant, who was a German, replied that they had only a German cook, but inasmuch as she had a well-furnished house of her own in Hulme they were quite sure she would not take anything. After making a brief investigation I soon arrived at the conclusion that if anyone was committing these robberies it was the aforesaid German cook, who seemed by the way to enjoy in a very great degree the confidence of her mistress.

Having ascertained which was the house said to belong to the cook, I proceeded there the next day, but only to find that the woman had merely been lodging at the place for a short time, and that when she left she was in debt to the occupier. Thereupon I made up my mind to go and see this German cook myself. Accordingly I went at once to the house of her master and knocked at the door, which, as good luck would have it, was opened by the cook in person. I had learned her name from her master, and so I began with—

"Good morning, Miss ———."

"I don't know you," was her response.

"Never mind that," I said; "I have been in the house for the last week, for anything you know, watching you. There has been a good deal of money stolen within the last three weeks, and I have reason to believe that you have taken it."

She went off in a fit of hysterics, which only lasted a short time however, and as soon as she had quite recovered I informed her that I must go upstairs with the view of discovering where she had put the money. Accordingly we went up to her room, when she opened a drawer and showed me three sovereigns.

"You had a great deal more money in this drawer on Sunday last," I observed; and when I had said that she seemed to think that I knew all about it, and for a time she would say no more.

"Well, Miss ———," I then said, "you went out last Wednesday."

"Yes," she replied, at once. This I had of course previously learned from her master.

"Were you in Hulme?" I next asked, pretending to read from a piece of paper I had in my hand. She returned no answer, and I continued, "Will you just tell me, now, how many pawnshops you visited?"

"Well," she answered, after a little hesitation, "I only went to one."

"Only one!" I exclaimed.

"Well, I did go to two."

"Let me see," I further inquired, "if you can tell the truth. How many bundles did you bring home?"

"Only eight," she said.

"No more than eight?"

At last she admitted that she had brought ten, and I remarked, "I suppose you have pledged these when you have been hard up, or out of a situation?"

"Yes," said she.

"How long have you been here?"

"Three weeks."

"Have you drawn any wages?"

"No."

"Well, then," I asked, "where did you get the money to take these things out of pawn? I will find the rest of the stolen money if it is in the house, even if I should require to have all the carpets lifted."

Upon this she began screaming, and said that if I would take her to her mistress she would tell all the truth. I did so, and she began to make an appeal in German, but I told the lady that I would not allow this, and that she must speak English, which she could do perfectly well. Then she told her mistress that she had thrown the money through the window.

"Come, then," said I, "and let us see if I can find anything of it."

"Well, I will tell you the truth," she then declared, "it is hidden under the carpet in the kitchen."

Accordingly I went with her to the kitchen, and found under the carpet there about half of the money that had been stolen. The culprit was taken to the police station, and afterwards tried and sentenced to six months' imprisonment.

In about nine months from this time a foreigner who

resided in Rusholme came to me and said that he had been missing a good deal of property out of his house, and that he had been told that my experience amongst dishonest domestics had been exceptionally large. He accordingly desired that I should come and have a look at his servants. "With pleasure," I responded, and made an appointment for the same evening. Accordingly I went down to his place at the specified time, when lo and behold who should open the door in response to my knocking but Miss ———.

"Oh," I observed to the gentleman, "there is no wonder at you losing property when you have this lady here."

"You can go out," she retorted, "I will never tell you anything again."

Her master declined to prosecute, though he at once turned her out of the house.

A servant girl came to me at the police station early one Sunday evening, and reported that her master's house had lately been broken into, the thief or thieves having placed a long ladder against a bedroom window, lifted the sash, and stolen a writing desk containing £2. I proceeded to the house, and found that nothing was known by the other inmates either of the robbery or how it was committed. The girl took me upstairs and said that early in the day the window was fast, that the desk in question was placed on the table a short distance from it, and that while the people had been at chapel that evening she had gone upstairs and seen that all was right. She added that she had stood at a certain place on the stairs and saw the window fast and the desk in its place a very few minutes before the family returned from the evening service. She further said that a ladder had been placed against the window.

Not believing her statement, but suspecting, on the contrary, that she had herself committed the robbery, I asked her to show me where the ladder had been placed. We went outside and she pointed out two holes in the ground where she said that it must have rested. Upon examining the holes I found that the soil had been lifted up and not pressed down as would have been the case if a ladder had been used. This confirmed my suspicions, and when we got upstairs again I asked her how she really thought that the thief or thieves had got in. There was, she said, no doubt that they must have had a knife, and had therewith pushed back the catch. Then I told her to show me the exact spot where she had stood when she saw the writing desk which contained the money safe, but when I stood upon it I found that it was impossible to see the window. Upon that I turned round and accosted her sharply with—

"It is quite clear to me that you know how this house has been robbed, and I shall take you into custody on a charge of committing the theft."

A young lady who was in the house seemed very much annoyed at what I had said to the girl, but I informed her that I had been asked to inquire into the robbery, and that I should act on my own suspicion and authority, and apprehend the girl. Seeing that I was determined to take her, the servant confessed that she herself had taken the £2 out of the desk, which she had placed in the waste-paper basket. She was taken to the court, and sent to gaol for six months.

At another time I received a complaint from the landlady

of a public-house at Newton Heath of money being missed every morning from the till, and that she had every reason to believe that her servant was stealing it. Thereupon I marked some money for the landlady, and one of the officer's wives went the following morning and spent something near £1. When, however, the landlady examined the drawer after getting up she failed to find more than about four shillings altogether. Afterwards I went in and accused the girl of robbing her mistress, adding that I should be compelled to take her into custody. She steadfastly denied this, and threatened to have me prosecuted for defamation of character. I told her these threats would not be of any avail as I should certainly take her, and then I went into the back kitchen and found the missing money, some stuck into the soap, and the rest under some pots on the shelves. The girl ultimately pleaded guilty, and was sentenced to six months' imprisonment.

CHAPTER X.

BURGLARIES AND HOUSEBREAKINGS.

ONE Sunday evening, a house was broken into and entered at Moss Side, and amongst the property stolen were several bank notes. The case was put into my hands, and having given notice of the numbers to the bank, in a short time afterwards I received information that one of the notes had been tendered by a fish dealer, residing in Strangeways. From this person I learned that he had received the note from a poulterer living in the same neighbourhood. I accordingly apprehended the poulterer, who began to "bounce" a great deal, and, as often happens in such cases, said that I might expect to get into trouble for arresting him. However, I soon began to think that I was right. In answer to questions, he informed me that he had received the note from a gentleman about 5 feet 11 inches in height, with dark hair and bushy whiskers, to whom he had sold a fowl.

The prisoner was locked up at Old Trafford Police Station, and while he was there his shopman came down and informed me that he was present when his master took the note. I, of course, asked him to describe the individual who had tendered it, and he said he was a man of about 5 feet 6 inches in height, clean shaved, and dressed in a "pepper and salt" suit. Then I opened the door of the cell where the prisoner was confined, and asked him to describe, in the hearing of his servant, the gentleman who had given him the note, and he repeated that he was about 5 feet 11 inches in height, with black bushy whiskers, and added that he was dressed in black. Subsequently, I succeeded in obtaining other evidence, which clearly proved, to my mind, that the poulterer had committed the burglary and stolen the property.

He was committed for trial at the Liverpool Assizes, and when I was at St. George's Hall, in charge of the case, a very fast young man, who was in company with the prisoner's wife, came up to me, and threatened that it would be the last case in which I should ever give evidence if I said one word against the husband, but, as may be imagined, I did not allow this to deter me from doing my duty, and the poulterer was tried, and sentenced to, I believe, fifteen months' imprisonment.

Early one morning in June, 1861, I was standing near the railway arch, at Miles Platting, looking up in the direction of Newton Heath, when I saw in the distance two men come into the road opposite Ten Acre Lane, and from their manner I felt certain that they had been in some serious mischief. Daylight was just beginning to break, so I quietly pushed my hat off, slipped down and got some sludge, which I rubbed over my face, unbuttoned the front of my coat, and otherwise disarranged my clothing, and then, pretending to be very drunk, I walked on towards the place where I saw the men. The fact that I was staggering appeared to encourage them to come on in the direction of Manchester, so I pretended to look at the tops of the houses on the left, and for that purpose reeled across to the footpath where the two men came up quite close to me, laughing heartily, as they believed that I was drunk. I suddenly grabbed one of the men by the collar of his coat with my right hand, and seized the other in a similar way with my left hand, and seeing a chisel protruding out of the pocket of the man on the right, I immediately threw both together, and got hold of their coat collars with my left hand. Then, taking the chisel in my right hand, and backing the men into the hedge, and holding the tool in their faces, I cried out—

"I will run the chisel in the eye of the first man that moves."

Upon that the man on my left drew from his pocket a most murderous-looking jemmy, and was about to give me a blow on the head with it, when I caught his arm with the elbow of the same arm with which I was holding them, and the jerk threw the jemmy out of his hand.

"Now, I have you," I shouted out, "And the first man that makes another move I will most assuredly run the chisel through his eye."

The men lay on their backs, with me holding them with the weapon lifted for about a quarter of an hour, until a greengrocer's cart came up from the direction of Oldham. The man in charge of the vehicle was young, but thick and corpulent. I called to him for assistance, and seeing the position I was in he got down, but as he came towards us I noticed that he trembled from head to foot.

"Master," he inquired, "dost want me to houd one for thee."

"No," said I. "But come and sit on one," for I was afraid that a man who trembled so would not be able to hold one of the rough customers with whom I had to deal. He really did sit down on one, however, without any more asking or ado, and one of my hands having been thus liberated I used my whistle, and two of my men came running up to my assistance. Afterwards, I discovered that they had committed a burglary at the house of a Mr. Clegg, close to where I first saw them, and they were sent for trial at the Liverpool Assizes.

When I went before the grand jury, and gave my evidence, some of their number seemed rather incredulous as to my statement that I had held two men in the manner I had described. Lord Derby, who was in the chair, said—

"Officer, do you mean to say you caught these two men yourself?"

"Yes, my lord, I did," was my reply. His lordship then turned to the other grand jurors, but, addressing me, quickly remarked, "Well, you have done your duty."

As I was going down from the grand jury room into the Assize Court below, I heard some one following me, and, turning round, saw that it was a county J.P. who had recommended me for the force. My idea was that he was coming down to see if I would make a different statement before the judge from that which he had heard, and I noticed that he took his seat in the High Sheriff's box while the trial was proceeding.

The late Mr. J. B. Torr, Q.C., on rising to defend the prisoner, paid me the highest compliment imaginable, stating that he considered I was one of the best detective officers the country had ever produced, and that he would feel as safe, if I was on the beat where his house was situated, as if it were guarded by a regiment of soldiers. This, I of course, took for what it was worth. Having had previous experience of Mr. Torr's method of procedure in such cases, I could not help thinking that he made the observation in order to draw me out a bit. He then said he considered there was not a man in England who could point to a wider experience of burglary cases than myself. Having thus paved the way he turned to me, and rather adroitly put the question—

"Now, Sergeant Bent, with your experience of burglaries, did you not expect to find a bit of candle in one of my client's pockets?"

"Well," I replied, "I should not have been surprised to have found a piece, but as it is Midsummer it is scarcely ever dark. Besides, the prisoners had matches, and the house that had been broken into had the gas lit." This seemed to annoy the learned counsel, who turned round rather savagely and said—

"My clients tell me they found these instruments, which you have put in the witness-box, in the road."

"I don't think they did," I answered.

"Give me your reason," was his next remark.

Pointing to one of the prisoners I replied, "If that man has the same coat on now that he had the morning I apprehended him, you will find that he has a pocket up the side of the coat which this jemmy will just fit, and he has a bit of cloth to button over it, so that no one can see what the pocket contains."

Mr. Baron Martin called out at once, "Is that so?"

The prison warder examined the man's pocket, and

replied, "Yes, my lord. There is a pocket here like a staff pocket."

"Oh, they are confirmed burglars," was his lordship's comment.

Mr. Torr sat down, and the prisoners were convicted, and sentenced to penal servitude. I have the instrument still in my possession.

On another occasion I remember standing near to No. 2 School, Oldham Road, speaking to one of my men, when I heard a crash, as of glass breaking.

"There is a burst," I observed to the constable. "Keep quiet and follow me in the shade of the lamp." At the moment I could hear some distant footsteps near the spot whence the noise had proceeded, and approaching in my direction. This was just as the clock struck one. I went towards the spot where the sound, as of clogs, was coming from, and suddenly ran against two men, and I placed an arm round each man's neck and almost strangled them. My man, whether through fright or whether he had not seen them, I cannot say, ran a considerable distance beyond the spot where I found them. The fellows begged to be released, and I complied as soon as the officer had come back to my assistance. Then I found they had broken into the Post Office, and stolen a large number of stamps. The pane of glass which they had broken must, I think, have been three foot square. They were convicted at the Liverpool Assizes, and sentenced to long terms of imprisonment.

A Manchester officer once came to me at Newton Heath to ask for assistance in some matter or other, and when walking with him towards the city I came to the ground upon which the Rectory of St. John's Church, Miles Platting, is now situated. Glancing up the street which led to the back of the building I saw three men, and it so happened that just before I had said to my companion, " This is a rare place for thieves," and then looking up I said, " Begad, there are three now."

Off I ran as fast as I could go and caught one with each hand, while I called to the Manchester officer to take the other. Grasping the two men by their coat collars I sent my elbow against their ribs, and feeling something bulky I pushed the two men backwards against a cart that was just coming up, a distance of about a dozen or twenty yards. I secured them, and found that their pockets contained poultry. They had, it seemed, broken into a duck-cote a short distance away and killed the ducks, and were taking them away at the time I met them.

These men's characters were very bad, and they were each sentenced to penal servitude for seven years.

Having received a good many complaints of robberies in the neighbourhood of Moss Side, about the year 1879, I stationed a number of officers in plain clothes in different parts of the district. Soon after this arrangement had been made, one morning, about two o'clock, as Constable Leedale was standing in one of the streets in the neighbourhood, he saw a man who was wearing goloshes passing along very quickly. He followed the man and seized hold of him, when the fellow took out a knife and stabbed Leedale in the hand. The officer called for assistance, and Constable Potts, who had heard the cry, came running up and struck the man a severe blow on the head. It was subsequently discovered that he had committed two burglaries, and a number of burglars' implements were found in his possession. The prisoner was sent to the assizes for trial and received a sentence of ten years' penal servitude.

At Newton Heath, one morning about two o'clock, I overtook a man with a pretty large bundle under his arm. I stopped the man and questioned him as to the contents of the bundle. He replied to the effect that they comprised his Sunday clothing, and also some of his working apparel, and that he was going to a good situation in Bolton, and expected in the course of a week or so to be able to send for his wife and children, who were staying at Oldham. As I did not believe his statement I took him to the Police Station, and then asked him to put on one of the pairs of trousers which I had found in the bundle. After some difficulty he did draw them on, when I found they were much too tight for him. While he had them on I asked him to lace his boots, and finding he could not bend at all, he exclaimed—

"Man! I will give it up. You will find where they came from in the morning."

The articles which I had found upon him were the proceeds of two different burglaries committed in Newton Heath within two hours of the time I stopped him. His character was a very bad one, and as several previous convictions were proved against him, he was sent to penal servitude for seven years.

Early in 1886, a large number of housebreakings and robberies were reported to have been committed in the neighbourhood of Patricroft, Worsley, Eccles, Urmston,

Crofts Bank, and Heaton Chapel, and for a time the constables were totally at sea, although it was quite clear to me that they were the work of some person residing in the district. Ultimately, suspicion was directed against a man who resided in Patricroft, and some of the stolen property was found at a pawnshop there. Inquiry was made for the pledger, but he had decamped. His photograph was found in the house, and his full description published in the *Police Gazette* and other papers, but nothing was heard of him until one evening later on. A gentleman, living at Bolton, left his house for a short time without anyone in charge. Shortly after he had gone out, a next-door neighbour heard a noise in the house, and knowing that the family were absent, he went to the back door, which, after some difficulty, he forced open. Then he gave an alarm, and a number of persons rushed to the house and heard somebody run upstairs. This person proved to be a man named Gregory, who turned out to be the person we wanted for the robberies mentioned above. When the neighbours entered the house, he stood at the top of the stairs calling out that if any person interfered with him he would shoot them; but a constable having been sent for, he and two or three others ascended the stairs, when the burglar quietly gave himself into custody. He was then taken to the Borough Police Station, and then sent to the prison at Strangeways to await his trial for housebreaking. By permission of the governor of the gaol, I had an interview with Gregory, when he not only confessed to all the robberies that he had been charged with, but offered to go with me and point out the places where the stolen property had been pawned or sold. After a little delay, I obtained an order from the Home Secretary to have the prisoner delivered into my custody, with authority to take him wherever I thought proper. With this object in view, I may state that in Oldham, Manchester, Salford, Pendleton, Bolton, Farnworth, Wigan, Liverpool, Miles Platting, and other places, I found nearly the whole of the property that had been stolen.

From one place which Gregory had honoured with his attentions, a large quantity of jewellery had been taken away, including six silver salts and spoons, which had been a wedding present. The thief inquired if I had already recovered these, and I answered in the negative. He seemed incredulous, and asserted that I must have them, but I assured him that was not the case. Thereupon he made a statement to me to the effect that the morning after he had stolen them he went to a small jeweller's shop in Liverpool, and offered them for sale. The jeweller looked at them and said he had a "route" describing those salts, and asked the housebreaker if he could show a receipt. Gregory was too anxious to get away then, and promised that he would fetch a receipt. He went off, leaving the salts in the hands of the jeweller.

Upon this, I went to Liverpool with the prisoner, and he pointed out the shop to me. The jeweller was not on the premises, but his wife was, and the thief observed that she was present when her husband took the salts from him. This, however, she denied, and I then left the shop, but returned on the following day with a Liverpool detective. Then I saw the jeweller himself, and saluted him with—

"Good morning."

"This," said the Liverpool officer, "is Mr. Bent, the

superintendent of the Manchester Division, who has come to see you."

"Oh," queried the jeweller, "are you the gentleman who paid me a visit yesterday?"

"Yes," I answered, "I am, and I have come for some stolen property that was taken by you from that man," indicating the prisoner.

"Does that man say I bought them?" he asked.

"No," I replied, "but he says that you got them and retained them in your possession, and the Liverpool police say that you never reported anything about them to the authorities, and therefore I look upon it as a very bad case."

"Ah, well," he observed, "if he says I did not buy them I will give them up to you, but I had no right to tell the police about it. My duty was to keep them for twelve months, and then they would have become my property."

At that time, having only permission to use the thief as a guide to the place where I should find the property, I could not apprehend the jeweller, but I took the salts and told him he would probably hear from me again. Afterwards I applied for a summons against him with the view to have the case brought before the magistrates, but seeing, I presume, the serious mess which he had got into he had closed his shop and I was never able to find him.

For the offence the thief had committed at Bolton he received a sentence of nine months' imprisonment, and at the expiration of that period he was taken into custody on other charges to which he pleaded guilty. It was then found that he had been twice in trouble before, and he was sentenced to seven years' penal servitude and seven years' police supervision. There were at least twenty untried charges of housebreaking against him.

One morning, about two o'clock, a constable came to inform me that a pawnbroker's shop at Miles Platting, belonging to John Lukeman, had been broken into, and a large quantity of jewellery and other articles stolen. The constable also added that he had discovered a man sheltering in a doorway not far from the pawnshop in whose pocket he had found two rings, but as the man had given a satisfactory explanation of who he was he had allowed him to go. Of course I admonished the officer for having done anything of the sort, and told him he ought to have brought the person to me and allowed me to decide.

On the following day I made inquiry in Manchester and other places, and learned that the city police had got a watch which was part of the stolen property. I also learned from a beerhouse-keeper that on the morning of the robbery four men had been in his house spending money pretty freely, and that his daughter had seen one of them put something, which she believed were watches, up the chimney. Afterwards they had sent the servant to the pawnshop with some other property, and she had been taken into custody.

It is but fair to confess that I felt rather annoyed at the Manchester policemen, and particularly so when before the magistrates they stated that they knew all the persons who had been engaged in the burglary, and assured the bench that the second watch that was asked for, and other jewellery, had been sent out of England, entirely ignoring everything that I had to say on the subject. They laughed at the idea of my doing anything further in the matter, but as I was determined, if possible, to find the property, I proceeded to call at several pawnshops. The two Manchester officers who had got the watches were standing in Ancoats Lane as I passed along that way, and sneeringly told me that my search would be of no use. I was not satisfied with this, however, but went on with my investigation until I called upon a pawnbroker, who informed me that a similar inquiry had already been made from him.

"Do not answer any question" I observed, "until I have read this to you," and thereupon I read, in a distinct tone, the list of Luckman's missing property. When I came to describe the watches the man turned pale and I addressed him with—

"Now, be careful. Do you mean to tell me you have not one of these two watches in your shop?"

"Well, Mr. Bent," he responded, "to tell you the truth I think we have one of them."

"Then let me see it," I said; and he at once showed me the watch which the Manchester constables said had left England. I can assure you that I went out of the shop with much glee, and in a great hurry to show them the watch.

Next day I happened to be at the Police Court, and saw two big rough-looking fellows brought up on a charge of burglary at Stretford, and in my own mind I felt convinced from the description I had received that they were two of the gang who had broken into Luckman's shop. Then I saw a man go into the gallery, and afterwards into the court, who, to my thinking, seemed to be conveying information to someone, and the suspicion came across my mind that he also had to do with the burglary. I went to the constable on duty at the bottom of the steps leading from the court, and told him what I suspected, adding instructions that if anyone ran downstairs from the court he must close the gate until I got down. Then I returned to the court, fixed my eyes on the man I have alluded to, and stared at him steadily. He evidently began to feel alarmed, and ran out of the gallery, and I followed him. Mr. Trafford, the stipendiary, hearing a noise, remarked—

"Why yonder's Bent just dropped his hand on a man like a crow on a hot potato," and he called to me to bring the fellow up at once. This I did not wish to do, because in reality I only suspected my prisoner to be the person that I wanted, and I had no evidence whatever upon which I could ask for a remand. However, as the magistrate had directed I was bound to obey, and I placed the man in the dock. Mr. Trafford asked me what charge I had to bring against him.

"Oh," I replied, "I believe he is one of the men that broke into Luckman's shop, but I have not sufficient evidence yet. If he could be remanded until to-morrow, I think I could have evidence here."

Before going to the court that morning I asked the beerhouse-keeper referred to, and his little girl, to attend and see if they could identify the two men who were charged with the robbery at Stretford, and it appeared that while I was speaking to the stipendiary the girl and her mother came into court, and as soon as the former saw the man that I had caught in the dock, she exclaimed—

"That is the man who put those watches up our chimney."

"There's a witness now, no matter how it is," said Mr. Trafford, laughing, and then the child went on to state what part the prisoner had taken in the transaction. Then I went back to Newton Heath, and asked the constable who had told me that he had found a man sheltering near Luckman's shop about the time of the robbery, if he would know the person again.

"Yes," was the confident answer. "He has a mark upon him which I shall never forget."

I thereupon had the prisoner placed amongst several others, and the officer having at once identified him, he was committed for trial.

On taking this 'man and the beerhouse servant to Kirkdale, the latter told me where I could obtain the pawn-ticket for the remaining watch wanted. When I had got it I took it to the shop of the pawnbroker whose name it bore, and at whose place I had been some five or six times, when he always denied that he had ever seen the watch. When I produced the ticket he began to apologise, and said it must have been taken in by his assistant when he was at tea. This latter circumstance I have only mentioned to show how difficult it is at times for the police to recover stolen property.

The little girl, who had first identified the man I have been alluding to, told me that one of the others who had been to their house was called "Flash Mick," and she described him to me in a very intelligent manner. He was, I understood, a big, powerful Irishman, and I searched a great deal for him before I could find him. About two o'clock one Sunday morning, however, when I was going off duty, I went to Cross Street, off Swan Street, Shudehill, as I had heard that a man had been seen in that street answering the description of him wanted, two or three days before. I had resolved that I would give almost every house in the street a turn over rather than miss him, and I got the assistance of a very good constable, named Dennis, who consented to watch the back doors while I went to the front. Some people came to the window of the first house at which I knocked, and I inquired if a young man was staying there of the description I gave them. They told me in a very civil manner that they did not keep lodgers. Then I went to the next house, and put the same question there, when I was told by the person who answered my knock, that he had seen a man at the next door but one the night before, who answered the description I gave. To that door I went and knocked, and someone came to the window and asked what I wanted. I replied that it was a private matter, and that I wished to speak to him downstairs. He came down upon that and opened the door, when I at once turned on my light, and saw an old woman on a sofa, and a foot which certainly did not belong to her. I at once got hold of the big toe of the foot saying—

"Mrs., what have you got here?"

"Oh, it is only another old woman," she replied, when all at once, a strong, strapping man arose up behind her, and cried—

"I am Flash Mick, you villain. I have heard of you before."

A struggle ensued between us, but, ultimately, with the assistance of Constable Dennis, of the City Police, I succeeded in putting the handcuffs on him, and taking him to the station. He was afterwards clearly identified by the beer-house keeper, his wife, and little daughter; and he and the man I had apprehended in the Police Court were each sentenced to twenty years' penal servitude. The servant girl was acquitted.

Each prisoner was separately defended at the Assizes, and in passing sentence the Judge remaked that it appeared to him there was a sort of club formed in Manchester for the purpose of defending lawless criminals such as he had before him, and that he would do his part in breaking up that club.

In March and April, 1887, several burglaries and safe robberies had been committed within a short distance of Manchester, all of which bore evidence of having been committed by an experienced thief. One of these was a case of housebreaking at Worsley, where some underclothing and other things had been stolen. In another case the office of the London and North-Western Railway at Worsley had been broken into, the safe forced open, and £8 12s. 5d. stolen therefrom. In this last case the thief left behind him on the floor of the railway station a leather wedge, which was found by the police when examining the spot next day.

Sergeant Hartley, who had charge of the case, made a careful inquiry, and ultimately found that several suspicious circumstances pointed very strongly to the conclusion that the thief was an elderly man named Alfred Scarfe, who had for a short time previously been residing at Worsley (cohabiting with a young woman named Esmeralda Abbott), and who represented himself as a pensioner from the navy. This man had been seen by one or two constables near Worsley Railway Station on the night of the robbery, and next day himself and the young woman Abbott left the district, leaving their house locked up, and giving no hint to anyone as to where they were going.

The suspicions of the police respecting Scarfe were soon confirmed by the result of further search and inquiry, for on Scarfe's house being searched by Sergeant Hartley, though he did not find any stolen property there, he did find other things which gave ample proof that Scarfe must have been a most experienced burglar. Among other things found in his house were two dark lanterns, a steel drill frame, a pair of glass scales and weights for weighing gold, and two bottles of liquid for testing metals. It was also ascertained soon afterwards that Scarfe was an old returned convict, who had only recently been released after completing a sentence of twelve years' penal servitude for breaking into a jeweller's shop in Manchester, and stealing about £1,000 worth of jewellery therefrom. The search for Scarfe was now vigorously prosecuted, and Sergeant Hartley traced him to Liverpool, thence to Birkenhead, and then on to Blackburn, where he was ultimately apprehended by the Blackburn borough police. Here himself and the young woman Abbott, with whom he had cohabited at Worsley, occupied a small cottage on the outskirts of the town, and on Sergeant Hartley and the Blackburn police searching it they found in a hole in the wall, near the head of Scarfe's bed, a loaded revolver, some cartridges, and a formidable life preserver.

Scarfe was taken to Old Trafford, and though he still strongly protested his innocence of all wrongdoing in an interview I had with him, yet from his manner and what he did say in that interview, as well as from what I learned had been said by him to the woman Abbott, when he was apprehended at Blackburn, I came to the conclusion that not only had he committed the Worsley robberies, but that the woman

Abbott was cognisant of the fact, and that there was some other things which might bring these robberies home to him hidden away in the house at Blackburn, which had not yet come into the hands of the police.

I therefore directed Sergeant Hartley to proceed again to Blackburn, apprehend the woman Abbott, and again thoroughly search the house; and that in order to do so effectually he should pour some water over the flags forming the floor in the lower part of the house, as well as on the bedroom floor and the stairs, and to watch to see where the water sunk rapidly down, as he would no doubt there find some hiding place underneath.

Sergeant Hartley acted on my instructions to the letter, and found hidden under one of the boards of the stairhead one of the most complete sets of housebreaking implements I ever met with, comprising crowbars, life preservers, drills, wedges, muffled hammers, and numerous other things used by housebreakers, and skeleton keys in abundance. There was also in the same place a large rough oilskin cap, with ear-flaps, which would have the effect of giving the wearer of the cap a most ferocious-looking appearance if met by any person in the night time. And last of all he found a piece of leather trace, from which it was clearly seen the leather wedge had been cut, which was left by the thief on the floor of the railway station at Worsley when he had broken into the safe there.

In the possession of the female prisoner was found £17 in money, as well as the clothing which had been stolen from a dwelling-house at Worsley, although she strongly protested her entire innocence in the matter and her ignorance of Scarfe's burglarious habits.

When the case came up for hearing at Strangeways Police Court, on the 5th of July, 1887, Esmeralda Abbott was discharged, and Scarfe was sentenced to seven years' penal servitude and seven years' police supervision; and thus the country got rid, for a time at least, of one of the most determined thieves that had for many years come into the district.

Perhaps I may be permitted to say a few words here about burglars and burglaries. A burglary, it is well known, can only be committed between the hours of nine o'clock at night and six in the morning, and then only in a dwelling-house in which someone resides. It would not be a burglary to break into a warehouse, lock-up shop, or other such place. Burglaries are looked upon, in the eye of the law, as very serious offences—offences which can only be tried, as the law stands, by one of Her Majesty's judges, and not at quarter sessions. These offences are often committed by desperate thieves, who frequently carry such dangerous weapons as life-preservers, knuckle-dusters, jemmies, or bars of iron, and sometimes revolvers. There are many methods adopted by the burglar fraternity of gaining an entrance to houses; but the commonest practice is by the insertion of a knife, or thin instrument, between the sashes of the window, and by this means pushing back the catch.

If the sashes are too close to admit a knife, as some of them are, then jemmies are used to force off the catch, but in the latter case, there is danger of the noise caused by the breaking of the catch being heard by the inmates. Sometimes it happens that the burglar, from some cause or other, not having provided himself with instruments for pushing back or forcing the catch, contents himself with placing a treacle plaster on the pane of glass under the catch, and then breaking the glass, which falls on the floor, but adhering to the plaster it causes little or no sound. When this is done, the operator can, with great ease, put his arm through the broken pane of glass and push back the catch. I have known it often to happen that people have been awakened out of their sleep by the noise caused through breaking of the window, but after lying awake a short time, without hearing any further sound, have concluded they had been dreaming, and again given way to the influence of the somnolent god, only to find in the morning, to their disgust, that the house had been burglariously entered and their property carried away. Had they had the presence of mind, when they heard the noise, to have got up and examined the house, the burglary would, no doubt, have been prevented. It is well known that immediately after a burglar has made a noise he lies down on the ground, or holds his ear to the window frame for some time with a view to see if the household has been disturbed. I have known one or two cases in which burglars, finding they had disturbed the inmates, have not run away, but have gone to the door and knocked as loud as they could, and when the inmates have come to the window they have been asked a simple question, such as where Mr. Jones or somebody else lives. The inmates would answer the question, put down the window and go to sleep, and the burglar, after sufficient time had elapsed, would enter the house and finish his work.

I would recommend a person who may be disturbed at night to go downstairs and examine his house, however annoying it might be to do so, taking with him one of the bedroom chairs, which is very valuable as a weapon of defence, or as a shield. If he finds anyone armed with knife or bludgeon let him grasp the chair back and run at the burglar. He need not be afraid of doing so, because the leverage a person with a chair would have over his opponent would be three times that of the burglar, and he could with any firmness at all force the burglar's head into the chair bottom.

Again, if he had to follow the burglar upstairs, the chair is the very best thing he could use. Placing the chair on the top of his head with the back to his face, he could walk upstairs without fear of any attack the burglar might make upon him; for, the moment the intruder would come near, the holder of the chair could lay hold of his feet. I have tried this plan myself on many occasions, and have never known it to fail—not only in cases of burglars, but against dogs supposed to be mad, as well as against lunatics. But another person should never be allowed to get hold of the back of the chair while you thus hold it, as by doing so you reduce your power very much, as both would not pull the same way.

To prevent burglaries by forcing windows I would recommend small brass plates at each side of the window sash, which I have occasionally seen used, and which to my knowledge have prevented many burglaries. They are so placed as to adjust themselves every time the sash is put down, and I have known part of the bottom sash broken off by bars, but the plates have successfully resisted the pressure.

There are other means of preventing the window-sashes from being raised, or the catch pushed back—that is, by putting a bolt through into each sash, but this gives too much trouble, and servants and others are liable to forget them. Not so with the catch I have named, because if the sashes are put down the catches must take their proper place.

I have known several cases of bedrooms being entered by burglars when the inmates have been in their bed, although they had taken the precaution of locking their bedroom doors, and left the key in the door, not knowing that by so doing they had made matters easy for the burglar to come with a housebreaking instrument in the form of a pair of lady's curling tongs (but both prongs are hollow), by which he can take hold of the end of the key and quietly unlock the bedroom door. If you take the key out, then skeletons are used. If you put a chain on, then the thief can so wedge the door that you cannot get out of your bedroom, unless you jump through the window, which is very often a dangerous game; but if you use a chair, and place the back under the door handle, then the bedroom cannot be entered from the outside without disturbing you, when you are better prepared to receive an intruder, and can either raise an alarm or prepare for defence or attack. If you do not use this precaution, you continue sleeping until the usual hour for rising, whilst the burglars have ransacked your pockets, and taken money, watches, and other valuables. In exchange they often leave an ordinary dark lantern, so fixed as to throw the light on the sleeper's face, who when awaking is bewildered by the glaring light.

About the year 1850 a number of robberies were committed at Old Swan near Liverpool, and representatives of the force were sent there from the different divisions to perform special duty in plain clothing, and I was one of them. Being very young then, I was told as soon as I arrived that I might consider myself transferred from the Manchester to the Old Swan Division permanently, but I objected to be so transferred, and at the expiration of about three weeks I was allowed to return to my station.

During my stay there I established an acquaintance with a tollbar-keeper, who kept a rather savage dog, but the animal appeared to have grown quite familiar with me, and would follow me all round my beat whenever it saw me. One afternoon I remember seeing a respectable-looking young man resting on the road sitting on a small jewellery-box, and recalling the old saying of "always believe everybody guilty until you prove them innocent" I began to stare steadily in his face when I got within about twenty yards of him. Whether or not he suspected that I knew him I cannot say, but he suddenly jumped up and ran off as fast as his legs would carry him. I at once gave chase, but as he was a slim young fellow he gained ground for a time but ultimately he slackened speed a little and then started off again. The dog which was with me then ran forward, and, pinning the runaway by the leg, threw him down upon the roadway. Afterwards I discovered that the box which he had with him, and which he claimed as his own, had been stolen by means of housebreaking from the library in a gentleman's residence not far from the spot where I had found it.

It so happened that this robbery was committed within the boundary of the borough of Liverpool, and its youthful perpetrator, who declined to give any account of himself, was sent for six months to gaol. I am happy to say for some time these robberies ceased, and there was good reason to believe this young man had a hand in committing them.

Between nine and ten o'clock on a Saturday evening, when stationed at Newton Heath, I was passing Roslin Terrace, when I saw that a pane of glass under the catch in the front window of one of the houses had been broken, and one of the neighbours thought that he had heard a noise in the house. I lifted the sash and went into the front room. The place was quite dark. Not finding anyone inside that room I proceeded to the kitchen, closing the door after me. I tried to open the door of the kitchen, but could not do so. However, after shaking it a little, I was enabled to press it open, when I felt a man whom I at once seized by the throat. He turned out to be named George Johnson, who had then been in penal servitude twice. I asked him what he was doing there, and he replied, "I thought the people that lived here had gone to Manchester, and I would mind the house until they came back." He had packed up everything he could find worth taking in the house. He was tried at Liverpool Assizes, and was sentenced to eight years' penal servitude.

CHAPTER XI.

EVENTS AND CASES—GRAVE AND GAY.

ABOUT the year 1868 a person named Travis resided in Gagsfields, Newton Heath. He was a hawker of blacking, and on Sundays he invariably went out fishing. Some Sabbatarians, however, got hold of him, and asked him how much he got by fishing on the day of rest. He told them about eighteenpence, whereupon they promised that they would give him that amount weekly if he would leave off Sunday fishing and go to chapel. This he agreed to, but as the payments dropped off in about two or three months he resorted to his piscatorial pursuits again.

His wife was an inmate of Prestwich Lunatic Asylum, and in her absence he had formed an alliance with a woman who kept a small shop near to where he resided. To me it was pretty clear that he had a desire, if possible, to get his wife out of the way.

One day he went to visit the unfortunate woman at the asylum, taking with him two or three Eccles cakes, which he gave to her. Shortly after he had left, his wife and another inmate went to a lavatory in the asylum to eat these cakes, when it was discovered that inside of each there was a dozen pins bent in the shape of fish-hooks. The two women at once showed the matron what they had found in the cakes, and I was sent for. I apprehended Travis, and then took the cakes to be analysed, and as it was found that they contained antimony in addition to the bent pins he was sent for trial on a charge of attempting to murder his wife.

Whilst he was awaiting his trial the fellow sent me a memorial. I cannot now remember all that he said, but amongst other things he implored forgiveness, and declared that he had never done any harm to anyone in his life, adding that for two years he had been a "locomotive" preacher. I went to the woman with whom it was said he had cohabited, and asked if she would kindly show me a bonnet the old blacking chap had bought her. At first she denied having one, but ultimately I found it concealed on the top of a cupboard. This she afterwards gave me to understand was to have been the wedding bonnet if ever she and Travis were to get married. I do not suppose that the chance could ever present itself, as the blacking man was sentenced to penal servitude for twenty years.

I had, I should think, a thousand applications for the dozen pins that were found in the Eccles cakes, and after I had given them all away I found so much pressure put upon me that I doubled up another fifty and handed them over to the first who asked for them. It is the usual way with relics or trophies.

When residing at Prestwich I was sent for by a cotton manufacturer carrying on business in Blackley, who told me that he had a very strong suspicion that a woman who worked at his mill was in the habit of stealing cotton almost every night, and desired that I should take her into custody. I pointed out to him that, unless I had some evidence, I had no power to apprehend the woman; and, after some conversation, I made a suggestion that I should go to the place where she resided, which was a cellar in Rochdale Road, and make a search, bargaining that, if I found no cotton cops, such as he described, the woman should go on working, and that I would keep an eye upon her. I added that I considered it would be a very great hardship if the suspected woman should be turned away from her work, seeing that she had three small children depending upon her, unless some better or, I should say stronger, evidence against her was forthcoming than that which had been adduced. At last this was agreed to, and accordingly I went to the woman's residence. A mixture of sleet and snow was descending as I proceeded, and the night was bitterly cold. I had no difficulty in finding the poor millhand's cellar, and into it I went; and there, alas! I found three little children standing before the fireplace, which had very little, if any, fire in it, while the only clothing that covered their nakedness was an old cotton frock for each. My heart was touched. The cellar was dark, except for the glimmer of the street lamps, which penetrated through the almost opaque windows. As soon as I opened the door the three children just casually looked round at me, and then turned their faces to the fireplace, without taking any further notice.

On approaching nearer to them I found that each one had a potato peeling hanging on the bar, and from their appearance I could easily see that these peelings, which the poor children were trying to roast, must have been taken from a neighbouring ashpit. There was no furniture in the house except a mattress, upon which the mother and the three children had to sleep.

After carefully looking through the cellar for stolen property and the cupboard for food, without finding either, I went and stood for a few minutes behind the children. The youngest appeared to be about eighteen months old, the next about two years and a half, and the third perhaps a year or a year and a half older. I asked them what they had to their breakfast, when they all at once replied, their tongues being no doubt sharpened by hunger—

"We had no breakfast."

Then I asked what they had to their dinner, when the youngest one called out—

"Only some salt and water."

Almost immediately afterwards they all three began to dance and sing or chant. "Mamma will bring home her wages. This is Friday night, and we shall have some supper." I asked the oldest if she would fetch me three penny cakes from a neighbouring shop. At the mention of this all three began to dance again, and the youngest to shout—

"Oh, don't break any off mine."

When the girl returned a cake each was given to the other two, and one to herself. I went out and bought a loaf and some other small articles of food and put them in the cupboard, telling the children to let their mother know when she returned from work that the relieving officer had called upon them, as I did not wish her to know that her house had been searched by a policeman.

After I had left the poor woman's cellar I thought it was my duty to find out if possible the relieving officer of the district, and try if something could not be done for these poor children. That night I failed to see him, but I took good care to go to his office the following morning, and to call his attention to what I considered a very deserving case. When I had finished my tale he coolly asked me what I wished him to do. My answer was—

"Put them in the workhouse, or do something; the children are starving to death."

The relieving officer burst out with a laugh.

"Why, look here, Mr. Bent," he commented on my suggestion, "if we were to take notice of cases of this sort, we should soon have the workhouse full, and that would not suit us. It would not do at all."

I left the office disgusted. I found out as time passed on that the woman whose cellar I had visited was kept at work by the master who had suspected her for a long time afterwards, and I never heard anything against her.

About two o'clock one morning I was in company with then Constable Whiteside, and we were approaching near the Bradley Wharf aqueduct, when I heard a moaning noise from the river, which I should think was about twenty yards below the place where we had been walking, and there we stopped. It was a clear frosty night, but the moon was overcast, and we could see nothing, though we continued to hear the moaning. We accordingly resolved to get down the embankment, which was very steep indeed, if possible to reach the spot where the wailing sounds proceeded from. No sooner said than done. When we got to the bottom we could see on some land in the middle of the river the form of a man apparently quite stiff and his limbs benumbed with cold, while, in fact, his feet and legs were actually immersed in the running water. He continued to moan, but could not speak, and after some trouble and personal risk, Whiteside and I got hold of him with a view to get him up the embankment.

He was like a log of wood that would neither bend nor yield in any direction, and several times, through the grass we had hold of breaking, we all three kept falling backwards, and had we tumbled all the way to the bottom we should have run a great risk of being killed. After great difficulty, we got the rescued individual into a small building used by boatmen, in which there was a good fire, and having got his clothes off, we began rubbing him, and continued to do so for about half-an-hour, until he regained consciousness, and began to use rather unparliamentary language in asking us what we were doing. As I could not well stand such insolence after what we had done for the fellow, I left him in charge of Whiteside and a sergeant, who had come up while we were going on with the rubbing process. From what I learned afterwards, it appeared that he had got drunk, lost his way, and rolled into the river, though by some means he had managed to get his body on to a bed of sand situated in the middle. I never knew of a narrower or more providential escape, nor one which resulted in such a trifling display of gratitude.

While taking a stroll in one of the streets off Lime Street, on one occasion when I was attending the Liverpool Assizes, I overheard a man ask an "unfortunate" if she would buy a pawn-ticket from him. She declined to have anything to do with it, and told him to go away, as she was not going to get into trouble on his account. I dodged about for some time until Inspector Stafford came up, and then told him that I believed if the man had a pawn-ticket at all it must relate to some stolen property, and that I intended to take him to the police station. Thereafter I approached the man in a jocular way, and bid him "good morning." In response to that he said—

"If you can find a house, I will stand drinks."

"Oh, yes," I replied, "I know two or three nice houses. Come along."

Observing a policeman in uniform at the moment, I went and acquainted him what my suspicions were, but he took no notice of me until I told him that if he did not take the suspected person into custody I would, and back I went to my would-be-treating friend with that intention. I unbuttoned his outer garments, and found that he was wearing three suits of clothes, one on top of the other. I also found, upon further investigation, that he had three "d's" marked under his arm, showing that he had been a soldier and had deserted three times. I took him to the Liverpool police station, and told the inspector in charge what my suspicions were. He seemed rather to pooh-pooh my idea, and was evidently disinclined to think much about it, and upon this hint the genius I had arrested began to threaten me with all sorts of actions for false imprisonment. He got into a great passion, and just as I was giving him to understand that all his shouting and threatening would be of no avail with me, two men came into the station, and stated that they had come from Ireland that afternoon in company with a soldier, with whom they struck up an acquaintance. When they got to Liverpool they had taken him, they said, into a public-house, and left him in charge of all they possessed, which consisted of a watch and about £15 worth of clothes. I asked them if their clothes were anything like the same the man had a little higher up—meaning the one I had taken into custody. With an oath they both declared that he was the same man they had left in charge of the box.

Upon further inquiry I found that this was the case, that one man had been left in the charge of the box, while the two others went to get a light cart to remove it, and that as soon as they had left by the front door the soldier stripped off his own clothes, put them in the box, and then dressing himself in the three suits, one over the other, walked quietly out into the yard, and then got away with the assistance of a cab.

Next morning at the Court, the officer, whom I had first called to my assistance, took very good care to give to the Bench his own version of what he had done in the matter, but when it became my turn to be examined it seemed to be thought that the other constable's testimony was of very little use. As in duty bound I at once reported the circumstance to the department of the Secretary of State for War and soon afterwards I received a reward of 20s. for the apprehension of the deserter, who received six months' imprisonment for his other crime.

Whilst stationed at Crofts Bank, I was going on one

occasion to Barton, when I saw a man who was very drunk lying on the top of a cart loaded with coals. He was just in the act of falling down head-foremost when I ran and caught him in my arms, and by that means prevented him from falling on the road, while I probably also prevented the wheel from going over him. Will it be believed that as soon as I let him go, the ruffian whom I had saved, took a running kick at me with his heavy boots, and broke the third finger of my left hand? He was taken into custody but escaped with the trifling punishment of a fine of £5.

Another man whom I caught in the act of assaulting his wife, and whom I was apprehending in duty bound, got my thumb in his mouth and bit it very severely. He was sent to the sessions for trial but got off with the reward rather than the punishment of one month's imprisonment.

A man of independent means, whom I shall name French, who was very fond of drinking gin, resided at Newton Heath while I was stationed there. He used to boast in fact that he never took less than fifty two-pennyworths every day. That was his least modicum, so far as the gin was concerned, but as a matter of fact, without reference to the total quantity, he sometimes had a pint of old ale between the gins, because, as he said, he thought it was best to mix it a little.

He had gone on in this way for a considerable time, until he began to play some curious tricks, and one night in the winter months having possessed himself of a pistol charged with powder only, and while his family were sitting round the evening fire, he blazed away with his weapon up the chimney with, I need hardly say the result, that every one present was covered with soot. The inmates were so much frightened that they sent for a policeman, and gave the offender into custody on the allegation that he was of unsound mind, and he was remanded for a week to Strangeways gaol.

On the first occasion when he was brought up I was not present, but when he appeared on remand one or two of his friends, who were very respectable people at Newton Heath, entreated me to do all in my power to prevent him from being sent to a lunatic asylum. The magistrates had not then come into court, and I thought I would just test my quondam friend, Mr. French. Therefore I said—

"Oh, Mr. F——, you will have to abandon all this work. It will kill you as sure as you are born. This drinking of gin to such an extent as you carry on is more than any human being can stand, and you will either be sent to a lunatic asylum, or you will kill yourself."

Clasping his hands together he exclaimed, "Oh, my God, sergeant, do get me out this time if you can, and I will promise you that I will never touch drink again while I draw breath."

"Oh," I said, "you won't keep your promises."

His reply was, "Oh, Mr. Bent, so help me God, I shall never touch drink again so long as I have breath."

I promised that I would do my best, and having left him for a few minutes I returned with a tumbler half full of water. Then I called to Mr. F——, and said, "Would you not like this drop of gin before your case comes on?"

"Oh, my God, Mr. Bent," he replied, "I should like a little drop," and he snatched the glass out of my hand.

I whispered to him to stoop down in the dock, so that if the magistrates came into the court they should not see him. He did so, and put the glass to his lips, but after taking one mouthful he called out—

"Oh, sergeant, there is no spirit nor fire in this," and he returned me the glass. Then I pointed out how soon his great resolve had been broken.

The poor fellow was discharged, but only to hasten his end by returning to his two-pennyworths. He had a brother in the same neighbourhood who was a publican, whom he occasionally went to see, when he would call for a pint. As a matter of course he looked upon all the pints he received as gifts, and never offered to pay. On one occasion he remarked to his brother—

"Joseph, this isn't as good ale as it should be;" to which Joseph made answer, "What the deuce does that matter to thee, tha never pays anything for it."

At one time a man named Taylor, residing at Whitefield, was wanted on a charge of obtaining goods to a considerable amount by false pretences from different tradesmen. These offences having been committed in Manchester, I was asked by Detective-Superintendent Maybury to assist his officers by all the means in my power. Twice or thrice I had gone near the suspected man's house, but found that he was not at home. One morning, however, I took with me Sergeant Smith, and placed him at the back-door of the house where I suspected Taylor was staying, while I went towards the front. Almost immediately afterwards he must have known of our presence, for he came from behind the house round the gable end a few yards away from me at full speed with the sergeant after him. I took up the chase as quickly as possible, but had only run a short distance when I was struck with a brick, which caught me on the left thigh, and at once disabled me, so that I had almost to be carried home.

I was attended by a medical gentleman and put to bed, but I was unable to return to duty for about three months. I suffered very great pain, and even at the present time, if I walk any great distance, I feel the effects of that injury. It was small consolation to me that the man I was after was subsequently caught and received a long term of imprisonment.

About two o'clock one morning, when stationed at Newton Heath, I was standing near the police station, when I heard a row (which is no unusual thing), between a man and a woman. They called each other thieves, and in the course of their altercation I heard the woman say, or rather shout, "You dirty scamp. You are going over to Northallerton for the watch you stole six months since."

"Ah, well," said the man, "I was tried for that, and got off."

"Aye," said the other, "you got off because they could not find the watch. I know where it is; it is buried on the brook side close to the go-by—meaning a stile—opposite the gas works."

I allowed them to continue their dialogue for some time, and then went and took them into the station, telling them that I would not have any bother in the street. Afterwards I let them go, but at the same time I telegraphed to the

Northallerton police the particulars of what I had heard, and telling them that the man was on his way to look for the watch. Strange to say the next day's post but one brought me a letter stating that the watch had been found; that it was only partially covered with grass; and that after it had been wound up it kept going for an hour, although it must have been lying there for about six months. It was further stated that nobody had been to look for it.

Two or three days afterwards, however, I met the man I have alluded to, and it appeared that he had gone to Northallerton for the watch, but not having found it had come away again. I took him into custody and telegraphed to Northallerton, and they sent an officer to take him away but I never ascertained the result of the trial. I heard that the same man and woman had been apprehended and convicted for shop-lifting.

I once had in my custody a man on a charge of drunkenness, who followed the profession of a rat-catcher, and when taking him to court the following morning he recounted to me a series of funny stories. Amongst others he mentioned that he had gone to a certain hall in Lancashire, the name of which would not matter, to follow his usual vocation. He had been fairly successful, and caught as many rodents as his cage would hold. He then asked what allowance he was to have, but the butler said he had no authority to give his master's liquor away without his permission. Thereupon the rat-catcher asked to see the master, but the butler answered that he was laid up with gout, and that he was just at that moment sitting before the fire reading the papers with his gouty leg on a stool. After a good deal of pressure the butler consented, however, to allow the rat-catcher to have an interview with the old gentleman. When the former was ushered into the old gentleman's presence he found him very comfortably settled down in an arm chair, dressed in a morning gown and night-cap, and with his foot on a cushion.

"Good morning," said the old gentleman, in a voice of great gravity. "What do you want?"

The intruder told him he wanted to know if there was to be any allowance for the rats he had caught.

"No, certainly not," replied the old gentleman. "Get out of my house as soon as you can. You have made quite enough out of me with the rats you have caught."

"I shall take nowt away as does not belong to me," returned the rat-catcher, and he opened his cage and let out all the disagreeable vermin, who soon swarmed all over the room, causing the old gentleman to dance upon chairs and tables, and then to seek safety in flight. The author of this somewhat cruel practical joke also thought it prudent to retire. Such he did without "standing upon the order of his going."

At an early hour one morning, when I was talking to a constable near to Broad Oak Toll Bar, I heard a rustling of leaves on the opposite side of the road. I asked the man to see what it meant. He seemed a bit tremulous, but he went across the road and came back with the answer: "It is a young gentleman who goes to Mrs. Hampson's." I told the constable that I was not quite satisfied with the reply, and so I crossed the road myself, stopped the man, and asked him what he was doing there at that time of the morning.

"I am a respectable man," he replied, with a very strong Scotch accent, "and well known about here. The policeman that is with you knows me."

"Well," I said, "you very much answer the description of a man I want for housebreaking at Crumpsall."

"If you say I am a housebreaker," he retorted, "I will make you pay for it," and again he added that he was a respectable man.

It struck me while I was talking to him that I had seen a photograph a week before and a "route" describing a soldier who had deserted from his regiment in Scotland, taking with him a large quantity of jewellery belonging to one of the officers, to whom he was servant. Finding that his dress and personal appearance, including smallpox marks, corresponded with the description of the thieving runaway, I taxed him with his desertion and delinquency, and searching his pockets, drew forth some small articles of jewellery, which, according to his account, belonged to his sister.

"Now then, look here," I said. "I honestly believe you to be the deserter I am in search of. If you deny the charge it will be my duty to ask you to go with me to Old Trafford Police Station, which is six miles from here at least; and we shall have to walk, as I shall have no means of getting my expenses for a conveyance. It will make no difference to you whether you say you are the man or not, because I can assure you that I will not leave you till someone comes from Scotland to see you. If you are the man, and say so, I will get a cab, because I can then get the expenses."

"I may as well tell you," he made answer, "that I am the man you are looking for."

"You can please yourself," I said, "whether you do or not, but before I get a cab you will have to give me the name of the person robbed"—and this he did at once.

I took the prisoner to Old Trafford, and then conveyed him to Edinburgh, where I handed him over to the authorities, but though I afterwards recovered several articles of the stolen jewellery in Manchester, I never learned what became of the dishonest deserter.

At the time of the Fenian scare in Manchester in 1867, I had been engaged with a number of other police officers on one occasion in searching a number of houses in the neighbourhood of Gorton, and was returning home to Prestwich by Higher Broughton about two o'clock in the morning, so tired that I could scarcely walk, when three men and a woman rushed out of one of the side streets just as I got to the first opening after I had passed the stables of the Manchester Carriage Company. I was armed with a loaded revolver, and a fixed dagger at the end of it, and one of the men came up and asked me what time it was. I very coolly took my watch out of my pocket with one hand, while I held the dagger at the end of the weapon with the other, remarking :—

"Look for yourself what time it is."

The moment I said so the party ran off down the road as fast as they could go, but I was too fagged to start in pursuit, and heard no more about them. I believe, however, that if I had not had the presence of mind to show the revolver in my hand, I should certainly have been overpowered, and if not severely beaten should have been robbed of my watch and the other things of value that I had about me.

On the 11th of February, 1888, a person called at a house

in Crumpsall, and asked that she might be allowed to leave a child, about three and a half years of age, till she went and saw her brother, who was a porter at the local railway station. The permission was granted, but the woman never returned for the little one. I made a good deal of inquiry, and had the facts published in the newspapers, but have not up to the present time discovered who it was who deserted the child.

About a week after the date mentioned a respectable lady and gentleman came to the station, and begged that they might be permitted to adopt the lost one. I told them I had no power to grant such permission, but ultimately I consented that they might have it and adopt it with all the authority I could give them, and so they took it home.

On the following Sunday a man and woman came from Bolton to the station at Crumpsall, desiring to see the child, which they said they believed to be one that had been stolen from them in Manchester, two years before. The sergeant on duty said he could tell them nothing about it, and that they had better apply to me at the Court on the Monday morning. I was at the Court, but neither the man nor woman put in an appearance, though about eight o'clock the same evening the latter came to the station in an intoxicated condition, when she had with her another little child which seemed to be almost starved to death. The woman then told me that she was quite sure the child which had been found at Crumpsall must be hers. I replied that in the condition in which she then was I would not tell her where it had been placed, and that if I had had it in my charge I could not have handed it over to her custody, as I thought she was too drunk to take proper charge of the one she had with her. Next night she and her husband again came to the station and demanded to know where the lost child was. They seemed both to be under the influence of drink, and so I answered that I would not tell them anything about the child that night, as from their manner I believed they would say any child was theirs that was shown to them. I promised, however, that I would make an appointment in the course of a day or two for them to see the deserted one, though I resolved that I would take good care that it was placed amongst other children of the same age. Afterwards I made an arrangement for them to meet me on the Saturday evening at Longsight Police Station.

Accordingly several children from the neighbourhood were brought to the station, and amongst these the lost one was placed, all being about the same size and age. The two persons, accompanied by a friend, came to the station, looked at the youngsters, and selected one, saying they believed that to be theirs. They picked the child up, kissed it, and were about to take it away, when the real mother, who lived in the vicinity, stepped up and disconcerted them with—

"That is my child, not yours."

Then the pair looked at one another, and said—

"This must be the one," pointing to another little one, which was in its turn examined, but when this had been done a policeman's wife stepped forward, observing—

"That is my child. I cannot allow you to have that."

Afterwards the couple went away, saying that if neither of the two children they had selected was theirs, none of the others were. The deserted child was again given over to the lady and gentleman who had adopted it, and I thought I had heard the last of the matter, but on the 27th of February the man came again to the station bringing a vaccination paper with him. I would have nothing to do with him, and told him that my opinion was the same as ever. I advised him to make his complaint, if he had any, to the magistrates, but he has not done so yet.

In my opinion it is a blessing that the lost child was not the one selected by these two persons, for no doubt it is being properly cared for and has a comfortable home with its present custodians.

On one occasion when I was on duty at Davyhulme, I saw a man going about begging. He had a slate in front of him and pretended to be deaf and dumb. Believing he was neither deaf nor dumb, I took him into custody for begging. In the morning I made a twitch—that is, I got a small piece of wood about four inches long and bored a hole at each end, through which I put a string, and tied it, leaving sufficient space through which I put the man's hand, and then twisted it until the string was tight around the wrist. When passing Eccles Church on my way to Court I gave the twitch another twist, which, no doubt, gave the man a good deal of pain, and he at once called out, with an oath, "Are you going to squeeze my hand off?" This I told the magistrate who tried him, and a rare bit of fun he had with him, before sending him to gaol for three months. After his release I found him begging again. He had on a pair of white trousers. One of his arms was in a sling, and a Davy lamp before him. He was sitting on the footpath, but as soon as he saw me he bolted, and I took no more notice of him.

One Sunday evening I was driving with my wife to Crofts Bank, and when near the Big Stone at Stretford I saw a tall fellow loitering on the highway. I had a suspicion from his hang-dog appearance that he was bent upon mischief, or some dishonest course or other. I therefore hurried on my journey, and arriving back again at the Big Stone, I found I was not wrong in my suspicions. I saw the man, but quite a transformation had been made in his appearance. He had taken off his shoes and put his hands in them, and had also obtained some haybands, and wrapped them round his knees. Thus made up, he was walking on his hands and knees with his feet upraised. He had his hat in his mouth, and a good deal of copper had been thrown into it. Taking him altogether I never saw a more pitiable-looking object. I at once alighted from my conveyance, and went up to the man and told him that if he did not get up and go away I would use my whip to him. There were a number of ladies and gentlemen around who sympathised with him, and who raised their voices against me, for what they called my harsh conduct. However, as the man would not get up and go away, I struck him a rather sharp blow on the soles of his feet. This mild form of bastinado had the effect of causing him to jump up and run away as fast as he could, to the disgust of the bystanders, who had been gulled by his imposture.

On one occasion I was returning from Manchester to Newton Heath attired in plain clothes, and when near Albion Street I saw a large number of persons gathered together in one of the side streets. I went to see what was the cause, and observed a young man with his hands on the ground, by this means dragging his body slowly along.

He was begging, and held in his mouth his cap, which seemed to be half full of coppers. On inquiry I was told that the man's lower limbs were paralysed, and that by the means of locomotion he had adopted, he could only cover a distance of a few yards in an hour.

Being incredulous, I went up to the alleged cripple and whispered to him—

"There is a bobby watching you. He says you can walk, and that he intends to lock you up. If you will get up and run with me I will show you how he will miss you." The young man at once rose to his feet, and we ran together for some distance, when he stopped and asked me where the bobby was. Pointing to myself, I replied, "He is here." He looked rather crestfallen. However, I took him to the station, where he told me he had been six weeks in learning the trick. On my way to the court on the Monday I went by way of Shudehill, and when I got to where the Buxton omnibus started from, the driver called out, "I have carried that fellow a score of times and put him on my 'bus, and the last time, whilst I was not looking, he jumped off." He was sent to gaol for six weeks.

Having on one occasion given great satisfaction to one of our magistrates who had a place at Rudheath, in Cheshire, he asked me if I would like a day's rabbit shooting. I replied that although I was not a shot, I should like it very much, and it was arranged that I should go on a certain day, and take a friend along with me. When we got to London Road Station, about half-past six in the morning, my attention was drawn to two gentlemen, each carrying a gun. One wore knickerbockers, and had a knapsack slung on his back, and had got himself up as much like a real sportsman as it is possible to imagine. He walked backwards and forwards, taking aim with his gun at the carriages, and acting so foolishly that I remarked to my friend that I should be sorry to go shooting within half-a-mile of him. To my surprise, however, the man at last walked towards us, and addressing me, said—

"You are Mr. Bent, I presume."

"Yes, I am," I replied.

"Ah!" he went on, "I believe you and I are going shooting together this morning."

"I sincerely hope not," was my involuntary answer, and I at once started to go away, but my friend persuaded me to remain, and suggested that when we got to the other end we might induce the keeper to go with us, and to send his assistant with the other two. Whilst we were on our journey we chatted away friendly enough, and having arrived at Holmes Chapel, on our way to Rudheath, we breakfasted together. At the urgent request of my friend I consented to join the lot, but made up my mind to keep an eye upon the would-be sportsman.

The keeper placed us in order, the sportsman, if I may continue to call him so, being on my left, my friend on my right, and the sportsman's friend on my extreme right. A ferret was put into one of the rabbit burrows, and every man stood ready with his gun. Shortly afterwards the ferret came out again, and the sportsman shot at, but missed it. Upon this, I pointed out to him the necessity of being more careful, as if he shot ferrets, instead of rabbits, his sport might become expensive. As soon as he had re-loaded, and we were again standing in order, a rabbit bolted, and the sportsman fired immediately, threw down his gun, and ran after the coney for a considerable distance. On his return I remarked that it was rather foolish on his part to run after the rabbit unless he had hit it, as it was sure to get into a hole, and out of his reach; but he persisted in saying that it had been hit, and that it could not have gone far down the hole. After this, I had a consultation with the keeper, and he removed us to some hedge-bank, placing my friend and me on one side of the hedge, and the sportsman and his friend on the other, and I distinctly heard him tell the former that if a rabbit came on the top of the hedge-bank, he must not fire, as if he did, he would shoot either Mr. Bent or his friend. Almost immediately afterwards, a young rabbit made its appearance on the top of the hedge-bank, and, I suppose the sportsman could not resist the temptation, for he fired, with the result that about seven or eight pellets entered my body, while sixteen were received by my friend. I need not say that we both jumped about four or five feet high. I threw down my gun and went to the sportsman, but, to my surprise, he argued that he was doing perfectly right, seeing that the rabbit was there. I told him then that if he talked in that strain I should certainly forget the position I held, and give him as much as he had given me. The pain caused by an accident of this sort can, of course, only be imagined by those who have had to go through the same experience. Although I suffered a good deal that afternoon, I felt it my duty to keep up my friend's spirits, for he was certainly much worse than I was. One or two of the pellets had gone into his elbow, and he had to keep his bed afterwards for a considerable time.

When we got back to Manchester, we called at the White Bear, in Piccadilly, and there saw two doctors from the Infirmary. I related to them what had taken place, and they invited me and my friend to go across to the institution, and they would see what they could do for us I was the first to be examined, and was advised to undergo no further punishment, but to allow the pellets to make their own exit. When it came to the case of my friend, it was considered that the pellets were too deeply imbedded in the flesh to be taken out with the forceps, and with a view to create a little bit of merriment, one of the doctors quietly made the observation—

"Some of these pellets will have to be melted out."

Thereupon my friend descended from the board on which he had been lying while being examined a great deal quicker than he got on to it, and he told the doctors that whatever suffering he might have to go through, he certainly would not have the pellets extracted by the melting process.

At the police court after this adventure the stipendiary magistrate appeared to have noticed, or, perhaps, some friend of mine had told him, that I could not very well sit down, and one day he asked me, with a smile, what was to do, that I did not occupy a seat as I usually did. Upon this I had, of course, to tell him how the whole thing occurred, but, as may be guessed, I got very little sympathy either from him or anybody else, and so far as I was able I kept the story secret from those who had not already been made acquainted with it by others.

The only other accident I ever met with in this way was at Holmes Chapel, where I was invited by a friend to go and have a little rabbit shooting. I should think I was quite one hundred yards away from the party, looking into a pit, and was just coming from behind a tree, when a shot was fired by one of my friends, and one of the pellets caught me just on the edge of the bone over the left eye. The wound bled pretty freely of course, and for a time I felt a good deal of pain, but I am happy to say that it passed off without any serious injury to my sight.

CHAPTER XII.

BEERHOUSE OFFENCES.

IT sometimes happened to be my duty to endeavour to detect beerhouse-keepers who were suspected of selling liquor during illegal hours. I remember on one occasion, at Newton Heath, one of the fraternity who, I think, had made up his mind to defy the law in every possible and imaginable way, by selling during prohibited hours, gambling with all sorts of instruments, permitting drunkenness and disorderly conduct, and so forth. He had been fined the full penalty of £5 several times, but this did not appear to have any deterrent effect upon him. One day I caught him offending, and he was summoned for a breach of his licence and again fined £5 and costs, and although he seemed sharp enough to evade the police on a great many occasions, I think that in the case I have mentioned he was rather outwitted.

He was allowed a month in which to pay his fine and costs, and at the expiration of that time he came to the Police Station just as I was going to bed, bringing £5 11s. in penny-pieces. Naturally, I felt very angry at this, but as he insisted upon a receipt, there was nothing left for me to do but to sit down and count the copper. Being annoyed by the man's evident desire to cause me as much trouble as possible, I determined, if I could possibly manage it, to pay him back in his own coin. I therefore commenced to count the coins, and as soon as I got up to 10s., I told him I was afraid I had made a mistake, and that I must go over it again, which I accordingly did. All the while he kept repeating that he was in a hurry to get home, and that he had other business to attend to. I replied that unless he waited until I had finished counting the money, I could give him no receipt, and would not do so.

Having taken about an hour to count the money, I then picked out about twenty pennies, which I showed him were bright with pitching on the table, and about fifty others which were not legible and which I could not accept, he had consequently to be at the trouble of going home for the value of these fifty pennies in silver. And then I gave him clearly to understand that he would be watched in the future; and that if he allowed any pitching on the table for money or money's worth he would be punished for it, as it was distinctly illegal. He informed me then that he had been to a lawyer, who had told him that the law was in such a state that if he were to pay the amount of his fine in pennies he could never be called upon to pay any further penalty, and that afterwards, so far as his house was concerned, the licensing laws would be null and void. He found that the lawyer's advice was not sound, however, for within a short time from that day he was caught again and fined a similar sum.

At another beerhouse, off Holland Street, Newton Heath,

I found a place, adjoining the licensed premises, where theatrical performances were going on nightly; and several of our men, suspecting that all was not right, went into the room after legal hours, but could find nothing. Feeling sure, however, that there must really be something wrong, I went to the place myself, and found that the wall which divided the beerhouse from the room had been painted like a scene. I went and knocked at different parts of the wall, and ultimately found that I was knocking against a board, and not on the bricks; and with very little trouble I was able to move it away, when I discovered a proper bar fitted up in one of the bedrooms of the beerhouse. By this means the beerhouse-keeper had been selling liquor until one and two o'clock in the morning, I believe, for months, if not for years.

A conviction followed my discovery, and shortly afterwards the house was closed up altogether, as without the bar in question it was useless.

On another occasion I was standing in a passage, near to a beerhouse, also in Newton Heath, when I saw two men come up to a side door. One remained there, and the other walked into the entry but as soon as the latter saw me he stood as if he had been mesmerised. Apparently he could not stir nor do anything but stare at me, while I kept my eyes fixed upon him. I heard the other man scratch the door three times, and he was answered by a similar sign. The door was then opened from the inside, and the man called out "a gallon." He received his gallon, and not until he had received it did his companion move an inch from the spot where he seemed rooted, gazing at me. At a whistle from the one who had obtained the beer the spell seemed to have been broken, and he walked away. Then I went to the side door of the beerhouse and scratched three times. It was opened from the inside, and I said—

"Two gallons."

"Go to the devil for it then," replied the beerhouse-keeper.

I then hurried after the two men, and entered the house where they resided almost as soon as they did, and after they had poured out some beer, I told them to be sure and take back the bottle as soon as they had done with it. I need not say that I caused a row in that house, for the man who had obtained the beer believed that his friend had told me all about it. The beerhouse-keeper was convicted and fined £5 and costs.

CHAPTER XIII.

POLICE EXPERIENCES AND PLEASANTRIES.—THE STORY OF A WHISTLE.

WHEN I was first sent on duty from headquarters I was attached to the Pendleton section for four or five months, and my attention was specially directed to the numerous beggars in the district. A constable's uniform was not made to fit so particularly well in those days as is the case now. Perhaps a man who was rather short-necked (like myself) would receive a coat that formerly belonged to a man with a long neck, and *vice versa*, and this happened to be so in my case. I had an overcoat, the collar of which was about four inches too high, and no doubt I looked very comical, as I was often laughed at as I passed along the street. This, as may be guessed, was very annoying to a new-fledged policeman. However, such was the case, and I had to bear it the best way I could.

One day I observed a man going from door to door begging, and, as I said before, my orders were to take every mendicant I found to the police station for further instructions. In those days the police court sat at eleven o'clock, and as

I had happened to apprehend the prisoner about a quarter before that hour, I was directed to take him at once to the New Bailey for trial. It was a very warm morning, and as I had my topcoat buttoned up, and had to walk rapidly, for I had only a short time in which to reach the court, I began to perspire very much, and no doubt I looked a "guy." When we arrived at our destination, the man who had charge of the gates wanted to know if I was going to church?

In my opinion, I had got a very serious case, and one the detection of which might help in securing for me promotion, but to my surprise the magistrate sympathised very much with my first prisoner, and gave him a shilling to go on the road with. I thought then that would be the last beggar I would apprehend, and I did not feel quite sure whether the justice ought to be allowed to have his name retained on the commission of the peace after treating my case in the manner he did.

When I was stationed at Croft's Bank I received instructions from my sergeant at Stretford, one morning, to take all the stolen and unclaimed property under my charge to Pendleton, the headquarters of the division. It so happened that there was some lead—the very lead, I believe, that Jack had carried for me, as narrated elsewhere—and I should think that, what with lead, iron, and so forth, the goods would weigh at least 2cwt. These I had to take in a wheelbarrow, and I had not gone very far before I found I could hardly stick to the wheelbarrow shafts, as my grip had gone. I borrowed a piece of rope and made a pair of slings; but even with this help, when I got to the Pendleton end of Cross Lane I felt quite exhausted, and really could not wheel the barrow any further.

Just then I noticed a young recruit from headquarters on his beat, and therefore went on the footpath with the wheelbarrow. The policeman, not knowing me, came up and asked me to take the wheelbarrow off the footpath or he would take it from me. I replied that I should not take it off for anybody. Feeling a bit annoyed at this, he pushed me on one side, and wheeled the barrow, with a rest or two on the road, all the way to the police station, a distance of about half a mile. Of course he took good care to keep me in front of the barrow, so that he would be ready to give chase if I offered to run away. When we got to the station the inspector opened the door, and asked the officer what he had got there, when I saved him the trouble of answering by explaining the matter myself, adding that I was really so done up that I could not wheel the load any further than I did. That policeman, as my readers may imagine, was subjected to a good deal of chaff from his comrades, and for this reason he had occasion to remember the incident for a long time.

Soon after I attained the rank of sergeant and was sent to Newton Heath. I observed that the men under me were very anxious to see the inside of the letters that were sent to me if I did not happen to be about to open them myself, so I thought I would just play a practical joke that might, perhaps, cure them of this propensity. I therefore procured a soot whistle, similar to those which I remember having seen and used when I was a boy. It consisted of a piece of gaspipe, bent over, and an opening made to give it the appearance of an ordinary whistle. This was filled with soot, and the pipe turned over, so that those who blew into the instrument were sure to receive the contents in their eyes. Having secured an invention of this kind, and an old pistol, I tied them together, and labelled them: "This pistol and whistle were found near to Philips Park, and are supposed to belong to thieves." Along with them I placed a sealed letter, and left them on the table; and hearing one of my men come in, I slipped into the lobby out of sight until he walked into the office. Then I watched his movements through a chink in the door, and saw him first look at the letter, hold it up to the gas, and put it down again; then he got hold of the whistle, and, after reading the label, gave it a tremendous blow, and immediately his eyes and nose were full of soot. He threw it down and shouted out—

"Begad, it is just what I expected."

"Oh, dear me," said I, stepping up to him at once, "you have spoiled my whistle."

He asked me if I would lead him to the sink till he could wash his face, but before I did so I took very good care to have the soap removed, and I left him to his scrubbing, which lasted the best part of an hour before he could get the soot off. This was rather too good a trick to be soon forgotten by the victim, and he afterwards refilled the whistle and left it on the table again in the state in which he found it. Later on in the evening another of our constables came in, whom we watched carefully through the window, it being dark at the time. He examined the pistol and the whistle, and evidently thinking the latter might sound too loudly, he went to the door and blew with might and main. Instantly thereafter he was calling to the first man who had been "sold" to guide him to the sink in turn, and although I, as sergeant, pretended not to know anything about it, I discovered, nevertheless, that the first sufferer had removed the soap just as I had done from him before. This, I suppose, is human nature. When a man gets hoaxed he likes to serve some other person in a similar way.

On the following night I went on duty, and was on till about half-past five next morning, when I took a man into custody, whom I found with about ten shillings' worth of copper in his pocket. I suspected that he had robbed some shop till, and when I got him to the police station I directed a constable to proceed to Oldham inquiring at all the shops on the way, and another to make search in the village of Newton Heath. I also left instructions with the man who had last blown the whistle to remain on reserve with the prisoner, and if nothing more was heard of the money to let him go. Then I took my boots off, pretending that I was going to bed, but instead of doing so I got close to the office door, when I heard the constable say—

"See, old man, you should have had a whistle like this, and if you had blown it when you saw the sergeant, the sound would have rebounded so that he would have missed you and gone the other way."

"May I just try it?" said the prisoner to the officer.

"You may just give it one blow," was the answer, "and no more."

Thereupon the man gave a tremendous blow, which filled his eyes, nose, and mouth with soot, as the constable had charged it rather too heavily.

"I think there is a bit of dirt in it," he remarked, as he gazed at the prisoner.

"No," said the prisoner, "I have blown it all out."

The poor fellow had no pocket handkerchief, but made use of a newspaper by spitting on it and trying to get the soot out of his eyes. No information of any robbery having been received the prisoner was released at seven o'clock, and he made his way down to one of the divisional police stations in a street off Oldham Road, when he met a gentleman who persuaded him to go and report me at once for allowing him to blow the whistle. When he got to the station the inspector asked him if he had come down the chimney.

"No," he replied. "I have come to report Sergeant Bent for making me this figure."

"Has he thrown soot in your face?" queried the official.

"No," the man answered; "but one of the force under him has let me blow at a whistle."

"Well, you were a fool for blowing it," was all the consolation he got. "What had Sergeant Bent to do with it?"

The inspector, who was himself fond of a practical jokes wrote me an account of what had taken place, and asked me to let him see the whistle. I accordingly went down with it to Swan Street, where he was on duty, and explained the whole thing to him, which seemed to give him great satisfaction. I placed the whistle on the counter, and just at that momen a detective inspector and sergeant came in, and, of course, two men so inquisitive as detectives generally are at once set about examining the instrument.

"I believe I have heard this whistle many a time," said the inspector. "I will try it."

He blew it accordingly, and at once both his eyes and

mouth were filled with dust, and he stood almost unable to articulate a word. When he did find his voice he swore that he would stand there until the chief constable came, so I snatched the whistle from him, and said I should have to go home, as the chief might not come that day.

On another occasion a medical man came to my house, and seeing the pistol and whistle, he manifested considerable interest in them, took the latter to the door with a view to see what sort of a sound it would make, and blew both loud and shrill, but, unfortunately, got served like the rest of them. In his case, however, I found some soap.

Of course, the properties of this whistle soon got noised abroad. A friend of mine came to borrow it, after he had paid the penalty, and went into a barber's shop at Newton Heath, kept by a very inquisitive old shaver indeed, who seemed to understand everybody's business better than his own. My friend placed the pistol and whistle on a table, and told the owner of the shop that he must not allow anyone to touch them.

"Well," said the barber, who was rather a droll fellow, "Aw should like t'have a peep at th' whistle, if it maks no difference."

"You may just have one blow," responded my friend; "but only blow once. If you blow twice you'll have Bent here."

There can be no doubt that he did give it a blow to some purpose, for in five minutes afterwards his shutters were up, and he had gone to bed. Next morning I threw myself in the barber's way, and I noticed that his eyes were still bloodshot. In my friend's hurry to get the soot I fancy that he must have scraped some mortar out of the chimney.

"Well, Bob, how are you?" I inquired.

"Eh, my goodness, sergeant!" he replied "Aw've summat to tell yo'. Did yo' lend James a whistle last neet?"

"Well," I answered, "I am not quite sure"—though I recollected in an instant that it was on the previous night I had lent it. "Well," I continued, "what about it?"

He then detailed his experiences with the whistle, and added—

"Eh, sergeant, if ar' Sarah had na sucked my een o neet, aw should na se'n yo' agen."

"You must have turned the wrong end up," I remarked. "But it will be as well, if you should blow it again, to take care to have your eyes shut."

About this time I had to attend the Liverpool Assizes, and one day I went to a public-house in that town kept by a friend, taking good care to have the whistle hanging out of my pocket. I turned my back to give my friend an opportunity of stealing my whistle, and almost immediately afterwards I felt him drawing it out of my pocket, but without pretending to know anything about the matter I walked out from the smoke-room into the tap-room. Almost immediately I heard a laugh amongst the people in the room I had left, whereupon I turned back and found the landlord covered with soot. This annoyed him the more because he had just put on a clean shirt for opening time. He was some time before he could find his way out, none of the men there who were interested in the plot being willing to lead him; but as soon as he got washed and re-fitted up, like previous victims, he expressed a strong desire to see the game practised upon someone else.

Accordingly the whistle was charged with lamp-black, some of which the landlord happened to have in the house, and just about this time a lady called and asked for a Mr. Johnson, whom she was to meet there by appointment. She was told that he was expected almost every minute, and sat down to wait. Now this Johnson was a man well-stricken in years, and extremely fond of a practical joke, and it was agreed between the landlord and myself that when he did arrive every facility should be afforded him for taking the whistle out of my pocket. Shortly afterwards he came into the room, and having shaken hands with the lady who had asked for him, he took a seat. I leaned over the table with my back towards Mr. Johnson, and I had not done so more than a moment when I felt my whistle being taken out of my pocket, and of course there seemed to be a general laugh, seeing that I, as a police-officer, was having my pocket picked, but I took no notice. I went out into the yard where I could see through the window what took place in the room. Mr. Johnson, I observed, turned round, and I could hear him say to the lady—

"I beg your pardon, ma'am, that is a police officer. I have only taken the whistle for fun, and now I'll whistle for him as hard as I can."

Some of the company called out, "Whistle twice," but he replied that he thought once would be sufficient. Then he stood up, holding the whistle with both hands, put it to his mouth, and if ever a man did inflate his lungs in this world it was Johnson on that occasion, for he gave a blow that almost forced the whistle out of his hand, and immediately nothing could be seen of his face but his red lips, swearing what he would do if he could find me. Everyone in the room enjoyed this very much, of course including the lady, who had come to meet the old fellow; but in this case, as in all the others, I had an opportunity of taking the whistle from him before he could open his eyes.

When I was stationed at Davyhulme, as a constable, I had a beat extending to about nine miles in length. Davyhulme Hall was on my round, and was a place which required a great deal of watching. When I got there in snowy weather I used to walk two or three times round the house, for I knew that Mr. Norreys would count my footsteps the next morning, and I invariably walked backwards a distance of several hundred yards, with a view to lead anyone who might wish to go to the house for the purpose of plunder to suppose that I had never come back again. One night I was about the premises, when I fancied I heard the sound of steps coming to "The Jaw Bones," which is known as the back entrance to Davyhulme Hall. I concealed myself close to the entrance, and, while standing there, my old friend Jack, who has been named before in connection with fowl stealing, came up, and exclaimed to himself:—

"See, by jingo, Bent's gone up there twice to-night, and has not come back yet. See his toes go that road, but where are his heels?"

Upon that he walked away, and then I went home, believing the fowls would be safe for that night at any rate. Often in the night time, when I came to detached houses, I was wont to put a bit of stick or stone or anything handy between the gates or the door, so that when I came round again, if I found the article so used still in its place, I knew that nobody had entered. I need not add that if it had been removed that particular house got a thorough good look round.

At that time there were a good many poachers living at Flixton, and I had naturally a great desire to discover in what direction they had gone when away on their night expeditions. The plan which I adopted was to get a bobbin of fine weaver's silk, and fasten it across the door of the dwelling of a supposed poacher, so that when he came out he would carry it away with him for some distance, and by that simple means I could very often guess his whereabouts.

After a month's probation at Preston, when I first joined the force, I was stationed at Pendleton, as I have said; but having been previously accustomed to go to bed at a regular hour, I found it hard at first to keep awake in the night time. My beat was what is known as an hour and a half one, and being very timid at the time, I was really afraid of going to the backs of some of the houses. On one occasion, however, I found what I thought was a favourable chance of having a good snooze at a dyeworks near Cock Robin Bridge. Into this place I went, and took my seat on an improvised settle a short distance from the fire. I had not been there many minutes before I was disturbed by one thing after another falling on the top of my hat, and on making an inspection I found that it was covered with cockroaches. Out I ran upon this discovery, and I need hardly say that, though the night was bitterly cold, I divested myself of my clothes, and subjected them to a close inspection. Later on, I met a friend at Charlestown, who was watchman at another dyeworks, and pointing out how difficult it was for me to get sleep in the daytime, expressed a wish that he would let me lie down for an hour and a half occasionally, on the understanding that he would call me at the end of the time prescribed. I availed myself of this indulgence more than once, till I found that my sergeant had grown suspicious, and so I gave my pleasant practice up.

On a very dark, cold, winter's night, which I well remember, even yet, when there was, moreover, a good deal of snow on the ground, and when my feet were so benumbed that I was hardly able to walk, I made up my mind to go once more to the dyeworks, and ask my friend the watchman to allow me to warm myself. I sat down to the fire in comfortable enjoyment, when presently I felt such a smell of burning leather that I looked up, and found to my dismay that my hat had got in contact with a stove, and had been quite doubled up and burned into a state of uselessness. I had to go out with the not very pleasant reflection that I should get into trouble over the occurrence. It was not long before I heard the sound of the sergeant's stick, and his first question naturally was—

"Why don't you put on your hat?"

"I am warm with walking," was all that I was able to reply.

I was afraid I should get discharged for this if the truth came out, and was utterly at a loss what to do. Next day my wife went to Shudehill Market to see if she could secure the top of an old hat, but she failed in her mission. I tried an adjoining saddler with the same result; and just as I was beginning to despair one of my comrades reminded me of an old soldier's hat which had been thrown aside in the superintendent's hayloft. This I soon obtained, but it so happened that the flange came down an inch too far; and, how it was I cannot tell, I had not the presence of mind to cut it off. On the following day I paraded with this hat on, along with the other men before the superintendent, who was a good-hearted man, though very hot-tempered.

"Bent," he called out, "what the deuce have you got on your head?"

"Best hat, sir," said I.

"Best be blowed. It is a disgrace for you to come here with that; and by Jove I shall make a row about it at headquarters."

I never heard anything more about the matter, but that was the last time upon which I encroached upon the hospitality of the watchman at Charlestown.

Whilst I was stationed at Newton Heath I received a divisional order from the clerk to the superintendent at Eccles, directing that all found and unclaimed property should be forwarded there immediately in exactly the same state in which it had been discovered. So imperatively did he give this order that he frightened some of the sergeants so that they scarcely knew what to do. However, I thought I would play him a practical joke, whatever was the consequence. As it happened, very shortly after I had received the general order, the Rochdale Canal was let off, and at the bottom was found a rope about ten yards long that had been covered with mud, &c. I had this wrapped up in the state in which it was found, and addressed it to the superintendent's office at Eccles, with the additional particulars that it was to be carried with care, and kept "this side up." I knew that the clerk's inquisitive nature would cause him to immediately open the parcel at the superintendent's office. It happened that two other persons were in the superintendent's office when the parcel arrived. After the clerk had looked at the parcel he directed the two constables to examine its contents, but, lo and behold! the constables had not been out of the office one minute when the dirty rope came whizzing across the yard with all the force the clerk could give it. I was sent for by the superintendent to give some account of sending in the rope in such a dirty state. My only defence was the divisional order I had received. The superintendent tried to give me a blow-up, but he could not do it, as he burst out in roars of laughter, and the clerk went out digusted. In a week afterwards the order was cancelled.

About the same time I had a great deal of trouble with a sergeant, who appeared from his manner to have more authority than the chief himself, and who was continually giving directions about matters which his superior had never heard of. For instance, he would send a "route" from one station to another about the simplest affairs imaginable, which necessarily caused the men to neglect their ordinary duty. He had even given an order that when a "route" was put into the hands of one constable he must walk on until he met another to whom he could give it, who must in turn pass it on after writing on the envelope the time at which he received it, and so on until it reached its destination. The annoyance of these messages lay chiefly in their triviality.

I well remember the case of one poor fellow who received in the night time a "route" of this class at Pendlebury. When he got to Prestwich he was unable to find another officer, and had therefore to go on to Crumpsall. As it happened, he did not know an inch of the road; but when he got to Scholes Lane, which verges on Bury Old Road, he came across a finger-post with two or three score of hooks driven into it to prevent the boys from climbing. He was afraid of being late, and the night being dark, he determined to climb up the finger post with the view of ascertaining in what direction Crumpsall lay, but to his great surprise, after getting to the top, he found that he could not get easily down again. The hooks had caught his trousers and torn them, and he had to walk in a very uncomfortable state to Newton Heath, where I received the "route," which was really of no importance, about half-past five in the morning.

Sometime in the year 1856, whilst I was stationed as a constable at Davyhulme, I met the constable, who was doing duty on the adjoining beat at Flixton, one evening about eleven o'clock. We had a walk round Croft's Bank, and when we were passing the Nag's Head public-house, Mrs. Pearson, the landlady, came out and informed us that she was leaving the house on the following morning, and asked if myself and my companion would step in and have a parting glass. It was a very cold night, with snow lying nearly a foot deep in every part of the lane, so I at once accepted her offer, and we walked into the kitchen and seated ourselves before a blazing fire. The landlady brought each of us a pint of spiced beer, into which she had put about half a noggin of whisky, and there we were drinking this dangerous concoction seated before a warm fire after getting out of the cold. This made us very comfortable with one another, and John Bull like I ordered another round, which was to include the landlady. I remembered commencing the second glass, but to be candid, I have no recollection of finishing it, though this much is certain, that I found myself in bed the next morning suffering from rather a severe headache. By no effort of memory could I recall the fact of leaving the Nag's Head, and my first thoughts were naturally given to poor B., who had about two miles to walk, and I felt sure that, though I had escaped, he must have been caught, which would ultimately lead to my being found out as well. I got up and dressed, but I could not touch any breakfast.

On leaving home, I went down Davyhulme in the direction of Flixton, with the view of making a little private inquiry by the way, and while I was doing so a man came out of his house, and asked me if there had been some row with the police the previous night. I asked him why he put the question, and he told me that he had found a hat, a belt, and a logwood stick on the road.

"Oh," I replied at once, "there was not much of a row, but the Flixton policeman was after a suspicious character, and in order to disguise himself, he must have thrown away his hat, belt, and stick."

"I thought so," was his answer. "They are here," indicating his house. "What shall I do with them?"

I asked him to give them to me, which he did, and I took them home, and then went again in search of B., whom I met in Davyhulme Lane. His head was hanging down, and he wore a plain hat, with his uniform coat, but had no belt.

"B., whatever is the matter?" I asked.

"Oh, my goodness," he replied. "I am done this time. I have lost my hat, belt, and stick. Dost know aught about them?"

I told him they were all right, which really relieved the poor man's mind so much that he hardly appeared to be the same individual, as the disconsolate look he had worn immediately vanished.

"Well, B.," I remarked, in joke, though with apparent seriousness, "I believe the sergeant followed you home."

"If he did," said B., "he went a deuce of a way round, for I found myself about five miles away in Cheshire, in the middle of a field, and nearly starved to death. If there has been a robbery on my beat it has not been committed by me, for I have not seen it for the last four and twenty hours."

The sergeant had, I believe, seen us in the public-house, but he went home and made no report.

As soon as I was first stationed at Davyhulme I discovered that the constable I had succeeded had possessed no power whatever over the roughs in the district. In fact, he used to get out of the way if he saw two or three of them together, while it so happened that the officer on the adjoining beat was a man of the same stamp. A simultaneous change was, however, made on the Flixton beat, and during the night the new man there and myself generally patrolled together. As I was parting with him about five o'clock one morning, near my house, from which he had about two miles to walk, by some means or other his foot slipped off the pathway, and in the act of saving himself from falling his face came in contact with my elbow, and he at once called out—

"Oh, curse it, you have given me a black eye."

He started rubbing the injured optic, and continued to do so for a minute or two, when, being desirous of a bit of fun, I put my fingers in the chimney of my lamp, which was generally covered with soot, and asked him to let me feel his eye. I touched up the one and then the other with the black substance, and afterwards, while my hand was in, I made him a moustache, and he actually said, "Good morning," and went away without knowing the ridiculous "guy" he had been made to appear. The next day I met the sergeant at Urmston, about a quarter of an hour prior to the time when the Flixton man was due to be there, but as there were some "routes" of a robbery to be read to the men, I was told that I must remain until D. came up. I waited, and shortly afterwards he came in sight, when, in order that the sergeant might not suspect anything, I told him a story, which caused him to laugh, but this only tended to enrage my comrade, who thought I had been recounting the previous night's experiences. He came up with his teeth clenched, and his stick grasped, making use of ugly words, and was about to strike me when the sergeant prevented him, and asked what was to do.

"Do!" he cried. "That fellow has been telling you all about it."

"All about what?" asked the sergeant. "I am determined to know what this scene is all about."

Thereupon he described the artistic embellishment of his visage I had attempted, and added :—

"I met a great many folk on going home, and as they looked and laughed, I did not know what was to do with me. In fact, I knew nothing about it until my wife came with my breakfast this morning, and she wanted to know where I had been."

I could see that he was not cooling down, and stole away

as quickly as possible, and I did not see him for a week afterwards, and by that time he was all right again. This poor fellow had three children, and as wages were then very low in the police force, he was not able to support his family properly, and used to earn a few shillings now and then by mending shoes for his neighbours when he ought to have been in bed, and thus it was often the case that when night came on I could scarcely keep him awake, especially when we called at his house or mine. Once, when I was doing a little writing, he came into my house and fell asleep in an armchair. I put a table before him with a large can of water on it, and a frying pan on the top of that, blew the candle out, shut the front door, and then made a row in the street by shouting and knocking my stick. In a minute I heard the table, frying pan, and can falling, and my mate crying out—

"Jim, where are you?"

The water came flowing under the door, and I at once opened it, as if nothing had been wrong, and cast the light of my lamp upon the scene.

"You confounded fool," he exclaimed. "What have you been doing to me?" He was then full length on the floor amongst the water, and declared that if ever I treated him so again he would break my head with his stick.

At another time we went into the firehole from which the vineries at Davyhulme Hall were heated, and where there was an old wooden chair. I got that and sat down upon it, and for lack of something better my comrade seated himself upon a very large flower pot. I tried to get him to talk a little, but he soon went to sleep, and I had no one to converse with. I thought that I would try again to cure him of his drowsy propensity, and finding a heavy clinker near the fire-place, I threw it at the flower-pot with all the force I possessed, and smashed it to atoms, while D. dropped to the bottom, and his trousers were torn in two or three places. Out I ran into the darkness, and I could hear him giving vent to very unparliamentary language; but what annoyed him most was that he had to carry away every bit of the flower-pot, as he was afraid that the owner would find out about its being broken. The officer in question, I may add, has been pensioned off for many years.

CHAPTER XIV.

TALES OF TIMIDITY.

IT is but fair to confess that I was not exactly well fitted for the calling of a policeman at the time I joined the force. I was timid rather than bold, and—as the effect of reading cheap trashy literature—was rather afraid of ghosts and hobgoblins, and dared scarcely venture out of the house at night. I was, however, very careful not to let my wife see how easily frightened I was in connection with matters supernatural. I have a vivid remembrance of one Friday night, when my "better half" had gone out shopping, that I began to read some of the penny-dreadful stuff which was popular in those days; and although I lived in a house with only two small apartments down and two upstairs, with cottages on either side of me, I dared not venture to sit by myself without having the door wide open, through being afraid of something "uncanny" coming out of the kitchen or down the chimney, while I would occasionally get up from my chair and go to the door to look to the right and left to see if anyone was passing.

At last I found my candle getting low; and though I knew that we had a supply of "farthing dips" in the small kitchen, it was a long time before I could muster up courage to go and fetch one. It so happened, however, that having seen two persons coming in the direction of our house, I took my nearly-exhausted light, walked backwards feeling for the candles, and having found them, I seized one quickly, and having burned the string attaching it to the rest of the candles, I bolted back into the house. Thinking I had achieved some great feat, I sat down again to finish the article I was reading, when I was suddenly startled by a tremendous crash in the kitchen. Of course, in the circumstances, this was much more than I could stand; so I ran out of the house and stood at the door whistling, and trying to make it appear that nothing was wrong, but now and then peeping into the house to see if anything had really come out of the kitchen or down the chimney; and in that condition I remained till Mrs. Bent returned.

As it was a cold winter's night, when my wife saw me standing there without any covering on my head, she naturally inquired what I was doing; but, of course, it was not likely that I was going to tell her that I had been frightened out of the house. I merely told her that something had dropped off the shelf in the kitchen, and that she had better see what it was. Mrs. Bent thereupon made a search, and found that the candles had fallen into the frying-pan. When she told me, I laughed to myself at what I had done; but I did not tell her that I dared not go into the kitchen to see what was the matter.

This sort of feeling lasted, I may say, for some time after I had been enrolled into the force; so it may be judged how much I was then fit to be a policeman.

Recruits, when taken on at Preston, were wont to be employed to sit in one of the rooms, with a view to answering the bell if any call was made during the night, one man remaining until two o'clock in the morning, when he would be relieved by another who would be on duty until six or seven. On one occasion a number of policemen, myself amongst the number, were seated at the fire just after they had finished their dinners, when one of the men remarked to the others—

"It is a long time since these offices were a nunnery"— an observation which was sufficient to make me fidget, though I pretended to smile.

"Aye," said another, "all their spirits are in the convent," and this again sent the blood to my head, and I began to wish that I was back at the little cottage in Patricroft, where I had resided. The conversation was continued, however, and another of the party went on with—

"I remember when we came here at first, before the wires were attached to the bells, they all began ringing one night just as it struck twelve o'clock, and the man that was on the watch was almost frightened out of his senses, for all the lights went out, and it was a long time before they could get the burners re-lit."

"Ah," put in another, "I remember an old soldier who joined the force at that time, and he said if they would lend him a sword he would watch in that room all night; so they gave him a cutlass. The sergeant went to visit him about one o'clock in the morning, when he found the old veteran in one corner, with his sword in his hand, and his hair standing on end to such an extent that his hat would not stop on his head. The old soldier said that just before the sergeant came in the lids of two baskets that were filled with old boots, and were in the room, had come off, and that the boots had come out and been dancing on the floor. The old soldier threw down his sword, pulled on his hat, and was never seen again."

Stories of this kind got my mind into such a state that it was almost a question with me whether I should not sneak out at the back door and set off for Patricroft; but I determined to remain a little bit longer, and adopted the same course the following evening, when it was my duty to be in the office. When the man whom I had relieved left me, I took a thick stick in my hand, one that I had given sixpence for, closed the door and sat down behind it; but though I shut my eyes, many a time did I feel my heart creeping up to my mouth, and I was so much afraid to stir that I believe if the bell had rung I dared not have answered the outer door.

Next day the conservation again turned upon ghosts, and the queer sights that had been seen about the yard and in different parts of the building, and, strange to say, foolish though it was of me, I was but too anxious to listen to these stories, as the others were only too willing to tell them. At night I took good care to keep the men as long as I possibly could, and promised if they would sit with me I would tell them everything that I had seen in my lifetime. I even went so far as to follow one of my comrades with the view of asking him to stay with me, but, luckily, my heart failed me, and I turned back without telling him the purpose for which I wanted him.

In about half an hour, when the lights were turned out in the office, I took my accustomed place behind the door, armed with my stick, and my eyes closed. Presently, I thought I felt something pressing against the door, and I pushed too, and soon found it was a reality. The door was forced open about an inch; and as I found that there was too much pressure outside, I had to give way, and the door was opened by a man who had been talking to me shortly before. He was covered with a sheet; and as soon as he came into the room, I clutched my stick and gave him a crack on the head which was almost sufficient to kill him. No sooner had I struck the blow than he called out at the top of his voice, "My goodness! What do you mean? It was only nonsense"; and he pulled the sheet off his head, upon which a lump nearly the size of an egg very soon made its appearance.

"It was only a bit of nonsense, man," he said.

"By Jove," I replied, "but you must not play tricks upon me!"

When we were seated at dinner next day the conversation turned upon the incident; and the sergeant, laughing heartily at the predicament the would-be ghost had found himself in, said, referring to me, "That fellow's hair is too red for him to be frightened." But he little knew the state of mind I was in at that moment, even after the lapse of twelve hours.

After this I began to gain courage and to lose my faith in ghosts; and having made up my mind that no child of mine should ever be brought to a similar state of nervousness by reading trashy books, I have never allowed literature of that kind to have a place in my house.

At the time I was stationed at Prestwich as an inspector, there was a very powerful fellow in the neighbourhood—a navvy, who often gave way to drink. He was an awfully wicked man so far as language went, and when in drink he was extremely pugnacious—in fact, he was a terror to other people, and often swore that nothing could frighten him in he world, and declared—to use his own words—that he "cared for neither dog nor devil."

In those days there were no lamps in Prestwich, and near Gardener's Lane the trees overhung the footpath, so that it was very dark during the winter months. One morning, about two o'clock, I had got under these trees, when I heard this navvy coming towards me, and as it happened he was cursing and making a great noise, I thought I would try whether he was as brave as he professed to be, and I therefore put a strong logwood stick, which I generally carried with me, against my stomach, and pointed it towards the man. Coming up, he ran against the other end of the stick without seeing me. After feeling around and under and over the obstruction, but in vain, for some tangible evidence of what was pressing against him, he retired a few paces, and exclaimed loudly: "Are you from heaven or from hell?" Receiving no answer, he ran away as fast as his legs would carry him, screaming with terror, thus showing that he was only a coward at heart, with all his empty boasting.

I have frankly confessed, at my own expense, that I was too timid to be a policeman at the time I became one, though it was not long before I got over the feeling. More than ten years after all trace of timidity had left me, I thought I would try if anyone was as easily frightened as I had been. When I was a sergeant at Newton Heath, there were two constables lodging with me, who were not by a long way so cleanly in their habits as I should have liked them to be. One, named Patrick Kelly, had been a soldier, and I thought I would try, if I possibly could, to frighten him. His beat at this time lay through the cemetery, down Kilshaw Brow, and by, I may say, one of the most dismal parts of Newton Heath. One winter night, when it was raining heavily and extremely boisterous, I quietly asked him—

"Paddy, do you see anything when you are on that beat?"

"No sergeant," he answered, "what is there to be seen?"

"Oh, nothing," said I, "You have been a soldier, or else I would not have mentioned it."

This did not satisfy him, so he came to me again, and asked the same question.

"Well, to tell you the truth," I replied, "they do say two persons were found murdered under that culvert, near to the cemetery, and that every night, between twelve and one o'clock, there is something white springs up from under it. Never mind," I added. "Shut your eyes and walk straight through. You have never done anything to make you afraid, and it will be all right for you. That is what I always do myself. It is a funny feeling, but you being an old soldier will never think anything about it."

"Oh, no," he responded, "I am not afraid,"

I took no further notice, but about five minutes afterwards Kelly came to me saying—

"Sergeant, would you mind getting someone to change beats with me?"

"No," I made answer. "I do not think any man in the division would have that beat only an old soldier. But never mind, Paddy. There is nothing of any moment."

"I will never go out again at night," he returned, "if I have nothing to defend myself with but a baton."

He then began to strip off his uniform, and all I could do with the view of inducing him to put it on again had no effect. He was not, he said, going to shut his eyes if anything was coming in front of him. Kelly actually left the service, and I heard that he had rejoined his regiment.

In my young days, when I lived at Eccles, which, as I have said, was my birthplace, most of the dead from a very large district were, I remember, interred in Eccles Churchyard. This was in the days of the "Resurrectionists," as they were called, and watch clubs were formed, and the members were appointed by turns, two at a time, to keep nightly vigil over a grave for about a fortnight after a funeral. This, of course, was done with the view of preventing body-snatchers from removing the corpses and selling them to the doctors, or medical students. There is a public-house on the high-road, opposite Eccles Church, which was then kept by a woman named Alice Fish, and she used to allow these watchmen the use of the taproom during the night. It was sometimes the case, too, that before Mrs. Fish retired to bed these men obtained supplies of rum and other spirits sufficient to last them the whole night through.

Two of them got very drunk on one occasion, when they had to watch a grave adjoining an open one, which was ten feet deep. In those days the gravedigger received a remuneration at the rate of a shilling per foot after a depth of six feet had been reached, but at any rate the one I am alluding to was ten feet deep. About two o'clock in the morning, one of these drunken watchmen went out to make an examination to see if all was right, but somehow he got too near to the open grave and tumbled in. The fellow called out very lustily for his companion, who was in the public-house, but could not make him hear, and so he coolly went to sleep in the grave.

During the time he was in the excavation, a man named Joe Griffiths, a very timid sort of person, who resided in Vickers Street, found that he was rather late in going to his work; and it became a question with him whether he should run across the churchyard, which was the nearest way to the mill where he was employed, or go round by the road. He thought that if he dared go across the churchyard he would just be in time; but if he went by the road he would be late and consequently fined. Accordingly, he determined to take the short way, and keep his eyes on the factory windows, which were lit up, opposite the churchyard, so that he should not be frightened. This he did, but unfortunately dropped into the grave where the watchman was, when the occupant cried out—

"What the d—— dost thou mean?"

It is said that Joe Griffiths, although only about 5ft. 5in. in height, jumped out of the grave very easily, and he certainly was never known to cross the churchyard again during the dark hours of night.

This Griffiths once told me a very amusing story, to the

following effect: His wife had been seriously ill, when a clergyman, whom he named, called to see her; and, on leaving, asked him to come to the vicarage, or whatever might be its designation, and he would send the sick woman something tasty. Joe shaved himself, put on his best clothes, and went to the house with a saucer, which he had been told to bring with him, when, to his intense surprise, the clergyman made him a present of two pickled onions! Upon his honour, Joe assured me that this instance of parsonic waggery was a veritable fact.

Soon after joining the force I was on detective duty at Newton Races. The racecourse was some distance from a barber's shop. I was in need of a shave, and I saw a travelling barber going about the course. It was early in the day, before the races had begun, and there were few people on the ground. The man invited me to have a shave, and everything appearing favourable I agreed, though not without hesitation. I sat on a tub, and after a copious lathering the barber rubbed his razor briskly on his hand, and proceeded to apply the implement to my chin. I shall never forget the agony of that shave, for the razor-edge was as nearly like a saw as anything I could think of. The pain was intense, and the misery of having to allow the fellow to finish the business was something to remember. I determined to see another victim if possible, so kept my barber in view, until a rough, navvy-looking man accosted the barber and requested him to give him a shave. The preliminary lathering passed off all right; but, on the first stroke of the razor, the navvy jumped up, and with his fist dealt the barber a tremendous blow on the head, which knocked him down. The navvy wiped off the lather with his coat-sleeve, and with an oath asked the barber if he was using a grater. This incident of the navvy quite satisfied me, and I went on my duty.

Some years ago, I remember, an abstainer went to Irlam to address a meeting in a school on "Total Abstinence." The school was crowded when the lecturer arrived, and amongst the audience there was a man who was very fond of beer, and who would at any time undertake to drink half a gallon of that liquor at one draught. The lecturer commenced by asking if any person would like to taste a quart of beer out of which he said he intended to burn blue devils, just to show that there was no deception. The man replied, "I don't mind trying it, just to see what it is like." The lecturer handed him the jug, and he drank every drop of the beer, and, smacking his lips, observed, "Aye, and gradely good ale it is. I wish I had another quart." Of course, another quart had to be obtained for the lecturer to perform upon, but he declined to let Tommy try it. This trick rather damaged the lecturer, as the audience did nothing but laugh.

To give the people's mind a turn from the beer, the lecturer produced a number of herbs, and amongst these there were two kinds of nettles—one, the red, or rank nettle, which bears a red flower and will sting very keenly, and the other a nettle bearing a white flower which does not sting. While the lecturer was describing the qualities of some small flowers, Tommy and another man got behind him with a gum pot, and took the red flowers from the rank nettles and gummed them on the white nettles, from which they took the white flowers and put them on the red stalks. Shortly after the lecturer, who was not aware what the two men had done, picked up one of the red nettles, turned up his coat sleeve, bared his arm, and said: " Now, ladies and gentlemen, this is what is called the dead or white nettle. You see this will not sting;" and then dashed the nettle on his arm. He had no sooner done so than blisters rose on his skin, and the lecturer, in pain, yelled, " Rat it, but it does sting though! I can say no more on this subject to-night," and he packed up and went away.

CHAPTER XV.

FEMININE ATTEMPTS AT EXTORTION.

THERE are some women in the world, and by no means few in number, who appear to make a living by preying upon the fears of the opposite sex.

A young gentleman of means, who had not been long married to a lady in his own rank of life, wrote to me on one occasion to ask if I would kindly give him a call the next time I passed his house. Having known him for a number of years, I did so, as a matter of course; and, after a brief preliminary conversation, he asked me if I knew a Mrs. S., who was said to be the wife of a sea-captain, who sometimes left her alone on shore for three or even six months at a time. My reply was that I did know her, but that I did not regard her with very high respect. She was "fast," whilst I did not think she was as respectable as she ought to be—that, in fact, she was what would be called a "high-stepper," and was by no means fit to be trusted.

After some further conversation, my friend confessed to me that there had been an intimacy between them prior to his marriage, and that he was afraid that if this got to the ears of his young wife it might be the means of causing them great unhappiness, if not even leading to a separation. He added that the thought of this had almost driven him mad, and that the woman had been threatening of late to expose him if he did not pay down a certain sum of money, whilst she declared that she had given birth to a child, of which he was the father.

I asked him how he knew she had been delivered of a baby; and he informed me that she had sent for him to a public-house on the previous Tuesday to look at it, but that he did not go. My advice to him was not to see her or make any compromise at all in the matter if he had reason to believe that he was not the father of the child. He assured me that he was not, and also that he had not seen the woman for a year or two. He seemed very despondent; and as I knew the lady he had married, I made up my mind to assist him by every means in my power.

Accordingly, I asked my superintendent for a day's leave of absence; and, after some inquiry, I discovered that the person referred to was living in rather a low part of Manchester. It had so happened, however, that at the Assizes held at Manchester, prior to the interview referred to, I had found this woman and a man in a part of the Court where they ought not to have been, and had ordered them out, so that I was afraid that she would not speak to me if I chanced to meet her. All the same, I thought I would try.

I failed to ascertain the number of the house in the street

in which I had been told she lived, but after I had passed up and down it, I saw a man whom I knew to be a returned convict standing at a cottage door, and while my attention was turned towards him, lo and behold! the object of my search came to the door of the same house, and to my surprise called out—

"Mr. Bent, how are you?"

We entered into conversation, and immediately afterwards the man went away, leaving the woman and myself chatting at the door. She asked me if I was going to stand treat, and I said "Yes," and gave her money to fetch a pint of stout, as she said she could drink one. We soon got to talking about the locality where the gentleman to whom I have referred resided, and in the course of our conversation she asked me if I knew him well.

"Yes," I replied, "I have known him for many years—in fact almost since I joined the police force."

"I do not think you know so much about him as I do," she returned. "Have you seen the large house he has got? Do you know what a lot of money he has got with his wife?" and before I could answer she went on with, "I mean to have some of that. I will frighten his soul out of him."

"Oh," I remarked upon that, "I do not quite know what you mean, but I hear you have had a baby."

"Yes," she responded, "and a pretty little thing too."

Then I asked if the skipper, meaning her husband, had seen it.

"Oh, yes," she answered, "he was delighted with it. It was scarcely ever off his lap."

I felt then in my own mind that my friend would be clear

as far as the baby was concerned. We continued chatting for some time longer, and then I observed:—

"I suppose you had a nice bit of fun last week?"—and I named the night on which she had sent for my friend to see the baby at an hotel. "I think you had a nice bit of fun," I continued. "I saw you, and I thought you were at some of your old tricks."

"What do you mean?" she earnestly inquired.

"Why," I replied, "did you not see me there? You had taken rather too much drink, no doubt; but I noticed you let that wooden dummy drop which you had brought for the gentleman to see."

"Oh, my goodness!" she cried. "Do you know about it?"

"Yes," I replied, "I do. I know all about it. And now let me tell you, as a friend, that if you do not mind you will get into very serious trouble. I saw the young man you let out of this house just now. I know him to be a returned convict, and therefore I have some idea as to the life you are leading. Now do you really know the seriousness of the course you are adopting with regard to the gentleman you have named?" I saw her change colour from white to red and from red to white, but as I proceeded with, "Are you aware that anyone endeavouring to extort money by threats is liable to fifteen years' penal servitude? and I may tell you, as a police officer, that if this gentleman only laid a charge against you to me for endeavouring to obtain money by threats, I should certainly apprehend you without waiting for a warrant. It is a most serious matter, and I am exceedingly sorry that you should have carried it so far as you have done;

but so long as you keep company with such men as the one I have just seen leave your house, it is only conduct of this kind that may be expected on your part."

Ultimately she began to cry, and confessing that the plot had been made up between herself and others, begged earnestly that I would forgive her. Thereupon I told her that so far as I was concerned I would take no further notice of the matter, unless I was compelled to do so by the gentleman from whom she had been endeavouring to extort money. I added that I sincerely hoped she would leave the house and the street in which she lived, and no longer keep company with returned convicts.

I returned to the gentleman who had sought my services and made my report, which, no doubt, greatly relieved his mind, and never from that day to this have I, to my knowledge, seen the woman or heard anything about her.

Having occasion at one time to be engaged at the Assize Courts in a case of perjury, I was accosted by a gentleman who asked me if I knew a certain young woman named Miss B., who lived in the village where I then resided. I replied that I had seen her, but that I had been such a short time in the district that I did not know much about her. He told me that he had kept company with her, but that she knew as well as he did that he never intended to marry her. He was about to be married to a very respectable lady, but Miss B. had sent him a number of threatening letters, and he was afraid that if this came to the knowledge of his betrothed it would give rise to a great deal of unpleasantness, and she not only declared that she would raise an action for breach of promise, but that she would be present at his wedding and kick up a tremendous row.

I asked him if he had ever promised her marriage, or had paid her money to give him up, or, in fact, made any arrangement whatever? He assured me that he never had, and I then said that I would see if I could assist him. On the same evening I went to Miss B.'s door and as soon as she saw me in police uniform she demanded in a loud voice to know my business.

"Quite right, Miss B.," I said. "If you want me to tell my business in the hearing of passers-by, I shall do so; but if you wish me to talk to you in private, I am willing to do that; and I should advise you to adopt the latter course."

"Mr. Bent, will you come in?" she then responded. I complied with the invitation, and opened fire at once by stating to her that I had been informed she was in the habit of sending threatening letters to the gentleman I have alluded to, to the effect that if he did not pay certain sums of money she would expose him. "Now," I went on, "I think, as a neighbour, I may fairly tell you that you are adopting a very foolish and dangerous course. Indeed Mr. C. can, if he thinks fit, produce these letters to the bench to-morrow, and apply for a warrant for your apprehension on a charge of endeavouring to extort money by threats, and I think I ought to advise you to stop this sort of thing. If you consider you have any legal claim, put your case in the hands of a solicitor, but do not send any more threatening letters, for if you do you will get into very serious trouble indeed."

She at once began to cry, and calling in her mother, asked her, in my presence, if Mr. C. was not the only gentleman she had kept company with in all her life.

"Of course he is," answered the mother. "Yes, I am sure he is."

Upon this, Miss B. ceased crying, and, becoming very lively, told me of a great number of offers which had been made to her, all of which she had refused, as she thought there was no man like the one I was representing. She thanked me for my advice, however, and promised that she would not send any more threatening letters, nor go to the wedding—a promise which I have reason to believe she afterwards kept.

During our conversation she asked me if I knew a certain solicitor in Manchester, and I replied that I knew him very well.

"Oh, Mr. Bent," she commented, "he is a rum fellow. I know many a solicitor in Manchester."

Whether she intended this as a sort of threat for me, because I had spoken to her on the other subject I cannot say, but at the Assize Courts on the following day I saw the solicitor she had named, and told him in a sort of chaffing way, and for a bit of nonsense, that Miss B. had sent him her compliments, although in reality she had done nothing of the sort. My legal friend was rather indignant, and told me he did not want her compliments.

"It is all right," said I. "I will tell her when I see her."

Later in the day, however, he came to me and said—

"Oh, Bent, I will tell you what I know about that Miss B. A friend of mine got into her company a time or two when he was drunk. Some time after this, my friend, who was also my client, was about to get married to a highly estimable lady, whereupon Miss B. sent him a number of letters saying that he had promised her marriage, and that she would destroy herself if he did not carry out his promise. Finding that this method of procedure was of no avail, she began to be abusive, and ultimately ended by sending some very bad letters, threatening what she would do if he did not send her a certain sum of money, and stating that any letters bearing on the subject must be sent to her through her solicitor. A man came to my office after that, but not being a solicitor I refused to see him; but I informed him in a letter that I would certainly take proceedings if she sent any more threatening missives, and from that day to this I have never heard anything more about the matter."

I asked the lawyer when this happened, and he said that it was about eighteen months or two years before. Then I told him my story about Mr. C., which seemed to be quite on a parallel with his, and showed clearly enough to me that Miss B.'s heart had been won by two men at the same time. I suggested to my friend that he should employ the solicitor I have been alluding to, and he did so. Afterwards the legal gentleman showed me a letter which he had forwarded to Miss B. in the following terms:—

"Madam,—Having heard that your heart has been stolen twice about the same time by different men, I am instructed by Mr. C. to take the case in hand, and all letters relating to this matter must please be forwarded to me. Kindly remember, as I told you on a former occasion, I do not deal with persons not duly qualified as solicitors."

I need hardly add that no other letters were found to be necessary, though I regret to say that the same young woman, if I am rightly informed—and I believe I am—was involved in many other cases of the kind.

While a constable, I had occasion to go to Liverpool, to apprehend a person, but did not succeed till nearly midnight— too late to return to Manchester. I asked a policeman where

I could get a clean bed for the night, and he took me to a provision shop. At about one o'clock I was shown my bedroom—an attic—the window of which I was unable to open. Not feeling satisfied of the perfect cleanliness of the place, I determined not to go to bed, and sat looking out of the window. Just as daylight began to break I heard a noise in the street, and presently saw a well-dressed young woman come out of a house and go up the street, and immediately I heard a scream. A respectable-looking man, wearing a white hat, frilled shirt, and otherwise well-dressed, came running up to her, and asked the woman what he could do for her. She replied, "My pa has come home in drink, and for God's sake do come and prevent him from killing ma." She then ran into the house, followed by the gentleman, who was not there more than two minutes when he was pushed out backwards by the woman. He was without hat or necktie, and his shirt front was torn out. The woman said, "Pay for the room! pay for the room! you mean scoundrel!" The man replied, "I have had no room. I will fetch a policeman." He went away, and presently returned with a policeman, to whom the man explained the circumstances which led him into the house. In answer to the policeman's knock, the young woman came to the door and complained that the gentleman having met her in the street had gone with her to her house, and had afterwards refused to pay for the room. Notwithstanding the gentleman's protestations of innocence the policeman was evidently inclined to believe the woman, and told the man he ought to pay. The man repeated the story how he had been deceived; and the policeman, to put an end to the matter, said to the young woman, "Give him his hat."

She brought the hat, and smashed it between her hands. She then threw it at the owner, calling him a "shabby devil." The poor man went his way much dilapidated as regarded his wearing apparel, his dresscoat having the laps torn off, and the rest of his fine clothes much damaged, and, no doubt, much hurt in his mind—a victim of circumstantial evidence.

The foregoing cases of female extortion which I have just narrated are only three out of a great many which could be given, as they are of frequent occurrence, but for the sake of morality I need not further enlarge upon them. The cases I have given, however, serve to show how very easily men can be ensnared and duped by designing women, and unthinkingly bring upon themselves misery and trouble. In such cases it very often happens that instead of at once taking proceedings against the person demanding money, and by this means extricating himself from the toils into which he has been entrapped, the victim will again and again submit to the demands made upon him, rather than face the exposure and disgrace which the female harpy into whose clutches he has fallen threatens to bring upon him, and this, too, even when, as in the case last mentioned, there is not the slightest foundation for the alleged wrongdoing.

CHAPTER XVI.

MISCELLANEOUS—PHASES OF DRUNKENNESS.

ON the first day when I attended the New Bailey court after my appointment to the rank of inspector, Mr. Trafford, the Stipendiary, seemed to be actuated by a desire to chaff me a little. The court was crowded when my predecessor, the late Mr. Superintendent Chadwick, introduced me to the bench as the newly-appointed inspector.

The magistrate at once turned round to me and said—

"Oh, you are now Mr. Inspector Bent, are you? I suppose the sergeants of the division, as well as the constables, will now have to salute you as Mr. Inspector Bent?"

Just at this moment a respectable lady came into the court and was inquiring from one of the officers how she was to go on. Mr. Trafford thereupon called out to me, "Mr. Inspector Bent, what does that lady want?" I said I was not aware, but I would inquire. "Very well," he responded, "Mr. Inspector Bent, do so," and he went on for some time in this manner, causing roars of laughter amongst the people who filled the court. I went to the lady and ascertained that she wanted a summons against the owner of a dog. When I returned to the witness box I was saluted by the stipendiary with—

"Well, Mr. Inspector Bent, what does the lady want?"

I replied that she had come for a summons against the owner of a dog by which she had been bitten. Turning to the lady, he said, "Well, ma'am, you may return. I only deal with puppies here," and the applicant went away apparently dissatisfied with the reception accorded to her.

A man named Jimmy Gayner, who had been imprisoned, perhaps, a hundred times, and who invariably tried the strength of every new officer coming into the district, was brought up one time before the Stipendiary on a charge of breach of the peace. Mr. Trafford was reading a newspaper when Gayner was brought in, but looked up at him and queried—

"Well, my old friend, you are here again?"

"Yes, Mr. Trafford, I am."

"Do you ever work, Gayner?" asked the magistrate.

"Sometimes," coolly responded the prisoner, "but I am a haymaker, and cannot work at this time of the year"—it was then about Christmas. This raised a laugh amongst the audience, but Mr. Trafford did not seem inclined to be treated in that way, and his reply was—

"Well, my friend, we shall need no haymakers for the next three months, so how it is, so I will send you inside here."

Gayner, was accordingly committed for three months, in default of finding sureties—a thing which he was never able to do.

The same man was brought up on another occasion in the summer time, on a charge of disorderly conduct, and assaulting the police.

"Well, my old friend," said the stipendiary, addressing him. "I thought you were a haymaker, and that you would be busy at this time of the year? How did you get on last time. Did you find bail?"

"No, I did not."

"Oh, you could not, I suppose you mean? I think you are not a haymaker, Gayner. I think you are an ice-breaker; and I will therefore send you back again for another three months, and by that time perhaps the frost will have set in."

One Monday morning when I was stationed at Newton Heath, I looked into the cells and found three warehousemen all charged with having been drunk and disorderly during the previous night. Now, at this time Mr. Trafford always expected a prisoner to be handcuffed, no matter with what offence he was charged; but these men said they all had families, and pleaded with piteous earnestness that they might not be taken through the streets with snaps upon their wrists. For some time I told them I could not interfere, and that the constable would be responsible for their safe keeping until they were discharged by the magistrate.

Feeling sorry for them, and having a desire to prevent them from losing their situations, as they said they would do if it came to their employers' ears that they had been locked up for drunkenness, I thought the matter over, and a happy idea struck me. I looked at their trousers, and finding they were all pretty widely made round the waist, I said to them—

"Well, now this is a serious affair for me. If any of you men ran away I should lose my position."

They one and all protested they would not run away.

"Then," I observed, "I will take you to the court without handcuffing you upon one condition, and that is, if you will let me have your braces," for I knew very well that it would be impossible for them to run and hold their trousers up at the same time. This they agreed to, and I did not handcuff them. Each man put his hands in his trousers pockets, and we started off to the court, and they did not make the least attempt to give me the slip. When we got to the New Bailey Bridge it happened, however, that I met the stipendiary going in the opposite direction. When the case was over Mr. Trafford called me into the witness box and said—

"Bent, thóse three men I have just fined were not handcuffed."

"No, sir," I replied, "they were not."

"Well, then," he asked, "do you know what would have happened if any of them had escaped?"

"I know the responsibility I have taken upon myself," I returned, "and that they could not have run very far without being apprehended."

"What, young men like them not run?" exclaimed Mr. Trafford. "What would prevent them?"

"Well, sir," I answered, "they pleaded so earnestly not to be handcuffed that I agreed not to do so if they would each give me their braces. You may depend upon one thing, sir, they would not run very far nor very quick without their suspenders."

"Where are the braces?" inquired the stipendiary, very

sharply, and I took them out of my pocket and produced them to him. Mr. Trafford then leaned back in his chair, and laughed until he was almost in convulsions at the device I had resorted to. When he had somewhat recovered, he said to Mr. Rutter, the magistrates' clerk, that it was one of the best tricks he had ever known in his life.

Having had occasion to complain to the sergeant of the Old Trafford section about men loitering around the houses in the neighbourhood, and with a view to test how he was going on with respect to them, I dressed a dummy up, fixed it in my trap, and put it in the coachhouse. Then I said to the sergeant that it would not at all surprise me if I found a man in the stable or one of the outhouses next morning if I got up early enough. I then walked away, but not so far but that I could hear a conversation that afterwards passed between the sergeant and a constable. The former said he would take precious good care that no loiterer or vagrant was found about the yard, or he (the sergeant) would never hear the last of it, and he added, "I will go and look at it now." The coachhouse was dark, and almost as soon as he had opened the door I saw him jump about two yards back, crying out to the constable—

"Blowed if there isn't a man sitting there now!"

After some conversation between the two officers I heard the sergeant say, "I believe the fellow's asleep. I will fetch him off that box with my stick;" and suiting the action to the word, although I did not see it, he gave the dummy a tremendous blow on the back, which caused it to fall to the ground; but if he had jumped two yards away before, I am sure that he then jumped four.

About five years ago a baker came to the police-station at Old Trafford to serve the men with bread. He was a very decent fellow, but extremely talkative, and the constables used to argue with him and to tease him by every means in their power. One day his poor horse had been kept waiting in the yard for nearly an hour, when some of the men went out, took the horse and van into my coachhouse, unyoked the horse, and put him in the shafts again, but turned his head where his tail should have been. One of the officers who had gone out slipped in shortly afterwards, and remarked that he had met a bread van going at a quick pace down Union Street. The baker at once called out that it must be his, and rushed off in the direction indicated, but not finding any trace of it, he returned to the station, and it having occurred to him that the horse might be somewhere about the yard, he opened the coachhouse, and saw the van, but owing to its being very dark he could not see the horse.

"Oh," he cried out, "here it is;" and he went off to get hold of the horse's head, but at once shouted, "Somebody has cut its head off."

A laughable occurrence took place at Old Trafford Police-station one afternoon. A sergeant, since dead, who was then in a delicate state of health, came to the station in company with a drunken man. I at once discovered that the officer had taken too much liquor, and asked him what was the matter.

"Oh, sir," he answered, "I have come to report this man for interfering with me in the execution of my duty."

The man, who was standing by, and who was certainly very much under the influence of something stronger than water, cried out—

"That is a lie. He vexed me when I was in the beerhouse, and he ought to be locked up. I said nothing to the sergeant, but he came in and pulled me out."

"No," contradicted the sergeant. "I believe it was you that pulled me out."

I saw that it was impossible to tell which of the men began the row, so I let the stranger go, while the officer was reported and punished by the chief constable.

While I am writing on the subject of drunkenness, I may state that I have, in about three or four cases during my service in the police force, found men who had imbibed too freely of alcoholic stimulants walking backwards in the streets, and I have had the greatest difficulty in persuading or convincing them of the fact. They would pay no heed to my remonstrances until they fell, bringing their heads into contact with the ground. They invariably seemed all right after they regained the perpendicular. I mention this as a curious fact.

Once, when acting as a detective-constable, I found a man lying down on the ground intervening between Pomona Gardens and the river Irwell, with every pocket that he had crammed full of bottles, while he had actually put some up the legs of his trousers and secured them by a string tied at the bottom. He had fallen down, and could not by any means rise up again. As soon as I could relieve him of some of the bottles I took him back to the proprietor of Pomona Gardens, who declined to press any charge against him, and he had to be liberated, although he had taken at least two dozen bottles of beer from the premises.

Several times I have seen men who, though in a drunken

condition, could really walk very straight, stop suddenly and undress themselves, and then lie down in the road under the supposition that they had gone to bed. Even when I have spoken to them they have ordered me to leave their bedrooms, telling me I had no right there.

On one such occasion I was standing in Shudehill Market, when a man came walking through it and went down some cellar steps. When I and a constable entered the place we found him entirely naked. We told him to come out of the cellar, but his reply was—

"Even if you are policemen, you have no business in my bedroom. Get out."

Finding we could not drive any sense into him, we got him out of the cellar and took him to the Swan Street Police-station; but all the way he threatened us with a prosecution for entering his bedroom without a search warrant. After the poor fellow had slept a bit, he was allowed to go home.

A good many years ago an old lady, about sixty years of age, whom I shall call Mrs. M., was garotted near the Roman Catholic Chapel at Barton. Information was at once given to the sergeant and myself, and we made together a good deal of inquiry. A cap and belt, supposed to belong to the thief, were found at the spot where the robbery had taken place, and it then became our duty to discover to whom the articles belonged. We soon found out that their owner was a bricksetter's labourer, who had up to that time been residing in Barton, but who had decamped since the crime was committed. He was, however, followed and arrested.

Mr. M. himself was a retired gentleman, and he went by the name of "Billy Fairplay." He was rather a corpulent gentleman, and the reason he was honoured with the sobriquet named was because he used to take his rounds forenoon and afternoon, and "fairly" divide his custom among the different publicans of the district, for, having visited one and called for twopenny worth of gin, and having drunk it, he would toddle on to the next. All those, in fact, who held licences seemed to have a fair share of his patronage. He was rather deaf, and anyone having to speak to him had to do so in a loud tone of voice.

The day after the prisoner's apprehension being Mid-Lent Sunday, the sergeant and I agreed to meet in Eccles on that day, but when the time came I found that my colleague had taken more drink than he was accustomed to. I stuck to him, however, and we walked about the place for a considerable time. Ultimately we met with Mr. M., and the sergeant accosted him with—

"Well, we have got some information."

"Very well," said Mr. M., "we must go to some public-house till you tell me what it is."

We accordingly did so, and went into a private room, and when the sergeant was asked what we were going to take he replied, "Brandy and soda." This was a rather more costly drink than the old gentleman was in the habit of calling for, and he looked at us with some amazement, but nevertheless he paid the reckoning, and then inquired what was the additional evidence we had got.

"The cap and belt can be sworn to," was the sergeant's reply.

"That is very good," commented Mr. M. "The vagabond will be convicted now."

After having drank off the brandies and sodas, we left Mr. M., but I soon found out that the potation had not sobered the sergeant very much. In the course of about half an hour we again met with our entertainer, when the sergeant, having forgot, I presume, that he had already seen him and told him about the evidence, said—

"Oh, Mr. M., we have some more information for you."

After some apparent hesitation, "Billy Fairplay" remarked that we would have again to go to some public-house. Having entered the establishment of this kind nearest to hand, Mr. M. again asked the sergeant what he would have, and his response was, "We will have brandies and sodas." Mr. M. seemed more staggered than ever to think that we should cause him to be at so much expense, but he paid frankly enough, though he had contented himself by calling for two-pennyworth of gin.

"Now, then," he asked, "what is this valuable information you have got this time?"

"Oh," returned the sergeant, unblushingly, "the cap and belt can be sworn to."

"Oh," cried Mr. M., in a loud voice, "the cap and belt could be sworn to before."

We all drank up, however, and left the public-house, but had not been away many minutes when the sergeant, no doubt forgetting all about what had taken place, met the old gentleman for the third time. He did not seem in a particularly good humour then, but not suspecting that my superior officer had taken too much, shook hands with him, and said to him—

"What have you fresh now?"

"We cannot tell you in the street," responded the sergeant. "We must go to some public-house, and then I will tell you."

"Can you not give me a hint?" returned the other, apparently not liking the idea of having to pay again for "brandies and sodas."

"No," said the sergeant, "we will have to tell you in some private place;" and after a little hesitation, "Billy Fairplay" observed, "Let us go into this public-house."

We went once more into a private room, and the same course of liquors was called for and consumed, while the sergeant reiterated the formula of the cap and belt being sworn to.

"Confound the cap and belt," yelled Mr. M. at the top of his voice. "They have been sworn to three times. I have had to pay three shillings for them, and I wish the d—— had them both."

I need not say that I found it necessary to stick very close to the sergeant after that, as I was afraid of his getting into trouble. At last I left him leaning up against the gable end of a house not far from the police-station. I ran there, and told the only constable on duty that he was to go up to a public-house in Eccles where there was a row, and then I rushed back for the sergeant, who had really become unable to stand, got him on my back, and took him to his own bedroom before the constable returned. Next morning, when I told him what had happened, he was very much ashamed of himself.

The owner of the cap and belt was sentenced to penal servitude for his offence, and I never heard of Mr. M. wanting any further information.

CHAPTER XVII.

SWINDLERS.

N one occasion, while stationed as sergeant at **Newton Heath**, a cattle dealer from Hereford called upon me in a very disconsolate state of mind.

He informed me that shortly before that time he had received a letter from Failsworth, giving him to understand that the writer of the letter was the proprietor of a very large estate there, and that while driving in his carriage through his grounds he had been informed by his bailiff that there was a large quantity of grass which it would be of advantage to have eaten off by some cows. The letter further went on to request the cattle dealer to send by rail, as soon as possible, to the address given at Failsworth, three of his best Ayrshire cows, for the purpose stated. The cattle dealer at once complied with this request, and the cows sent were valued at £30 each. But not receiving payment as readily as had been promised, the cattle dealer wrote several letters to the address given, but had them returned to him through the dead letter office. He now came himself, to see what could be done in the matter. From what the cattle dealer told me I at once concluded that the writer of the letter he received was a notorious swindler residing in Failsworth, and who, so far from having an estate, had not a yard of land he could call his own. He resided in a cottage, with a small backyard, having a shippon attached to it. When I told the cattle dealer the sort of man we had to deal with he was almost heartbroken. I cheered him up, however, as well as I could, and said I would go with him to the swindler's house, and see what could be done.

When we arrived there we examined the shippon, and found that it was locked up, but through the keyhole we could see a cow in the shippon which the cattle dealer believed to be his own cow. Having at that time no legal authority to force an entry, I did not attempt to break open the door of the shippon, but, as the cattle dealer was so distressed at the loss of his cows, and appealed to me as to what he should do in the matter, I told him he could please himself, but that if the cow was mine I should break open the door with a arge stone, to which I pointed, in the yard, and take the cow away. The cattle dealer acted on this hint, and got possession of his cow, which he put up at a public-house in the vicinity while we went in search of the others.

Having received information that a cow answering the description of those sent from Hereford had been seen at the farm of a relative of the swindler some distance away, the cattle dealer and I went to the place, and saw a cow chained up in a shippon, which the cattle dealer at once identified as his property. The farmer, however, stated that he had purchased and paid for the cow, and threatened to use violence to the cattle dealer if he attempted to remove the cow from the farm. The cattle dealer again appealed to me for advice as to what he should do, and, believing the farmer and the swindler were in collusion, I told the cattle dealer that if the cow was mine I should take no notice of the farmer's threats, but remove it at once, and that if he chose to do so I would protect him from violence, for if the farmer had bought the cow, as he stated, he could sue the person from whom he bought it for the amount paid. The cattle dealer acted on my advice, and having got the cow away, we marched it and the one we had seized at the swindler's house through the village, amidst the cheers of the inhabitants, who appeared to be deeply incensed against the swindler for his many heartless tricks on confiding people.

A short time after this the same swindler called at the Top King, Oldham Street, Manchester, and from a tailor who was in the habit of calling there to meet country customers and receive their orders, he ordered a new suit of clothes, value £5, to be ready for him by a certain date. The tailor did not then know what sort of man he had to deal with, but before the clothes were completed he was to some extent enlightened on that point. The swindler promised to call at the public house the following Saturday, and bring the money. He kept his appointment with the tailor, but did not offer to pay the money. On the contrary, he stood for some time at the door of the public house, talking away with the tailor, who stood with the suit of clothes in his hand, waiting to hand them over on receipt of the money. At this moment the Failsworth 'bus came driving past the door, and as this was just what the swindler was waiting for, he snatched the clothes from the tailor, jumped on to the 'bus, and got clear away. The tailor, however, next day applied for a warrant against the swindler for stealing the clothes, and as the offence was committed in the city, the Manchester police in the first instance tried to execute the warrant, but could not lay hands on the swindler. Ultimately the warrant came into my hands, and I found the man hiding in his own house. On the way to the police station he remarked—

"This is only a debt, Jimmy. You did not search the house, or you might have found something else."

"That is soon remedied," I replied, and marched my prisoner back again to the house, where I found a valuable skin rug, which was identified the following day as stolen property.

The man was tried at the following sessions for stealing the clothes out of the tailor's hands, and at the trial the tailor swore that he never intended to part with the goods to the swindler on credit, but intended the sale to be a ready-money transaction. The Recorder, in passing sentence, clearly explained that as the tailor looked upon the sale as a ready-money transaction, the swindler, in taking the clothes away in the manner stated, had been guilty of larceny, and accordingly sentenced him to seven years' penal servitude for the offence.

The methods adopted by dishonest persons for victimising the public are very many, and vary a good deal according to circumstances. For instance, it often happens during the winter months, when the frost is severe, that one of this class, having previously obtained the name of some respectable gentleman likely to have several spare suits of clothes, watches until he sees the gentleman leave his house. After allowing sufficient time to elapse, he then walks hurriedly up to the gentleman's residence with a well-concocted tale about the gentleman having inadvertently stepped on to some ice on a pond some little distance away, and the ice broke so that he fell into the water; or perhaps varies the tale by stating that the gentleman had gone to the assistance of some person who had thus fallen into the water, and by this means had got the clothes he was wearing quite wet, and had sent him, the messenger, for another suit of clothes to put on. Of course the lady of the house readily believes the tale, and at once complies with the request, only to find shortly afterwards that an ingenious fraud has been practised upon her, and that the gentleman has never been in the water at all.

I need not say that the clothes thus obtained are generally at once pledged, and the scamp who obtained them by false pretences clears out of the district to try the same trick at some other place.

Another fraud often practised is that of a man, ostensibly a knife and scissors grinder, who will hang about some respectable neighbourhood until he sees a lady or gentleman leave one of the houses. He will then go boldly up to the door of the house, and tell the servants that he has been directed by the lady or the gentleman, as the case may be, to call for the best carving knife and fork to sharpen. The servants, of course, having no reason to doubt the man's statement, will very often hand him the articles asked for, when he immediately decamps, and is never again seen unless the police manage to lay their hands on him, and bring him to justice for the offence.

I have simply mentioned the foregoing cases out of a great

many similar ones which often occur. Very often, too, the victim, imagining he has no remedy against the swindler but the county court, allows him to escape the punishment he so richly deserves, rather than go to the trouble and expense of prosecuting.

CHAPTER XVIII.

PAWNBROKERS.

I SHOULD like to avail myself of the opportunity which here presents itself of doing what I can to remove what seems to me a most unjust suspicion on a body of respectable men who are engaged in business as pawnbrokers. I know that some persons, even some of high standing, harbour the opinion that pawnbrokers as a class, if they do not aid and abet crime, at all events render felony more easy by providing a ready means for the disposal of such articles of value as would be the most likely to tempt the thief. I cannot but think that this opinion, if not hastily, is erroneously formed. Few men have had more extended or extensive dealings with the pawnbroking class than myself, and I am ready and glad to bear witness to the fact that the police are often indebted to them far more than the public would imagine for the speedy detection of crime, especially larcenies. The instances in which suspicious circumstances connected with a tender of goods in pledge are brought at once to the knowledge of the police authorities, but in which no definite evidence of wrongdoing is detected, are very numerous; and the cases in which the difficulties of the police would have been almost insuperable had it not been for the speedy assistance of the pawnbrokers to whom portions of the stolen property had been offered in pledge are not rare. I scarcely ever knew a case during the whole of my experience in which any respectable pawnbroker to whom application has been made for information has refused to give such information as it was in his power to give, but I have known many cases where great help has been voluntarily rendered to the police by the pawnbrokers which has led to the speedy arrest of the right man. Of course I would not be thought to desire to say that there are not among the numerous body of pawnbrokers men who are not quite so scrupulous as they ought to be in their rather dangerous calling, but taken as a body I am sure they endeavour to conduct their business in an honourable and honest way. Many suggestions have been made to me during the course of my long experience for the better regulation of this calling, but on the whole I cannot but think that pawnbrokers are already hedged about with restrictions quite sufficient. It must not be forgotten that pawnshops are established to supply a very great convenience to the needy poor, and to others in want of a temporary money loan; and as far as my experience goes I can say that the number of instances in which stolen property is offered in pledge successfully, bear such a small proportion to the total transactions over the pledge counter as to be utterly insignificant. The law, which, in the discretion of the court, imposes upon the pawnbroker, where the court considers want of care has been shown, the serious loss of the value of the loan, in the event of his taking in stolen goods, has no doubt a most wholesome effect on those who, in the absence of such a penalty, might be disposed to be rather lax; but I believe that the general result is in far greater measure due to a strong and continuous desire on the part of the vast majority of those engaged in the pawnbroking trade to do their duty honestly and uprightly before all men.

It should be borne in mind that if there were no pawnbrokers many persons who are in distress and requiring immediate help would be compelled to sell their clothing and other articles instead of pawning them, and therefore would be much worse off than they are at present, because they would have no chance of again redeeming them. The buyer would likely be some unscrupulous person, who probably would not give more than a third of their value, while some pawnbrokers would in many cases advance two-thirds of the value as a temporary loan.

I may further remark that were it not for the existence of the pawnbroking trade it would often be an impossibility for the police to find stolen property after the lapse of a few days from the committal of the robbery, as they would be quite at a loss to know where they should commence their search, or how to conduct it with any prospect of success. Thieves and receivers of stolen property, or " fences " as they are called, would soon become hand and glove in their felonious operations in vastly increased numbers, and recovery of stolen property would in that case become as rare an occurrence as it is at present quite the reverse. To prove this I may give an example of what I have more than once seen myself. Some suspicious person would drop a bundle at the stall or shop door of someone suspected of being a receiver of stolen property, and then walk away. It has been clear to me on such occasions that an understanding existed between the parties, as almost immediately after the person who left the bundle had gone away some person would come out of the shop, pick up the bundle, and go inside. If the bundle contained clothing, &c., some person kept in readiness inside would soon alter the articles and give them such a different appearance that if the original owner entered the shop a few minutes afterwards he would not know his own garments. After allowing time for this to be done, the thief would return to the shop and get from the "fence" whatever he thought proper to give him, which is generally the merest trifle, but whether small or great the thief has to be contented with it, as, of course, he has no means of retaliating. In cases where the thief is not sufficiently acquainted with a "fence" himself, he must employ an older and more experienced thief, who will take the stolen property to some "fence" with whom he is acquainted, get whatever the "fence" chooses to give him, and then, after charging a commission for his risk and trouble, he will hand whatever small balance there may be to the first thief who handed him the stolen goods. If he cannot find an old thief to act for him, he is either driven to sell it in the street, or low beerhouse, or as a last resource, try his luck at a pawnbroker's shop.

In the case of such stolen property as gold, silver, and other articles of jewellery, the "fence" adopts a different plan than he does in the case of stolen clothing. He has in readiness a crucible or melting pot, into which nearly all valuable metal is generally thrown as soon as received, and by this means, of course, all chance of the owner identifying it again is gone.

With watches still another plan is sometimes adopted—the works are taken out and put into other cases, and the original cases are melted down, unless they are found to have no distinguishing marks upon them, in which case they are again used after the works of some other watch are put into them.

I have known as much as £50 worth of this class of stolen property to be sold for as many shillings, and receivers never give any information to the police, because, of course, by doing so they compromise themselves, as they scout the idea of having any dealings with thieves until they are found out.

With pawnbrokers the case is quite the reverse, and almost the only chance the police have of recovering stolen property, after the lapse of a few days, is by its coming into the hands of pawnbrokers.

I have heard remarks made to the effect that the small amount for which stolen property is often pledged should be sufficient to arouse the suspicion of pawnbrokers, but I entirely differ from such notions. It should be borne in mind that as a rule the working classes are the persons who usually take advantage of the pawnshops to pledge goods, and I have known many cases in which such persons would feel it a great hardship to be deprived of the privilege afforded them thereby. For instance, though it might be impossible for them to buy new clothing out of their weekly wages, yet by getting the clothes, and then pledging them for about two-thirds or so of their value on Monday, taking them out of pledge on Saturday, and reducing the amount by weekly instalments, the clothing, &c., soon becomes their own property.

It may thus be seen that the pawnbroking trade is not only a necessary institution in the country, but one that, conducted as it is at present by the respectable portion of those engaged in it, may be considered a positive boon to the community.

CHAPTER XIX.

GARROTTERS.

IT was about the year 1865 that not only in Manchester and Salford, but throughout the neighbourhood, and all over Lancashire, a new danger was added to those which had beset pedestrians in the more lonely streets and lanes after nightfall. This new outrage became known as garrotting. The number of instances of this form of attack grew so rapidly that it soon became almost unsafe for any person to walk alone through any but the best lighted and most frequented thoroughfares of our towns. At any moment it might be that the arms of the garrotter would be thrown round your neck from behind, while an accomplice seized such valuables as were obtainable. The difficulty of dealing with this class of outrage was caused by the fact that three were generally engaged in one attack, the third one, generally a woman, being detached to watch for the approach of the police, so as to warn her accomplices in time to effect their escape. The prevalence of this class of outrage became so great that it became necessary to use some more than ordinary means to secure its repression. Fortunately the law was strong enough to deal with this evil, and it only wanted the courageous hand of a strong administrator to bring its effects into play. That hand was found in Mr. Justice Lush, who at the Assizes held in Manchester in the month of, I think, August, 1865, seeing the necessity of crushing the outrage, brought to bear the "cat." It was not until after long consideration that bodily punishment was deemed to be the only means of bringing home to the ruffians to be dealt with the fact that the law was strong enough to deal with them. Imprisonment had no terror. Many, if not most, of the persons guilty of this offence had spent most of their time in confinement—some had suffered transportation, some had undergone penal servitude until penal servitude contained for them no dread. Twenty-three such criminals were at this one assize arraigned before Mr. Justice Lush for punishment. Every one of them was sent into penal servitude, some for longer periods than others, and every one of them was ordered to make the acquaintance of the "cat." According to the violence of which they had been guilty, so were they to experience in their turn a measure of violence. Some of the most desperate villains were ordered to be flogged three times at the commencement of their term of servitude; others were allowed to escape into the confinement of the penal settlement after tasting twice the punishment of flogging; and others again but once had to bare their shoulders to the thongs. But none of them escaped. The scene which was witnessed in the court when the sentence was passed is one that neither I myself, nor probably any who saw it, will ever forget. It fell to my lot to assist the prison warders to handcuff some of the prisoners upon whom the law was shortly to bring to bear one of its strongest arms of punishment. I never saw human beings more utterly cowed. The dread of pain is to such persons their only fear, and from that dread they will shrink like a whipped cur. So it was on this occasion. When the day came for the sentence to be carried out I was very glad it did not fall to my lot to be present. It is never a pleasant thing to see suffering humanity, and to me it is always especially painful, but an eyewitness informed me that, as the thongs fell on the bare shoulders of the ruffians who had not hesitated to inflict unknown cruelty upon their victims, it was piteous to hear their cries for mercy. A few of them, putting on the air of bravado, which desperate men driven to earth sometimes assume, would pretend during the first stroke or two that they would be able to bear the blows without shrinking. "Lay it on," "My mother could do more than that," "You wouldn't do for a schoolmaster," and similar epithets were indulged in; but as the blows continued to fall, first there would be silence, and then the cry for mercy would burst forth from the recently boastful lips, ending in utter collapse. I shall never forget how, on the day they received their sentence, I was besought by them for a bit of my boot lace, that they might put it between their teeth whilst they were being flogged, because they said it would to some extent alleviate the pain. I never experienced a more convincing proof of the efficacy of the application of bodily punishment to the class of criminal which was then to be dealt with. There was not one of this gang of desperadoes who did not say that he would rather be twice "boated" (that is, sent into penal servitude) than once "bashed," (that is, flogged); and as soon as the lash became the instrument of punishment, we can most of us remember how speedily the crime diminished, and it is now almost a thing of the past.

CHAPTER XX.

SCUTTLERS.

FOR many years past an outrage locally known as "scuttling" (though what the derivation of the term may be I cannot say) has become very prevalent, not only in some parts of the county round about Manchester, but more especially in the lower parts of Manchester, as well as in Salford. I am not aware that it is at all known in other large Lancashire towns, and certainly it is quite unknown in other parts of the country.

"Scuttling" partakes a good deal of the tribal hatred or clan animosity which led to many a bloody fray in bygone times. In some of the districts on the borders of Manchester, such as Miles Platting, Bradford, Gorton, Beswick, and occasionally Openshaw, this outrage has given the police a vast amount of trouble. A gang of boys, ranging in their ages from ten years to manhood, form themselves into a body of ruffians, who wage war against any one person or district they may fix upon. Sometimes they will attack an individual, and sometimes (more frequently) they will direct their violence against another gang of ruffians hailing from a neighbouring district, and formed into a band actuated by the same motives and violent propensities as themselves. It is a noticeable fact that their object seems to be the indulgence of the brute passions only, rather than robbery, which has never been charged against them as a purpose in view when making their attacks either upon individuals or upon what may be described as their rivals and opponents.

The mode of proceeding and the description of weapons adopted by "scuttlers" seem always the same, and although they are often found provided with sticks, stones, bricks, and even knives on such occasions, yet their favourite instrument of violence is a strong leather belt, such as is commonly worn by persons of their class in lieu of braces for the support of their nether garments. Armed with these effective weapons, they will sally forth in the darkness of the evening, forty or fifty strong, eager for an affray. If a wayfarer should meet them on their way, woe be to him—that is, if they think he belongs to the district with which they may happen to be at variance. All sense of fear and all fear of consequences for the time being seems to abandon the "scuttlers," and as often as not the object of their wanton attack will be left, so far as they are concerned, or care, to die in the road. Sometimes, but not always, the knife comes into play, and on many occasions wounds of a most serious nature have been inflicted in the *melée* between two such rival factions. The heavy brass buckle attached to the leather belt is a most fearful weapon in the hands of a strong unscrupulous youth, and this instrument they will use upon each other without thought or care as to what may ensue. It is difficult to imagine the origin of this sort of outrage on law and order; nevertheless, in the districts where it has prevailed, the inhabitants have lived very often in a state bordering upon terror, and the police have had added to their responsibilities another evil with which it has been found difficult to deal effectively, not only because it is never known at what spot in a wide district the scuttlers may suddenly assemble, but also on account of the formidable opposition with which a body of fifty or so such reckless men may meet them. Not very long ago a very eminent medical man told me that scarcely a day passed without someone being brought into the Manchester Infirmary in consequence of violence used in these "scuttling" affrays. The youths taking part in them have had every possible chance given them by the magistrates before proceeding to extreme measures. In some cases they have been cautioned; in other cases they have been fined; and in some cases short terms of imprisonment have been tried. But all such mild dealings have proved of no avail. When released from the police court or from gaol they have been looked upon by their comrades as heroes worthy of imitation; and it was not until they were sent for trial at the Sessions, and there made the acquaintance of Mr. Higgin, Q.C., chairman of the Quarter Sessions, that a most effective check was put upon them. As it was formerly, when Mr. Justice Lush cured the garrotters, so Mr. Higgin put down scuttling in this district by passing upon the offenders such severe sentences as to effectually stamp it out in the districts where previously it had been quite prevalent. It may be further remarked that in some cases, since the heavy sentences referred to were passed, when scuttling affrays have commenced, the appearance of even two or three constables on the scene has been sufficient to make as many as fifty scuttlers decamp very speedily; but this no doubt has been in consequence of knowing what they had to expect if apprehended and sent for trial. It is to be hoped, however, that, though these strong measures have been found absolutely necessary in dealing with this evil in the past, yet as education advances the energies which have run riot in such reprehensible and evil practices will aspire to something better, and "scuttling," like garrotting, will become a thing of the past.

CHAPTER XXI.

THE HARPURHEY MURDER.

THE crimes I am about to recount in this and the succeeding chapters might each be made to form the basis or to constitute the plot of an interesting romance. Any of them would afford ample scope for the pen of an ingenious and imaginative or descriptive writer, who, out of the materials at my disposal, might construct an elaborate and graphic narrative. Such, however, is not my purpose, and I shall merely give to my readers a "plain unvarnished tale" of the events connected with these tragedies which caused a great sensation at the time of their occurrence.

About nine o'clock on the evening of 7th January, 1879, I was informed by Police-constable, now Sergeant, Lever, who was then stationed at Harpurhey, that a dreadful murder had been committed that evening at the house of a Mr. Greenwood, at Harpurhey. I at once proceeded to the place, and began to make inquiries, and learned from Police-sergeant Moses Thompson, who had been obtaining information prior to my arrival on the scene, that Mrs. Greenwood had for some time been lying dangerously ill, and that, although she was still very low and weak, she was rather better than she had been, and had that night for the first time been able to sit up in bed.

Afterwards, I went up into Mrs. Greenwood's room, where I found her seated before the fire wrapped in a blanket; and in answer to my questions she told me that she had been bedfast for a considerable time, and that for the first time she had got up that day. She also said that early in the forenoon a friend of theirs named Cooper, who, as I subsequently ascertained, kept Mr. Greenwood's books, happened to come to the house by the front door, and when closing it he saw a letter addressed to Mr. Greenwood. This letter I read, a *facsimile* of which appears on pages 230 and 231.

Mrs. Greenwood further informed me that her husband had, at her request, gone to the Three Tuns to meet the writer, and that a short time after tea she and her servant, the unfortunate Sarah Jane Roberts, were sitting by the fireside in the bedroom, when the girl got up and said she would go downstairs and wash the tea things. A shor time after she had gone below, Mrs. Greenwood heard someone knock at the front door and the servant go to answer it, and then she heard the steps of two persons pass through the lobby into the kitchen and the closing of the kitchen door. From the manner in which they went into the kitchen Mrs. Greenwood concluded it was some friend of the servant come to visit her. In a few minutes after this she was alarmed by a scream, when she at once came to the conclusion that Jane must have been lifting something from the mantelpiece and her clothing had caught fire. In a few minutes afterwards she heard a second scream, whereupon she ran downstairs, past the kitchen door and into the street, where she said she called loudly for help.

As Mrs. Greenwood was in a very weak state, I had but a poor opportunity of questioning her closely. No one could speak more highly of the murdered girl for steadiness, truthfulness, and attentiveness than Mrs. Greenwood did.

A strict investigation was of course made in every part of the district, with the view of tracing the murderer. Some suspected one person and some another, but to my mind not one of those upon whom suspicion was cast had taken any actual part in the perpetration of the crime. It will be understood that the letter I have quoted was written for a ruse of some kind, for the writer never appeared at the Three Tuns to keep the appointment he proposed.

Day after day I was engaged along with the available inspectors, sergeants, and constables in doing everything that lay in our power to unravel the mystery, and every police force far and near had bills sent to them offering a large reward for such information as would lead to the apprehension of the murderer or murderers, also a free pardon to any person not being the actual murderer who would give such information, but without any good result. All sorts of suggestions were made from varied and numerous sources as to the criminal; but, as is usual in such cases, with outside and inexperienced opinion, they were mostly wide of the mark. Many embraced the idea that the object of the murder had been robbery, but if such was the case the assassin appears to have made no attempt to effect his object, as he did not appear to have gone farther than the kitchen, and no money

Mr Greenwood

Mr Grinwood,
Jan 1779

I want to take that land near the cockpyard behind the shipsprints shop Queens Rd I will pay either monthly Quarterly or yearly and will pay in advance and I will meet you to sign it at the Three Inns corner of Chennet st and will tell you all particulars I don't know your address or I would have posted it

Yours &c
W. Mclean
Chatham Rd

was missed. Some said the poor girl had been murdered because she would not submit to undue familiarities—in fact, theory and speculation ran riot in the public mind. Many people came in for a more or less share of suspicion on the part of the neighbours, and for a considerable length of time every suspected person was looked upon as guilty until his or her innocence had been proved beyond the shadow of a doubt.

Visitors without number called upon me, including a great many ladies, who were imbued with a desire to throw light on the matter, and to render some assistance in the apprehension of the murderer. For instance, when I was tired and wearied out, after having been up night after night, a gentle tap would come to the door, and when it was opened, some lady or other person would enter and, beginning with an apology for troubling me, proceed to relate how a great many people who had committed murders had been discovered and captured in consequence of dreams. My visitor, usually a lady, as I have said, had in dreamland invariably seen the stairs, the position in which the dead girl's assailant stood, and the very manner in which the instrument of death was used, but I noticed that the recital was generally commenced with or preceded by questions as to what was the size of the kitchen, how the bedroom stood in relation to the lobby and staircase, and where the room was situated in which Mr. Greenwood kept his money. At these points the dreams seem to have failed, and it happened many times when I declined to say where the money was, I seemed to some extent to cause vexation to my visitor. No matter how fagged I was during these interviews, nor how much inclined to go to sleep, I had often not only to listen to the dream with which the lady had been favoured on the previous night, but to the narration of a great many of her other visions of the night, by which stolen property had been recovered and murderers traced. Perhaps, before the dreamer had left me, another lady would be waiting to tell me that she was a spirit-rapper, or medium, or something; and then, again, although tired, and used up for want of sleep and rest, I had to listen to an account of a number of crimes that had been detected in consequence of what had been heard and seen at spiritualistic seances; till, what with one thing and another, I sometimes wished myself entirely out of the country.

Everything was done that could possibly be done to track the murderer, and a *facsimile* of the letter given was produced and published in all the Manchester newspapers, and exhibited in a room where limelights were being shown, but without success. Hundreds of letters reached me, giving me some reason or other why I should suspect a person's handwriting, some of whose manuscript had just been discovered amongst their papers. From some I received dozens of communications, pointing out that the "i's" were dotted in the same way, and from others similar assurances that the "t's" were crossed in an exactly similar fashion; but nothing ever caused me to think that those so forwarded were in any way similar to the handwriting of the letter.

Some people thought it would be wise to take a photograph of the murdered woman as she lay in her coffin, as they believed that if the eyes as presented in the picture were examined by a powerful microscope the figure of the murderer would appear. In order to try this chance, and to satisfy those who proposed it, I had the lid of the coffin taken off, just before the funeral started for the church, and the corpse of the girl was photographed, but no such figure could be seen in the pupil of the eye. All this was done under the direction of an eminent medical man, but it was of no avail.

The inquest was duly held, and the facts, as I have stated them, were spoken to by Mrs. Greenwood and other witnesses.

As before stated, all sorts of rumours were prevalent on the subject at the time. I have little doubt in my own mind as to who murdered Sarah Jane Roberts, but I am unable to bring forward evidence for the purpose of obtaining a legal conviction for such a terrible and awful crime.

CHAPTER XXII.

THE MURDER OF CONSTABLE COCK.

AS in the case of the Harpurhey murder, so in regard to that of Police-constable Cock, which is perhaps most widely known as the Habron murder case, I shall only write a clear and simple narrative of it, without attempting to colour the facts by the aid of highflown language. On the 26th of July, 1875, two brothers named William and John Habron, were summoned before the magistrates, at the County Police Court, on a charge of drunkenness by a constable named Cock, who was then stationed at Chorlton-cum-Hardy, and the case, as far as John was concerned, was adjourned until the following Thursday, August 2nd. On that day I was called into my private office by a gentleman in the court, who told me that he thought Constable Cock was mistaken as to the identity of John Habron, and asked me if I would withdraw the case. I replied that if I thought the officer was wrong I would certainly do so, but that I would call Cock into the room and see what he had to say. At my request, Constable Cock at once came into my office, and I said to him in the hearing of the gentleman—

"Cock, this gentleman says you are mistaken as to the identity of John Habron. If that is so, say that you are mistaken, as it is possible for any one to be."

"I am not mistaken, Mr. Bent," replied Cock, "and the gentleman knows it. He came to me when I had my arms round them, and asked me to let them go, and he would give me their names, which he did."

I then observed, "Well, the case must go into court. I shall not interfere in the matter."

Shortly after this the constable came to me and said, "Mr. Bent, I know these men very well. They have threatened several times to shoot me within the last few months, if ever I summoned them."

"Well, Cock, you are not afraid," I answered, not for a moment believing that the men intended to do him any serious harm.

Cock replied, "No, I am not afraid; but I thought I would tell you what they have said."

The case was proceeded with in the court, and after the evidence had been given, Mr. Haworth Ashton, who heard it, said—

"I'll give the defendant the benefit of the doubt. He has been up twice, and I will now discharge him."

Later on, John Habron left the court, and Constable Cock came to me saying—

"Mr. Bent, John Habron has just told me that he will shoot me before twelve o'clock to-night."

"Cock, are you really afraid of him?" I asked.

"No," he replied, "I don't know that I am;" but he nevertheless seemed a little troubled in his mind.

It was nearly twelve o'clock the same night, and I had just gone to bed, when the night bell was rung by one of the constables. Answering him, I inquired—

"What is the matter?"

"Cock is shot," was the man's reply.

What Cock had said to me at the court in the morning of course at once crossed my mind. I went without a moment's delay to the house of Dr. Dill, where the unfortunate constable was lying on a sofa in a dying state.

Besides Dr. Dill, I had another medical gentleman called in, but the poor fellow passed away without giving any intimation as to who was his murderer.

As soon as death had ensued, bearing in mind what I was informed had been said by the Habrons, I directed several constables to proceed with me to the outbuildings adjoining their employer's house, in which the brothers slept. Having arrived there, I caused the men to surround the house, and instructed them to remain quiet until my return. One of the sergeants came to me with the information that there was a light in the outbuildings. I then went and aroused their employer, and asked him to come downstairs.

"What is to do, Mr. Bent?" he inquired.

"Cock is shot," I answered.

"Who has done it?" he asked.

"Nay, I must ask you who has done it," said I.

"Oh, dear me," he then observed. "I told them to let it drop, and have no more bother about it." Next, he exclaimed, "Oh, my God, if it is any of these men it is that young one"—meaning William—"as he has the most abominable temper of any man I ever knew in my life."

I then said, "I am afraid that if these are the men that have murdered the constable—one of them having said they would do it before twelve o'clock to-night, and he has been murdered before that time—they may be prepared to shoot someone else rather than be taken. What I want you to do is this. Will you go quietly to this outbuilding, and let your voice be heard, so that they will know it is you, and then get them to open the door to speak to you, and I will rush into the room. I do not wish you to run any risk, unless you care to do so, but simply to make them believe that it is you at the door and not the police."

After a little hesitation he consented, and he and I were walking quietly towards the outbuilding, when the sergeant again came to me and informed me that the lights in the outbuildings had been blown out. I once more enjoined silence, and their master went to the door. He knocked, and shook the latch, but no one answered, although the bed was close to the door. He knocked a second time, more loudly, but still no answer. A third time he knocked, and again shook the door, calling out "Jack," and someone having opened the door, he cried out, "Superintendent Bent wants you."

Sergeant Gillanders, myself, and one or two others, at once rushed into the room. It was in complete darkness, but to be ready for such a contingency I had provided myself with a policeman's lantern. As soon as I got in, I put my hands on the three men who were in bed, and found that they were stark naked. Of course, I warned them against making any resistance. I then asked them to get up and dress in the same clothes they had worn before they went to bed that night, and each of them got up and dressed. When they were dressed I handcuffed them, and said by way of caution, "Now, mind what I am about to say to you. You three men are charged with the wilful murder of Constable Cock." Then I paused for a moment, when John Habron called out, "I was in bed at the time." No time had been mentioned by me or anyone else. William and Frank made no reply, and the three were removed in a cab to the Police Station at Old Trafford, their boots being taken along with them. I then went to the spot where Cock had been shot, and placed a number of constables there, to prevent any persons who might be passing from effacing the impressions of footmarks which might possibly have been left by the murderer or murderers. When it was daylight I found some impressions had been left on the ground, and as rain was beginning to fall I covered them with a box. I then sent for the boots of the prisoners; and their employer, and another man, a draughtsman, coming up about the same time, impressions were made, to see whether the boots, or any of them, tallied with the marks found, and the draughtsman at once said they were similar to those made by the Habrons. I afterwards returned to the police station, and saw the three prisoners separately, when they said one after another that they were in bed the previous night at nine o'clock. This I found out to be untrue, because they were drinking at a public-house, a very short distance from the outbuildings, until nearly eleven o'clock. Constable Cock would have to pass this very public-house at about five minutes past eleven, and walk to West Point, where he was afterwards found murdered.

In the course of prosecuting further inquiries I ascertained next morning, from a young man named Wilcock, a watchmaker, that the three Habrons, who were friends of his, had told him privately, "that if ever Cock brought them a summons they would shoot him dead." I also found that a beerseller, living near to their employer, had heard repeated threats from the Habrons that they would shoot the constable. Another person, named Brownhill, although he said nothing to the police before he got to the court, stated that John Habron had told him that he had to attend court as he had been summoned by Constable Cock, and had sworn to him that he would shoot Cock.

In addition to the foregoing evidence, two men employed in an ironmonger's shop in Oxford Road, Manchester, informed one of my officers, whom I had sent to make inquiries, that a man had been to their place about noon, on the day on which the murder was committed, trying to bargain for some cartridges, and that they had not sold him any, but that next morning, when the box was again examined, three cartridges had been missed. Both of these shopmen said that they would be able to identify the man if they saw him again, and were asked to go down to the court to look at some prisoners who were being brought up. They arrived at the court about ten minutes after the Habrons had been put into the dock, and one of them at once identified William as the person who had come to their shop, and the other witness also said he had very little doubt about it.

As it was suspected that the pistol with which Cock had been shot might possibly have been thrown into one of the ditches or pits at Chorlton-cum-Hardy, every available means were adopted to recover it. Pits were emptied, drains and ditches were searched, but no pistol could ever be found, and after several adjournments, two of the prisoners, William and John, were sent for trial at the assizes on the capital charge.

They were tried before Mr. Justice Lindley, Mr. W. H. Higgin, Q.C., chairman of the Salford Hundred Sessions, and Mr. John Addison, Q.C., conducting the prosecution on behalf of the police, while Mr. Leresche defended the prisoners. The substance of the evidence already stated was given, and at the close of the first day's proceedings, against the wish of their counsel, the prisoners determined to call witnesses. On the following day, several witnesses were accordingly placed in the box for the defence, but on being cross-examined by Mr. Higgin, the *alibi* which they endeavoured to prove was shattered to pieces, their statements being very different from those which they had signed at the time the Habrons were before the magistrates. In fact, I believe it was their contradictory statements which caused William Habron to be convicted, more than any evidence given by the police or the other persons who were examined for the prosecution.

Perhaps I may appropriately state here that while the prisoners were awaiting their trial I received numerous anonymous letters, some declaring that the Habrons were the right persons apprehended, and others that Cock had other enemies in Chorlton-cum-Hardy, while a third set used threats of violence if the men were not acquitted. After the liberation of John Habron, as I had grave doubts concerning his attitude towards several witnesses in the case,

I considered it my duty to tell him I had received so many complaints about his conduct and threatening peoples lives, that if any person who had given evidence in the case received any injury, I should hold him responsible, and would find him if he went to the other end of the world, as I felt sure that if he was not the person to do the harm himself he was certain to be its instigator. It is somewhat remarkable to state that the gentleman who had at first told me that William Habron was one of the most abominable tempered fellows he ever knew, began afterwards to paint him as one of the most innocent creatures that ever walked.

I do not hesitate for one moment to say that when the time arrived at which William Habron was discharged from gaol he had not a friend in the world more pleased to hear of his release than I was, and he came to see me at my house several times. I had no desire to see either him or any other person executed; and if the authorities were satisfied that he was not guilty, I had no right to be dissatisfied with the decision at which they had arrived. No man felt more grieved than I did when I heard of William Habron's subsequent troubles. I believe he would have done anything in his power that I wished him to do.

Had the Habrons not made use of the threats they were said to have done, they would not have been apprehended. It was not I nor the police who proved these threats, but private individuals. Of course, I was in duty bound to make every possible inquiry, which I did. Nor did I confine myself to finding evidence against the prisoners, but had frequently made inquiries before the trial on statements made by another brother of the Habrons who had not been mixed up in the affair at all, but all such statements were found on investigation to have no basis whatever.

The case afterwards assumed a highly-sensational aspect, through the confession of the notorious Charles Peace (who was under sentence of death for another crime) that he was Cock's murderer. This ultimately led to the release and pardon of William Habron, who received a considerable sum from the Crown as compensation for his supposed erroneous conviction.

In addition to this, several persons in different parts of the country confessed to having committed the murder; but on investigation, their statements were found to be without foundation.

CHAPTER XXIII.

THE MOSTON MURDER.

ON March 1st, 1888, a terrible murder was committed in Moston Lane, Moston, by a man named John Alfred Gell, a wheelwright not employed, who had for some time resided with a Mrs. Millar, a married woman, living apart from her husband.

Gell, it appeared, had been living at the house for a considerable time, but followed no employment and this caused Mrs. Millar to give him notice to quit several times. On the day in question he told Mrs. Millar and her daughter Isabella, who lived with her, that he had obtained a situation, and was going away. He left the house between eight and nine in the morning, but returned stealthily about 11-50. Entering the yard by the back door, he obtained possession of an axe, used by Mrs. Millar for breaking coal. The woman happened to be bending over a washing tub at the time, and Gell, surprising her, dealt several terrible blows about the head, almost killing her outright. The daughter, Isabella, who was in the front room, hearing the noise, got up to ascertain the cause. When Gell saw her he at once pursued her into the parlour, and dealt her a fearful blow on the head with the axe. She succeeded, however, in reaching the front door, and her screams brought several neighbours to the spot, who, after attending to the young woman, went into the yard, where they found Mrs. Millar in a dying state. Medical aid was immediately obtained, but Mrs. Millar was beyond help, and died a few minutes after the doctor's arrival. Her daughter, Isabella, was taken to the Royal Infirmary, Manchester, and her case appeared so hopeless that Mr. Leresche, stipendiary magistrate, attended at that institution to take her depositions on the evening of the same day.

Shortly after Gell had committed the murder, Police-constable Robinson, who had not then heard of the tragedy, was on duty in Moston, some distance from Mrs. Millar's house, when he saw a man running across a field without a hat on. Whilst Robinson stood watching him, a tradesman came up and told the constable that there had been a terrible murder in Moston a short time before. Robinson, suspecting the man he had seen running across the field, at once gave chase, and after pursuing him for some distance, Gell turned round, and meeting the constable, said, "Put the handcuffs on me." This request was at once complied with, and Gell was conveyed to the Harpurhey Police Station, where he was identified as the murderer of Mrs. Millar. Being charged with the offence, he made no reply.

Whilst waiting at the Infirmary, for the purpose of taking the daughter's depositions, Gell told me that the girl had been the cause of all the trouble. He knew that she hated the sight of him; that she had caused a good deal of unpleasantness between her mother and himself, and had many a time ordered him to leave the house; that he felt it very hard to leave one he loved so dearly as Mrs. Millar, but he believed she was not true to him. He further said that after he had struck Mrs. Millar on the head with the axe, his hands were covered with blood, and that when running away from the house he could not help licking the blood off them. He also said that he endeavoured to commit suicide before he was caught by drowning himself; that he had tried to get under the ice of a pit at Moston, but was unable to do so, and had hurt his hand by trying to break the ice.

This man was committed for trial on the capital charge, both by the coroner and the magistrates, and on April 27th, at Manchester Assizes, he was sentenced to death by Justice Charles, who held out no hope of mercy, and on Whit-Tuesday, May 22nd, he was executed.

CHAPTER XXIV.

THE ATHERTON MURDER.

ALTHOUGH what has now become known as the Atherton murder did not take place in this particular division of the county of Lancaster, yet as the murderer was not only apprehended here, but the first links of the strong chain of circumstantial evidence which finally encircled him were welded here also, I thought it only right to give a short account of the incidents connected with the crime and its detection.

On Monday, the 22nd July, 1889, it soon became generally known that a murder of a peculiarly savage character had that morning been committed at Atherton, the victim being a young man named Walter Davies, assistant to Mr. John Lowe, pawnbroker, there.

About half-past seven o'clock that morning Davies obtained from Mr. Lowe the keys of the shop, which he opened and swept out, and proceeded to get everything in readiness for business as usual. He was seen so engaged by some of the neighbours who were passing, and nothing unusual transpired until about ten minutes to nine, when the man who became the murderer entered the shop. This man, who was described by a witness who saw him, apparently bargaining across the counter with Davies respecting some silk handkerchiefs, was about five feet five inches in height, of respectable appearance, and was the last person who was seen with Davies before the murder was committed. About twenty minutes afterwards, a neighbour coming into the shop, not seeing Davies going about his work as usual, suspected something was wrong, and after shouting his name went to the top of a set of steps leading down to a cellar underneath the shop, and on going down the steps found Davies lying on his back in a dying state, and bleeding from several wounds about the head and face. Davies died almost immediately after being found by this neighbour, without being able to give the least hint as to who had committed the crime.

Davies had been a strong young man, though short in stature, and had he not been suddenly pounced upon by his murderer, and struck down before he had time to defend himself, he would no doubt have made a stronger resistance than he appeared to have done. How the murder was actually accomplished will probably never be known, but it is very probable that after endeavouring to sell the silk handkerchief referred to, and supposing that the man who had been examining them had gone away, Davies went down to the cellar, which was underneath the shop, to put it in order, as he had previously told his master he intended to do. Meantime the man, who had been waiting about, re-entered the shop, and finding no person in charge, proceeded quickly to lay his hands on several watches lying about, and in doing so made a slight noise, which was heard by Davies in the cellar. Thereupon Davies was coming up the cellar steps to see what caused the noise, when he was suddenly struck on the head by some blunt instrument before he could reach the top, and fell down to the bottom in consequence of the blow. Being, however, as I have said, a strong muscular young man, Davies would not be rendered quite unconscious by the blow, and would no doubt, in a half-dazed state, grapple with his assailant as the latter followed Davies into the cellar. He was then attacked with a knife, or some other sharp instrument, causing the wounds about the head and face which resulted in his death shortly afterwards.

After the discovery of the murder a careful examination was made to try and find some clue that would lead to the detection of the crime, but with the exception of the fact, soon discovered, that several watches were missing from the shop, and would sooner or later be offered in pledge, no clue could be formed. Not only had the murderer stolen the watches from the shop, but he also had the cool audacity and heartlessness to rifle the pockets of his victim as he lay bleeding to death at his feet, and stole his watch and chain, and took what little money he had in his pockets, leaving them turned inside out. In fact, so little effect on his mind did the awful crime he had committed seem to have, that within a few hours afterwards the murderer pledged the murdered man's watch and chain in Manchester, and then endeavoured, at other places, to dispose of the rest of the stolen goods under the name of "Mr. Fred Smith," which he wrote in the book handed him for that purpose by the pawnbroker.

Vigorous search and inquiry were at once made by the police in all directions, with a view to find some trace of the murderer, but for some time without any definite result; and, as very often happens in such cases, many of the public, gratuitously enlisting themselves for the time being as amateur detectives, tried to find, and suggest some reason for supposing that every suspicious-looking person they saw or heard about had something to do with the murder. Ultimately there were some grounds for supposing that the murderer was actually arrested. A man was apprehended on Wigan fair ground by one of the Manchester city detectives, who considered he had sufficient grounds for making the arrest and charging the man with the murder. But after being detained in custody sufficiently long to admit of full inquiry being made, it was conclusively shown that this man had nothing whatever to do with the murder, and, in fact, had been living in a different part of the country when the murder was committed, so he was discharged.

Meantime, justice was following hard in the tracks of the murderer, and inexorably reaching forth to lay its grasp upon him. He might easily at first have escaped to some foreign country, where he would probably be safe for a time, but no doubt feeling secure from danger, or from the natural audacity of his character, he chose to remain until the date of his apprehension, residing within about ten miles of the scene of the murder.

For some time both before and after the murder at Atherton, numerous robberies were continually occurring at various points on the London and North-Western Railway, such as Eccles, Manchester, Preston, Carlisle, Crewe, &c., the *modus operandi* being as follows:—

The thief, who appeared to be thoroughly acquainted with

all the stations on the London and North-Western Railway, would first of all, on entering the railway station, have a look round among the passengers, to see if any lady or gentleman among them had luggage with them which gave good promise of repaying him for his trouble and risk in getting the coveted property into his possession. After mentally selecting his victim, he would walk boldly up to the booking office, to ascertain for what place they took out a ticket. He would then get a ticket for himself for some station not quite so far away, and, obtaining a luggage label for the same station, he would by some means manage to fix it over the label previously placed on the luggage by the owner or by the railway officials. On arriving at the station at which he intended to decamp, the thief would walk up to the luggage van, boldly demand "his luggage" from the guard, and walk off with the stolen property. In one case, where he got possession of a lady's property in this manner, he actually got a railway porter to carry up the stolen property for him to a cheap hotel, where he put up for the day; and on arrival there he told the railway porter that unfortunately he had lost his keys, but that if the railway porter would be good enough to fetch a locksmith to open the box for him he would give him something for himself. This was done, and the railway porter actually stood by while the stolen box was forced open and the contents taken out by the thief, never dreaming there was anything wrong until long after the occurrence. In fact, so very respectable did this man, who represented himself as a commercial traveller, dress himself, that many of the guards and railway officials, with whom he was careful to keep on very friendly terms, were in the habit of saluting him as he travelled from place to place carrying out his nefarious practices, never dreaming for one moment that they were saluting a thief.

By-and-by, however, these mysterious railway robberies seemed in some unexplainable way to point to Eccles as the base of the thief's operations, and quiet inquiries were set a-going, with the result that on the 23rd of October, 1889, a man named William Chadwick was apprehended at Eccles, as he was trying to pledge some of the property stolen from the railway company.

He was locked up at Eccles, and on being searched there was found in his possession a gold watch stolen from the Cross Keys Hotel, Eccles, as well as things stolen from other places.

Search was made in the house where Chadwick resided at Eccles, and there more stolen property was found, as well as a great number of pawn tickets for stolen property pledged by him in Liverpool, Preston, Salford, Manchester, and other towns throughout the country, which was afterwards recovered, and which was found to be the proceeds of about thirty different robberies.

The total value of property which could be clearly traced as the handiwork of Chadwick amounted to about £1,000, and of this sum about £600 was recovered.

Chadwick was several times remanded in the custody of the police, and often in his journeys to and from the police court spoke on various subjects to Sergeant Chipchase, who had charge of the case. Among other things he remarked te Sergeant Chipchase—

"I expect Mr. Bent will charge me with the Atherton murder yet. I have been expecting it every day."

Sergeant Chipchase did not attach much importance to this remark the first time it was made, but as it was repeated, and Chadwick seemed afraid of having an interview with me, the sergeant began to think there was something under it that had not yet transpired. Besides, he remembered that when Chadwick was locked up in the cells at Eccles Police Station one of the constables heard him remarking, as he sat in the cell reading the account of the Atherton murder and the trial of the man who was afterwards found innocent—

"They have got the wrong man for that job. Pawnbrokers will swear to anything and anybody."

Sergeant Chipchase therefore brought the matter under my notice at Strangeways Police Court, as Chadwick stood in the dock for the railway and other robberies. I thereupon went over to the front of the dock, and, calling Chadwick to me, said to him—

"You may be prepared to be charged with a far more serious offence than has yet been preferred against you."

Chadwick at once replied—

"I knew, Mr. Bent, you would charge me with the Atherton murder as soon as you saw me."

Next day I had an interview with Chadwick in Strangeways Gaol, and on that occasion, as I entered the cell where he was confined, he said—

"Oh, Mr. Bent, I know you have come to charge me with the Atherton murder."

I remarked, "You have got a good deal to say about the Atherton murder."

Chadwick replied, "Well, you can let that man go that you have in custody. He is not guilty. He had nothing to do with it."

I then remarked, "Well, if you know he is not guilty, you must know something about it. Would you mind writing for me the name Fred Smith?" Chadwick at once got hold of the *Police Gazette* I held in my hand, and wrote on it "Mr. F. Smith." I then told him that what I wanted from him was to write "Fred Smith." He then wrote that name on the *Gazette*, and on comparing his writing with a *fac simile* of the name signed in the pawnbrokers' books by the pledger of the watches stolen from Atherton, I considered it my duty at once to send for Mr. Superintendent Weir, in whose division the murder had been committed, in order that he might allow the pawnbrokers with whom the stolen goods were found to see Chadwick. Mr. Weir lost no time in coming, and when I showed him the writing, and explained what had taken place, he at once took charge of the case, and I had very little further to do with it. The first steps having been thus taken, many more convincing evidences of Chadwick's guilt were soon brought to light.

On examining the pawn tickets found in his house, it was ascertained that when pledging the proceeds of railway robberies he had in several instances given the same names as had been given by the man who pledged the watches, &c., stolen from the shop where the murder had been committed at Atherton. There was also found in a portmanteau, which Chadwick acknowledged having pledged, a silk handkerchief of the same pattern as those stolen from the same shop, and a coat and vest which also formed part of the stolen property.

Not only so, but Chadwick was identified by several witnesses as having been seen by them at Atherton early on the morning the murder was committed. I need not, however, here enter into all the details of the evidence against Chadwick, but simply remark that when arraigned before Justice Mathews, at Liverpool Assizes, for the murder, the proofs of his guilt were so conclusive that the judge, in summing up, said, " The evidence pointed irresistibly to the conclusion that the prisoner was the unhappy man " (who had committed the murder).

The jury unanimously found him guilty, and on the 15th April, 1890, Chadwick was executed in Kirkdale Gaol.

When looking back into Chadwick's history, it may appear strange that he should so long pursue a career of crime, apparently with impunity; but that is easily explained, not only by his natural boldness and cunning, but also by the fact that he was in the habit of continually altering his appearance by the use of hair dyes and various cosmetics, and moving about from place to place, so that even his wife, to whom he had been married about nine months prior to the murder, really knew very little about him, as he only returned home from his predatory expeditions about once a week or so. Chadwick commenced his evil career early in life, and when only seventeen years of age made a murderous attack on a cashier at Radcliffe, whom he robbed, and who, some time afterwards, died from the effects of a blow on the head by Chadwick with a crowbar. For this offence Chadwick was sentenced to seven years' penal servitude.

CHAPTER XXV.

THE MAPP CASE.

BETWEEN eleven and twelve o'clock on Friday night, November 23rd, 1889, Police-sergeant Michael Lynn, stationed at Chorlton-cum-Hardy, found Elizabeth Mapp, age 22, asleep in a watchman's cabin at or near Chorlton-cum-Hardy. He wakened her up, asked her some questions, and then went away. In a short time after, not feeling satisfied, he went again to the cabin and aroused the girl. Observing that she had a small bundle, he asked her what was in it, and she said that it was some baby's clothes that had been given to her to alter. The bundle was examined, and found to contain a baby's frock and other articles, all of which smelled very strongly of medicine. She was taken to the police-station and there charged with sleeping out. She had also in her possession a gold watch, six shillings, and a few coppers.

She was brought to the police-court the next day, and a remand was granted. I asked her to give some account of herself, that inquiry might be made, and if her character was good she would get the benefit of it, but she absolutely refused to say anything about herself except that, for the last two years, she had been knocking about from one town to another, and she was quite firm that the baby's clothing found in her bundle had been given to her to alter, but declined to say by whom. I strongly suspected that she must have had a baby, and that she had by some means disposed of it. In the presence of the young woman I directed Sergeant Lynn, who had charge of the case, to go and take any number of men he desired, and search every piece of water in the neighbourhood of Withington and Chorlton-cum-Hardy. I could see by her manner that these instructions to the sergeant affected the young woman very much.

While visiting the neighbourhood of Eccles the same afternoon I received a telephonic message from Sergeant Lynn to the effect that Mapp desired to make a communication to me. I at once returned to Old Trafford, where she had been kept, and she told me she wished to make a statement. I gave her the usual caution, telling her that it was a very serious matter indeed, and that whatever she said to me bearing upon the case I should make known to the magistrates before whom she would be taken. However, she was determined to make a statement, and I allowed her to do so, which ran as follows :—

"I went to the workhouse at Stockport to be confined about seven months ago, and gave birth to a child there about six months ago. I came out of the workhouse on Tuesday last, taking with me my child. That night I slept in a closet. I then went to Kershaw's lodging-house at Stockport, and stayed there until yesterday. The child was very cross, and was crying night and day, and I got some infant's preservative, to keep it quiet, at Mrs. Cooper's, in Chestergate, for which I paid 1½d. The child cried so much that I had no peace, and was nearly fagged out. I did all that I could for it while I had it. I thought I would not like anyone else to have it. I thought I would like to know the end of it. I should not like to see anyone else ill-use the child. If I am taken I can find the child. I started on from Stockport and walked on for a long distance through fields. The poor little child was almost asleep, and I thought I would put it out of its misery. So I wrapped it up in a little shawl and threw it in, and it died almost in a minute. I stayed there about a quarter of an hour. I looked round and saw some lights in the distance—I went on in the direction and found they were only a few glimmering lamps, and then lost my way, and afterwards saw a man that was watching on the road in a cabin, and he told me I might wait in the cabin if I gave account of myself to the policeman when he came round. So I went into the cabin and waited there. "Elizabeth Mapp."

After I had read this statement aloud, I handed it to her, and said, "Can you read?"

She replied, "Yes."

"Well, read that; and if there is anything at all that you think ought not to be in, tell me, and I will take it out," I answered.

After reading the statement she said it was quite right, and signed it, and expressed a wish to show me where she put the child in the water, but, it being dark, I suggested we should go next morning, which we did, taking Sergeant Lynn with us. We alighted at Barlow Moor Hall, and Mapp walked in front until she came to the river Mersey; but before getting there she told me she had put an iron-spiked hurdle on one end, so that she would know where the place was. After searching about there for some time, and seeing that she could not find the baby, although we found the piece of hurdle, and she showed me where she sat when she threw the baby into the river, I brought her away, and on our way back she told me that the father of the child was a single young man, who earned about 18s. per week, and lived at Stockport; and she further told me she would have fathered the child, only he had told her that he would deny being the father, and that, nobody having seen them together, it would not be possible for her to prove her case. She also told me that the child would have two stockings on one foot, and had a little crimson coloured frock on when she threw it into the water.

She was several times remanded, whilst Sergeant Lynn and others were engaged in dragging the river; but at last a man, named James Johnson, on the 19th of December, passing along the side of the river Mersey at Urmston, found the body of the child fast to some stakes that were driven in at the waters edge to keep the embankment up.

On further inquiry Sergeant Lynn discovered that Mapp had left the Union Workhouse, at Stockport, on the 19th of November, and, after staying one night in a closet, she went and lodged with Mrs. Kershaw, who keeps a lodging-house in Stockport, where she remained two nights, and so far as could be ascertained she had behaved well to the child. She left the house on the 22nd November, under the pretence of going to the chemist's, where she had been the day before for medicine, but never returned; and it transpired that she had taken the tram from Stockport to Manchester and then from Manchester to Withington, where she turned down Barlow Moor Road, and made her way to the river, and from there to the watchman's cabin, where she was found by Sergeant Lynn.

The day following the finding of the body of the child, Mapp and the witnesses were taken to the Talbot Hotel, Stretford, to which place the body had been removed with a view to identity. As soon as Mapp saw the child she took it up, kissed it, and said it was hers.

The prisoner was committed for trial, on the charge of wilful murder, at the Manchester Assizes, and was sentenced to death by Mr. Justice Charles. The sentence was afterwards commuted to one of penal servitude for life.

Petitions were afterwards got up with a view to reducing the sentence, but up to the present time without effect.

CHAPTER XXVI.

POLICE COURT WITTICISMS BY THE LATE MR. TRAFFORD, STIPENDIARY MAGISTRATE FOR MANCHESTER DIVISION.

MUCH has been said of the late Mr. Trafford in these reminiscences that I thought I would include some of his pithy sayings to people attending the court, all of which I heard myself.

One morning a lady came into the court, and asked for a summons against another lady, who, she said, had been talking scandal about her.

Mr. Trafford told her he had no power to do anything in the matter.

"What must I do?"

"Prosecute her in the Ecclesiastical Court, and, if convicted according to an old law, she will have to stand barefoot at the church door covered only with a white sheet and in broad daylight with a burning candle in her hand. It may cost you some hundreds of pounds, but then the sight will be worth seeing, and perhaps you'll think it worth the money."

A POT AND KETTLE BUSINESS.

It frequently happened that women were brought before the court charged with tearing each other's clothes, rolling each other in the dirt, and tearing the hair from each other's heads; and he would humorously order some police officers to compare the hair that was torn off with that which was not torn off, and then direct that the hair should be impounded for the benefit of the women's hair sofa, which he would be able to make some day, and he would often address them thus—

"Well, this is a pot-and-kettle business. Which is the blackest is more than I can tell. However, you will both be bound over to keep the peace for some time to come."

TEETOTALISM.

A man was brought before him for outrageous conduct while drunk. He had been before the court several times, but not of late, and Mr. Trafford said to him—

"Good morning. Come to see me again, have you? We are old acquaintances, you know. Have you been a teetotaller while you have been away?"

"Yes, sir."

"I thought so, for whenever you teetotallers break out you are ten times worse than ever. Well, now, if I let you off easy this time what about the pledge?"

"Oh, I'll never break it again! I'll never come here any more—never."

"Ah! it is a good big long promise. I'm afraid you won't keep it; but go and try."

COMMITTING HIMSELF.

On one occasion, when a man had brought two lads before the court for pelting him with stones, he said—

"What did you bring them here for, and bother me with

it? Why did you not lay hold of them, and throw them into the nearest ditch?"

Seeing one of the reporters laughing and writing it down he called out from the bench—

"I say, Mr., don't you put that down. I don't want that in the paper. There'd be a row about it."

PARISH CONSTABLES.

He had a special contempt for these, and when they came once a year to be sworn in, it was a rare day of chaff. He would say to big, strong, middle-aged men—

"Ah, we shall feel safe now you are in our service."

If they were *fat*, he would ask them if they could *run* well, as it was the duty of the parish constable to do a good deal of *running*, when there was any *danger*. On one occasion one of them would not take an oath, as he did not believe in a future state of rewards and punishments.

"Here's a pretty go, Mr. Clerk. He don't believe in a devil. Shocking, isn't it? We couldn't take his oath if he'd give it."

Once a man asked him if he was to use his stave, and in return said—

"What do you want to know for?"

"Oh, some lads may get into my garden, as they have done afore, and I thought I'd give 'em a taste of it if they did."

"In that case I may have to give you a taste of something, and perhaps mine may not be sweetest, after all. Mind what you are about."

TAKING BAIL.

Sometimes he would refuse bail in this way: "I'll keep

you while I've got you. We may have some trouble to catch you if I let you go. We have plenty of room inside, a parson to preach to you, a doctor to physic you, and all the rest of it; and they may do you a power of good. I think I'll try it."

CONTRIBUTING TO THE COUNTY RATE.

When a publican or a drunkard had been fined several times he would say, "I must call on you for another contribution to the county rate. You are one of the best contributers we have; quite a patriot in this line of business. If you will break the law you must pay for it."

CROWING OVER HIM.

On one occasion a man was brought before him for stealing a number of fowls, which were brought in a bag for identification. When pulled out of the bag, one of them proved to be a gamecock; and being put into the witness box, he forthwith crowed lustily, as gamecocks will do, as much as to say, "I'll crow as well as you here." Whereupon the magistrate thus addressed him: "No crowing here, sir. I'm cock of the walk here. Don't crow over me, or I'll commit you for contempt of court."

QUACKERY AT THE LAWYERS' TABLE.

A man was brought before him for stealing some ducks. They were lifted out of a bag and put into the witness-box, and, being alarmed, they began to "quack, quack, quack," very loudly; whereupon the magistrate turned to them, and said, "No quackery here, if you please." And then, bowing to the lawyers at the table, he said, "We've enough quackery here without you."

A JEST AT DOCTRINE.

On one occasion, when a man applied for a summons against his employer for his wages, the following dialogue ensued—

"Why won't he pay you?"

"Don't know."

"Yes, you do. What does he say?"

"Must I tell you?"

"Yes, certainly. Go on, or go home."

"And *must* I tell you."

"You may lose your brass if I grant you a summons without knowing the reason of it. What does he say?"

"Well, he says—he says—he says he'll go to h—— in his old clogs first."

"Does he? Well, it don't matter which pair he goes in—old or new—they'll be sure to be frizzled when he gets there."

VERDICTS OF JURIES.

Lawyers would often say, for the defence of their clients, "No juries would convict upon this evidence, your worship."

"I don't know that," he would say: "there's no telling what juries will do. On one occasion, a man pleaded guilty to horse stealing, but the jury found him not guilty, for all that. They said he was such a liar nobody could believe him."

NICKNAMES.

He used to get some fun out of Irish cases. On one occasion he was addressed as "my lord."

"Nay," he said, "don't call me nicknames, sir. I'm not a lord; never shall be."

"But, please your reverence."

"No, I'm not a reverence either. Come, drop these fine names; don't think to come over me that way."

I now give two or three specimens of the serious side of his character:—

A SAD CASE.

On one occasion a young man was brought before him—a highly-respectable young man—charged with stealing a beer glass, while in a state of intoxication. When the evidence had been heard, and the publican urged punishment because he had lost so many beer glasses, he said to the young man—

"What have you to say to this?"

"What have I to say to it?" said the young man. "What matters it what I say now? I've disgraced myself, my friends; disgraced in the eyes of all who knew me; and if my friends ever have words with anybody here—there's a good many here—they'll throw it at them and me, and say 'He stole a beer glass, he did.' I was drunk for the first time in my life. I had been to a Christmas party, and I didn't know what I was doing. I'd plenty of beer glasses at home. I didn't want his beer glass, though it was found in my pocket, smashed to pieces. I never stole a beer glass from the man before. I never was in the house before that night. Settle it! settle it! It matters not what I say now."

Mr. Trafford interceded with the prosecutor, and the case was withdrawn.

HE IS TAKEN IN.

On one occasion a man was brought before him for robbing

a young woman, a public-house singer, of her earnings, between Oldham and Hollinwood, and committing a criminal assault upon her. The man was brought up as a prisoner, and the woman (in giving her evidence) seemed to have lost her wits from sheer fright. She wept, and screamed, and howled, so that nothing definite could be got out of her. He remanded the case for three days, to give her time to recover herself; but she didn't appear. The police-sergeant of the district said she couldn't come; her friends had pawned all her clothes, and she was in bed naked. Whereupon he said to the prisoner—

"I'm not to be done in this way. The woman shall come, or you shan't go."

Then he privately gave money to get the things out of pawn, and adjourned it for three days more. At the end of that time the man was brought up again, but the woman was not produced.

"How is this?" said he to the police-sergeant.

"Oh, they got the things out of pawn, your worship, and sent her off."

He adjourned the case again and again, but had to give it up at last, as a case in which he had been done for.

A SERIOUS POSITION.

On one occasion an old soldier was brought before the court, charged wth stabbing a man, and calling out as he did so, "Take that. I'm a Fenian."

Addressing the man, he said, "You are in a most serious position."

"I am, sir. I know it."

"The penalty may be death."

"It may, sir."

"Well, what have you to say?"

"I've been wounded in the head, sir, and spirits drove me mad. I hadn't touched them for years till this day, and do not know what Fenianism is."

AN OLD SOLDIER'S THREAT.

An old soldier was brought up before him, charged with begging.

"Why did you beg?"

"Better beg than steal."

"But why not work?"

"I can't work. I went into the army before I learned to work. Been there all my past days, and was sent off with £40 at last. It soon went in street hawking."

"Why don't you go to the relieving officer for a bed and a breakfast?"

"After fighting for my country, as I have done! Bundled off to get a bed and breakfast somewhere else is all the relieving officer will do for me."

"But you have a parish settlement somewhere?"

"No, I have not. I went where I was born. They said I didn't belong to them. I went to the place where I was an apprentice and run away to be a soldier. They said I didn't belong to them. And I've been to the place where I've been since I left the army, and they say I don't belong to them. I shan't be brought up for begging any more. I'll have what I want, where I can get it."

"I'm sorry for you. We ought to provide for such as you

better than we do. But don't carry out your threat; it will be worse for you."

A WELL-DESERVED REBUKE.

A man was brought before him charged with being under a bed in a public-house, with intent to commit a felony. He had been several times in prison for felony. On this occasion the woman who had lived with him as his wife was forced into the witness-box to give evidence against him. She cried bitterly, and the man himself was affected.

"What do you bring her here for? Isn't it bad enough without that?"

"You should have made her your wife, sir. You should have done her justice, and then the law would have provided she should say nothing against you. You did not do it, and must now take the consequences."

LIGHT WEIGHTS.

He was usually very *heavy* on persons brought before him for light weights. He would chaff them, and say—

"Of course, you know nothing about it; light-weight people never do. But it is a serious matter for your customers. You rob the poorest of the poor; and we'll give you something to help your memory in future, in the shape of a heavy fine to-day. Come here again, and you shall have a double dose."

He used to deal very heavily with servants for any petty theft of which they might be guilty, as though he had a special hatred against them. In spite of his wit and deep powers of penetration, he was a very passionate man; and if ever a complainant or defendant, witness or attorney, got on the wrong side of his temper, they had indeed to make out a good case to get a decision in their favour.

On one occasion when the stipendiary came into court he found a good many ladies there. Addressing the clerk, he said—

"Mr. Rutter, how is it there are so many ladies present? Is there a dirty case?" Then looking into the charge book, "Oh, yes, I see there is one. I will take it at once." Looking straight towards the gallery he called out, "All respectable women leave the court."

Some at once left, but many kept their seats, on which the stipendiary called out—

"Go on with the case. All respectable women have left the court," and the case was at once proceeded with.

On one occasion two men were brought up before Mr. H. L. Trafford, on a charge of being drunk and stealing a horse and cab. When the prisoners were asked what they had to say, one replied that he was drunk. It was only a lark, and he never intended to steal it. "Oh," replied the Stipendiary, "I have got a very nice cage for larks. I will have you put in that cage, and see if it will make you sing," and they were then remanded.

NOTE.

THE jargon which the predatory classes use in communicating with each other is curious in its way, but thoroughly unintelligible to the outside world. Here are a few examples of their vocabulary, with appended translations, which I have put in tabular form:—

Highland frisky	Whisky.
Break me	Breakfast.
Jimmy Skinner	Dinner.
Mary Blane	To meet a train.
Salvation	Station.
Twirls	Housebreaking implements.
Sighted it	I have seen it.
Dimmick, or Snide	Base coin.
Flimsy	A £5 note.
Long-tailed	£10 or £20 notes or higher.
Fence	A receiver of stolen property.
Took us on	He changed banknotes.
Rubs	Years of penal servitude.
Stiff	A letter.
Nine moon	Nine months.
Dutch Doll	A woman.
Peter	Portmanteau.

Smashed	Committed for trial.
Mouthpiece	A barrister.
Done for half a stretch	Six months.
Sundial	Photograph.
Square pross	Make it right with prosecutor.
Barrow run	Fined £5.
Eye me float	Coat.
Daisy roots	Boots.
Charles Brady	Hat.
Round my house	Trousers.
Charley Prescott	Waistcoat.
Tommy Roller	Collar.
Bushel and Peck	Neck.
Maks	Liquor.
Toke	Bread.
Packing	Food.
Snoute	Tobacco.

THIEF'S MESSAGE SENT BY ANOTHER THIEF.

"I have got 9 moon at the last pulley. When are you going out, Harry? I am going out 11th of next month. Will you go and tell Dutch Doll to come up to try and get me right twirl (good warder). Tell her that I am doing mats. I do not care for it. I am going to try to get into the cookhouse, and tell her to keep straight, and not fail in meaning another man. There is a twirl here from another stir. If he sees me I am sure to be balled for my super (supervision). You might tell her to go and do that place over. It is put up for £200. Go to mother, and tell her to take care of my Peter. Tell the Dutch to get that Jenny (watch) out, in case I am balled for my supper."

APPENDIX.

THE OLD TRAFFORD POLICE SOUP KITCHEN.

MORE than thirteen years have now elapsed since my attention was specially called to the extreme sufferings which prevail in severe weather amidst orphan and uncared-for children. I am not now referring to actual gutter children—those nomads of civilisation who pick up a precarious living in the streets, and who have no roof to shelter them upon which they have a claim. Their cases are very mournful, but they can only be satisfactorily dealt with in public institutions into which the little waifs and strays are received as inmates. In the case, however, of heartless and drunken parents, who heed not what becomes of their offspring—of orphans who are taken charge of by relations and others, and who are neglected, uncared-for, and starved—or even of those whose fathers and mothers, from want of employment, illness, or other causes over which they have no control, are unable to provide for their little ones, much good can be done, and has been done in other ways.

This has been the case, for instance, in connection with my soup kitchen in the drill hall at Old Trafford Police Station, where a vast amount of beneficial work has been done for the period I have named, at a strictly moderate expenditure. In order to convey some idea of the good actually done, I may mention that in the winter of 1887-88 no fewer than 155,010 meals were supplied, while about 1,000 pairs of clogs and 1,300 suits of clothing were given out in the more necessitous cases. This was all accomplished at what I may call the trifling cost of £867 3s. 1d.; but of course it will be understood that if more money were forthcoming than has hitherto been received more good would be done.

To go a little fuller into the matter, I may mention that during the thirteen years in which the system has been in operation at Old Trafford, 1,582,923 meals have been supplied, while since March, 1886, as many as 25,061 have been provided at Patricroft and 22,444 at Gorton, making a grand total of 1,582,923. During the past three years 3,350 pairs of clogs and 3,650 suits of clothing have also been given away. Since 1881 the amount expended has been no more than £5,856 7s. 2d., while there was a balance in hand at the date of the last audit of £95 19s. 10d. The average of meals given in the kitchen is now about 1,100 a day. It may be added that the charity is worked with laudable conciseness and regularity, and subscribers may rest assured that every penny contributed is the means of doing some real good, while the whole work is of very substantial advantage to a genuinely necessitous and usually deserving class. In this work I have been energetically and loyally aided by Sergeant Cameron and those officers of the force who are off duty when the children have to be attended to.

APPENDIX.

STATISTICS RESPECTING OLD TRAFFORD POLICE SOUP KITCHEN.

The kitchen was opened in January, 1878, and attention is directed to the following statistics relating to our operations since that time:—

NO. OF MEALS SUPPLIED IN THE

First Year		41,648
1878—1879		99,080
1879—1880		101,520
1880—1881		101,090
1881—1882		102,360
1882—1883		149,900
1883—1884		102,410
1884—1885		105,050
1885—1886	Old Trafford	152,410
	Patricroft	25,061
	Gorton	22,444
1886—1887		146,730
1887—1888		155,010
1888—1889		156,660
1889—1890		121,550

Attendance from commencement 1,582,923

Each year about 2,000 and upwards of the poorest children in Manchester and Salford are taken in boats for a trip and picnic, and about 1,000 pairs of clogs and 1,400 suits of clothing are given out to the most necessitous cases, after each article has been stamped with the word "POLICE."

FINANCIAL STATISTICS.

YEAR.	No. of Subscribers.	Balance from Previous Year.	Amount of Subscriptions.
		£ s. d.	£ s. d.
1881—1882	135	2 2 4	158 19 8
1882—1883	650	4 16 10	639 11 11
1883—1884	340	182 14 5	342 16 6
1884—1885	380	136 19 11	368 9 9
1885—1886	840	69 4 10	1066 12 1
1886—1887	500	123 4 11	839 18 0
1887—1888	600	95 19 10	869 6 9
1888—1889	580	126 12 6	1003 6 1
1889—1890	650	175 3 8	688 12 11

YEAR.	Total Amount Received.	Amount Expended.	Balance in hand.
	£ s. d.	£ s. d.	£ s. d.
1881—1882	161 2 0	156 5 2	4 16 10
1882—1883	644 8 9	461 14 4	182 14 5
1883—1884	525 10 11	388 11 0	136 19 11
1884—1885	505 9 8	436 4 10	69 4 10
1885—1886	1135 16 11	1012 12 0	123 4 11
1886—1887	963 2 11	867 3 1	95 19 10
1887—1888	965 6 7	838 14 1	126 12 6
1888—1889	1129 18 7	954 14 11	175 3 8
1889—1890	863 16 7	740 6 10	123 9 9

STATEMENT OF RECEIPTS AND PAYMENTS,

For the Season ending 30th September, 1890.

Dr.   £ s. d.

To Balance brought forward from last year 175 3 8

„ Voluntary subscriptions and donations, and proceeds of concerts as given by the Minnehaha Minstrels (£140 6s. 4d.), Children's Bazaars, &c., and £105 from Manchester Division of County Police 685 9 3

„ Bank interest received 3 3 8

£863 16 7

Cr.   £ s.

By Sundry payments for food, clothing, clogs, &c.......... 740 6 10

Balance on hand in banks, &c. 123 9 9

£863 16 7

APPENDIX.

HONORARY AUDITOR'S CERTIFICATE AND REPORT, 1890.

"I have examined the books and accounts relating to Mr. Superintendent Bent's Soup Kitchen up to the 30th September, 1890, and hereby certify that the amounts received and paid have been duly recorded and vouched. For the information of subscribers and the public, a list of subscriptions and donations is exhibited in the Police Office, at Old Trafford. I have ascertained by independent testimony the correctness of the amount to the credit of the charity with the bankers. During the season (1889-90) 121,550 meals, consisting of soup and bread, were supplied to poor children, at a cost of a little in excess of ½d. per head per meal.

"The donations resulting from the voluntary efforts of the Minnehaha Amateur Minstrels on behalf of the charity amounted to £140 6s. 4d. The Manchester Division of the County Police contributed 100 guineas to the funds. In addition to a sum of £50 contributed by Mr. James Benton, I find that he also paid direct in January last £125, being the cost of a Christmas dinner given to the waifs and strays frequenting the soup kitchen, and which sum forms no part of the £685 9s. 3d. shown in the statement of receipts and payments.

"The books have been well and carefully kept.

"JAMES BOARDMAN (Chartered Accountant),
Honorary Auditor.

"Manchester, 1st December, 1890."

I am proud to say that my soup kitchen has become not only one of the institutions but one of the sights of Manchester, as will be seen by the following letters which have appeared in the Manchester papers:—

Manchester has reason to be proud of its charities. It has numerous and admirably-conducted hospitals for the treatment of almost all the ills that flesh is heir to, and where the highest professional skill is always at hand for the relief of the unfortunate sufferers who are compelled to seek its aid. There are agencies for the relief of the deserving poor, and there are also homes for the reclamation of the waifs and strays who abound in our streets. All these institutions have done, and are doing, work which is entitled to the fullest recognition on the part of the public. To these must be added another institution, which, though not at all ambitious in its character, and which has, as it were, taken a line of its own, has nevertheless rendered valuable service to a certain portion of the population of this city. For the past ten years Mr. Superintendent Bent, of the county police, has unostentatiously carried on a mission of charity, his soup kitchen having supplied during the winter months the temporary needs of thousands of starving children. The story of how Mr. Bent was first induced to enter into this work has never been told, and a recital of the incident which led to his action may not be altogether uninteresting. It was during the bitterly cold winter of 1878, when snow lay on the ground a considerable time, that Mr. Bent, while walking one day from Belle Vue to Gorton, saw a lad, apparently about fourteen years of age, standing shivering in the snow. The boy, who appeared to be begging, was almost naked and shoeless. He appeared afraid of the superintendent, thinking probably that he would lock him up, but Mr.

Bent, feeling sorry for the lad, turned his head and walked away to remove his apprehensions. Mr. Bent, however, had not gone more than twenty or thirty yards when he decided to go back to the boy, take him to a clog shop, and buy him a pair of clogs. He returned to the place where he had last seen the lad, but he had vanished. Mr. Bent went home, thinking over what had occurred, and decided to try and keep about twenty children until the frost and snow had gone. Taking with him a sergeant, the two journeyed into Stretford Road, and purchased a quantity of ham and beef bones, and other necessary provisions, and made a quantity of soup. Then a difficulty arose. Here was the soup, but no children, and the police station was the last place to look for them. The difficulty was soon overcome by Mr. Bent, Sergeant Keighley, and others, going to the poorest dwellings in Hulme, notably the neighbourhood of Lord Street; and in some of the most miserable dens that the imagination of man could conceive, found children huddled together in the darkness, shaking with the cold, for in most of these places there was not a spark of fire. Mr. Bent and his men endeavoured to entice the children to go with them, but the poor things were suspicious of the officers, thinking they wanted to lock them up. Many of them cried: "Do you want to lock my daddy up?" The superintendent, not to be beaten, finally gained his object by promising to give each of them a penny if they would come to Old Trafford and have some soup, and directly after the officers were on their way back to Old Trafford with eighteen badly-clad children trotting after them. So benumbed, however, were they with the intense cold that at first they could scarcely hold the basins.

But the combined influence of the fire and soup soon had its effect, and when the expected pennies were placed in their hands the little ones went home, probably for the first time, in high glee, promising faithfully to return on the morrow. This was Mr. Bent's first experience of feeding the starving. His second, third, and subsequent days' experiences were rather startling. Instead of eighteen, there came on the second day 180, and on the third day 580 put in an appearance, so rapidly had the good news spread among the ragged and pinch-faced children of the neighbourhood. Such a sudden attack—like that of an invading army urged on by famine—for the moment bewildered the superintendent, who, while expecting a considerable addition to the numbers, had no idea that he would have his limited resources, as they were then, so severely taxed. None, however, were turned away, all were equally deserving, and Mr. Bent resolved to continue with his philanthropic project. The numbers asking relief continued to increase rapidly, until on one occasion, there were 1,750 children present, and at two later gatherings as many as 2,000 meals were served. By this time Mr. Bent was £50 out of pocket, but as he had from the outset come to the determination not to appeal to the public for anything he had, as he said, no expectation of a shilling being returned. Assistance, however, soon came. The value of the work Mr. Bent was carrying on became more widely known, and sufficient money came to hand to reimburse him for his outlay, and to buy a few clogs for the barefooted little ones. The kitchen was then closed for the first year, but on the commencement of the winter in 1879 it was again opened, Mr. Bent having obtained the permission of the chief constable. On this occasion, however, the operations were on a larger scale, a boiler being erected in the police drill ground to contain 200 gallons of soup, the Messrs. Jennison, of Belle Vue, kindly lending a sufficient number of tables and forms. Mr. Bent was thus able to feed 320 at one sitting, but was compelled to reduce the meals to one per day, instead of two as before. Since that time to the present Mr. Bent has continued his benevolent work at Old Trafford, the great majority of the children coming from Salford, Hulme, and the surrounding districts. At every gathering of the children the same sad scene was repeated. Many of the girls had only an old cotton frock or a shawl, which afforded no protection to the bitterly-cold weather, to cover them, and many of the boys were as inadequately clothed. Some idea may be formed of the relief the worthy superintendent has afforded by the following figures, which need no comment: Number of meals supplied in first year (opened in January, 1878), 41,648; 1878-9, 99,080; 1879-80, 101,520; 1880-1, 101,090; 1881-2, 102,360; 1882-3, 149,900; 1883-4, 102,410; 1884-5, 105,050; 1885-6, 152,410; 1886-7, 146,730; total, 1,102,198. About two years ago, as will be remembered, great distress prevailed at Patricroft and Gorton. Although Mr. Bent had his hands full at Old Trafford, his sympathy was moved for the distressed people, and he opened a soup kitchen at each place, distributing altogether 150,000 meals. Mr. Bent never seems to tire in his work. It is to him a labour of love which he delights in, his unremitting efforts on behalf of the poor children for so long a time proving how thoroughly he has thrown himself into the praiseworthy task of endeavouring to make the lives of the neglected little ones a little brighter and a little happier. There is one very interesting feature in connection with the kitchen, and that is, that nothing is paid for the making of the soup or the dispensing of it. Mr. Bent's own men have shown so great an interest in the work that they agreed to give an hour or so of their leisure time each evening to distribute the food to the children. If the whole of the men are engaged, some of the applicants for soup are selected to assist, in return for which they receive an extra bowl. It must also be mentioned that, in addition to the voluntary services rendered daily in connection with the distribution of the charity, and apart from the cost— £28 12s.—of a picnic for 1,800 children to Worsley Park last year, the staff of the Manchester division of the county police have given two donations amounting to £130 towards the funds of the kitchen, and that this same county police division, with the exception of 50s. received from a lady residing at Moss Side, paid out of their own pockets the whole of the expenses attendant upon a visit of 1,100 of the poorest children to the Manchester Exhibition a few weeks before its close.

Accepting a cordial invitation from Mr. Bent, I paid him a visit the other day, to see for myself what was being done at Old Trafford. On my arrival I found some scores of children already assembled, and more followed in rapid succession, until about 300 were gathered, this being the number which can be accommodated in the kitchen—a comfortable shed where the meals are served—at one time. The children were drawn up under the walls of the drill ground, and as they stood there, eagerly awaiting the meal which was ready for them, one could not fail to observe in their general appearance indications of the unseen misery which exists in Manchester. In most cases the clothing which these boys and girls were wearing was of the most wretched description, totally inadequate to produce any warmth; and had it not been for the timely assistance of Mr. Bent, their sufferings during the cold weather we have recently experienced must have been painful to contemplate. It was noticeable, however, that while the clothing—if the word can be applied—of most of the children was in rags and tatters, a considerable number of them instead of being shoeless, as some of their unfortunate companions, were wearing good stout clogs and stockings, a number of which Mr. Bent for several years past has been able to distribute. Questioning some of the little people who appeared to be the most intelligent the same story of poverty was told by all. One little fellow said he had neither father nor mother. He lived with his sister, and had gone without anything to eat for his dinner many a time. He had had no dinner that day. Another boy stated that his father, who was a bricklayer, had been out of work for a long time. Asked what he had had for dinner that day, the lad replied, "Taters in their jackets," adding that he often had "taters" for his dinner, and sometime got nothing at all. A third case was that of a lad from the City Road district. His father, he said, was a bricksetter. He had been out of employment for several months, but had that morning "got a job" to fix a firegrate. There were six children, the eldest fifteen and the youngest three. He had had no dinner that day, and only a bit of bread and butter for his breakfast. A pitiful tale was that of a lad who lives in Salford. His father, who had tried to eke out a living by hawking, had, for some cause the lad could not clearly explain, been unable to continue that calling, and had failed to find any employment since. That was three months ago. His mother was dead. To the query what he had had for dinner that day, the lad replied that he had had none at all, and often had to go without. A similar answer was returned by a lad living in Providence Street, whose father, a slater, had not had any work for three months. In another case a girl, also from Salford, stated that there were six children at home, the youngest being twelve months old. The father had been out of work for a long time, and the mother was compelled to go out washing. The child added that she had a " shive " (half a slice) of bread for dinner, the same at breakfast, the same every day. Another girl from Salford related a somewhat similar experience. There are seven children; the father, a slater, is not working, and has had no employment for some time, and the only support of the family is the small earnings of the elder brother. The child had a bit of bread for dinner. Probably the saddest case of all was that of a poor dejected-looking woman, with an infant in her arms. Her story was that her husband, a carter, who received at the last place where he was working 18s. a week, had now been without work a month. They had seven boys, the youngest being only seven months old, and the eldest thirteen in June next. The unfortunate woman declared that they had become so reduced that everything in the house had had to be pawned even down to the bedsteads. She added that had it not been for the kindness of Mr. Bent (six of the lads being regular attenders at the kitchen) they would have been compelled to apply to the guardians. The foregoing may be taken as a fair sample of the cases which come daily under the notice of Mr. Bent, and I was further assured, on the authority of the superintendent himself, that large numbers of the children never have, while the kitchen is open, anything to eat except what they receive at the kitchen, unless some kindly-disposed neighbour gives them a crust of bread.

At a given signal the 300 children marched in single file into the kitchen. There was no confusion. A staff of police officers, who on these occasions put off their uniforms and don civilan attire, were at hand to direct the little guests to their respective forms and to attend to their wants. In a few minutes all were seated. Grace was sung by the children in vigorous style, but so tempting was the savoury odour which arose from the steaming soup before them that more than one hungry little mortal commenced an attack upon the contents of the bowl before the singing of the grace was over. Each child had, in addition to the soup, a large piece of bread to accompany it. When the feast was in full swing the scene was a remarkable one. To the right and left, from the centre of the kitchen, stretched long benches full of the very poorest children of Manchester and Salford, the pick as it were of the slums, apparently forgetting—judging from the happy expression on all their faces—all thoughts of the miserable homes from which they had just come. The ages of the children varied from two to fourteen, the very small ones being brought by the brothers and sisters or friends. Several pathetic scenes were witnessed. In one case a little shivering fellow, who had gone to the table, was observed to pour his soup into a can, which he had placed beneath his knees to take it home to his mother. In another instance, three girls were observed to be concealing the pieces of bread allotted to them in their dirty and tattered dress, and when asked why they were doing that, all three replied that they had had nothing to eat that day, and they wanted to keep the bread for breakfast. After the meal was over, and the kitchen cleared of its first batch of guests, another relay of the same number, who had also assembled in the drill ground, marched in and took the vacant places. The same course of procedure was observed, and following these came two more relays, making altogether a total of over 1,100 children who partook of the bounty of Mr. Bent. But the bounty did not stop at the children. For some time past a number of the "unemployed" have presented themselves daily at the police station, and have had the soup that remained after the children had been supplied. There was no exception to what seemed to be now an established rule among these men on the occasion of my visit. Over 100 presented themselves, and waited patiently till the time for their turn came. It came at last, and the men, many of whom, it must be confessed, had a sort of out-of-work appearance about them, were served, as the children, with soup and bread.

Mr. Bent contemplates closing the kitchen in about a fortnight. It was opened on the 14th December, and up to Wednesday evening over 124,000 meals had been given. It should also be mentioned that the whole of the arrangements in connection with the kitchen are under the charge of Sergeant Cameron, who has been an efficient assistant of Mr. Bent. The closing day will be one of great moment to the children. Inquiries are already being made into the circumstances of the parents whose children attend the kitchen, and in all the cases in which the investigation is satisfactory the children will receive from Mr. Bent some clothing. At the same time a proper precaution is taken. There is every reason to suppose that in some instances the articles of clothing would be pawned or sold by the parents if no steps were taken to prevent this. A plan has been adopted, however, which has proved very successful. The plan is to brand the inside of every article of clothing given to the children with the word "Police." There is not the slightest intention in doing so to cast any reflection upon either parents or children, the sole object being to check effectually any attempt to deprive the latter of their clothes. It only remains to be added that Mr. Bent would be happy to receive any visitors who might desire to see what is being accomplished at Old Trafford Police Station.—*Manchester Courier*, *March* 23, 1888.

"READY TO PERISH."

Those who have sated themselves with the mirthful scenes and the bountiful feasts of the Christmas season, and require a little harmless diversion which shall restore to them the power of enjoyment and give a new zest to their food, as well as those who lament that there is no poetry in their lives, and who try by the aid of morbid poems and unwholesome novels to galvanise a sickly sensibility into vigorous life, may hear of a new source of pleasure. After the above ponderous sentence some of the readers of the *Courier* may be, like the Syrian general, disappointed with the humble nature of the prescription, when I say, "Go to Mr. Superintendent Bent's Soup-kitchen." A police-station is—very erroneously—

supposed to be a place utterly prosaic. But what can be said of a soup-kitchen attached to a police-station? I will try to show. The soup-kitchen of Mr. Bent when in full work does not present a spectacle so gorgeous as a Theatre Royal pantomime, or so imposingly respectable as a civic banquet. Its effect differs from that of either of these. I visited the Old Trafford Police Station on the evening of Saturday last, accompanied by a gentleman who takes as much interest in the success of such an undertaking as this as he does in the investigation of public accounts, and by another whose canvases are not unknown to the walls of the Royal Institution. We reached the police-station a little before five o'clock, and found a cluster of quiet and orderly men, though scantily dressed and with a lean and hungry look, waiting outside the yard, into which we passed. Immediately on our right was a large shed, with its front open to the capacious yard. The floor of the shed was taken up with long forms and deal tables, on which were placed rows of basins, each accompanied with a spoon and a piece of bread. The atmosphere of the shed was impregnated with a most fragrant and appetising smell. Ranged along the wall of the yard were some hundreds of little children not to be distinguished each from another in the darkness. Presently, however, the police officers who, being off duty, had come in their own time, and in plain clothes, to wait upon their little guests, completed their task of filling every basin. A signal was given, and the children marched in single file into the shed and took their seats until every steaming basin and "chunk" of bread was confronted by a shivering and eager little boy or girl. The others remained in the yard to wait their turn. Not a spoon was lifted, however, except in the case of a three-year-old little girl, who could barely reach the table, and whose pinched and shrivelled little face was a study for our artist friend, and excited the pity of us all. No joys of home had ever brightened the existence of that little morsel of humanity. All the juices of her nature had been dried out of her at that early age; and her first great need, physical, moral, and spiritual, was—soup. But, by this time, Mr. Bent had appeared on the scene and given us a hearty welcome. Conducting us to one end of the shed, we bared our heads, and every child rose to its feet. I have felt the subduing and reference-inspiring effect of cathedral music when the "pealing organ" is answered by "the full-voiced choir below," and I have heard the children of the Foundling Hospital sing, looking as clean and dainty and well cared-for as possible. But the singing of one verse by 300 hungry and unwashed little choristers, with a "prosaic" police-superintendent as their precentor, had an effect different from either of these. Mr. Bent's sonorous voice gave the keynote of the "Old Hundredth;" and some with voices sweet and strong, and some with voices shrill, reedy, piping, and weak, the children took up the tune to "Be present at our table, Lord." If that invocation was ever heard and answered, surely it was then. The "Father of the fatherless" heard that weak and wavering song, and was present with even the "least of these little ones;" and that murky police-shed was in very deed a sacred temple.

It need not be said that the children did eat their meat with gladness, the grave and kind Sergeant Cameron and his brother officers moving about among the little ones and seeing to their wants. We also moved about among the children, and noted their pale faces—except where washing was obviously a thing of the remote past—their scanty clothing, and their unnaturally weary and care-worn looks. "Where do you live, my little man?" we questioned one little lad rather brighter looking than the rest. "Off Rochdale Road, sir." "What does your father do?" "He's a cabinet-maker, sir; but he hasn't done nothin' for three months." "What does your mother do?" "Please, sir, she goes out washin' when she can get a chance." "How many brothers and sisters have you?" "Two brothers and one sister, sir." "What had you for dinner to-day?" "Nothin', sir." "What for breakfast?" "A 'butty.'" "What had you for dinner yesterday?" "Nothin,' sir, till I come here." Another had had some cold potatoes for dinner, several had had none at all, while one whose mother was dead, and whose father was a navvy who had had his foot crushed and could not work, had shared with his little brother and sister, who were there present, and under their brother's right and left wings respectively, "a bit o' meat as a lady bringed us." Several of the children had lost their fathers; and their mothers "went out charin'." We noticed that while some were shoeless, and others little better off in that respect, some wore stout serviceable clogs and warm stockings. These, Mr. Bent informed us, he had been able to distribute to the number of 50 pairs of each, out of subscriptions which had been sent or brought to him; but 50 was a small number among 700 or 800 children. On the previous (Friday) evening the number of children, women with children, women without children, and men, who sat down in the order named, in relays of 300, and were each supplied with a basin of soup and a piece of bread, was over 1,000, more than three-fourths of whom were children. From the time Mr. Bent opened his "kitchen," about three weeks ago, up to last Saturday night, 11,450 basins of soup and bread had been dispensed with, many of the recipients, of course, coming regularly, in addition to which the afore-mentioned clogs and stockings and some second-hand clothes have been distributed to those who needed them most. I may mention that the clogs are all branded on the wooden sole, "Old Trafford Police Station," so that there is little fear of their being converted into merchandise by unscrupulous parents.

After the two relays of children had been served—some of whom had brought cans and jugs, so that if any soup were left over they could take some home—a small cluster of women who had been standing silent and shivering, making the most of their flimsy clothes, sat down, and these were followed by the men, to one of whom I spoke. He was a blacksmith, 68 years old. He had left his last place because his striker had learnt all that he knew, and, being a younger man, could do the work better. He had tasted no food on that day. He had waited two hours for his basin of soup and bread. He did not know where he should lodge that night. His clothes were so many playthings for the cold wind, and the salt rheum of age and of cold dimmed his eyes "I don't want to go into the Union, because I can do a day's work yet, sir," he said. His lodgings were insured for him for one night at least, and he went to his single meal. The men who are relieved are not of the class who are "known to the police" in any way unfavourably—in fact,

Mr. Bent is the last gentleman in the world those people would wish to see—and neither man nor woman is permitted to sit down who shows any sign of intoxicating drink. But Mr. Bent's efforts are chiefly made on behalf of the children —the little uncared-for wretches who have broken no principle of social economy except being born, and who aer pining and dying in want and misery through no unthrift of their own. To such, in this bitter weather, it is an act of the highest kind of charity to supply warm and nourishing food. The soup is, indeed, excellent. I tasted some, and would gladly have finished the contents of the basin, but that I had the fear of my auditorial friend before my eyes, who would doubtless have condemned my needless and illegitimate banquetting.

Let those who seek a new excitement pay a visit to Mr. Bent. Let them see in the pinched faces and the bare shrunken limbs of a thousand little children something of the unseen misery of Manchester. Let them see how much can be done by a little expenditure and a little trouble, prompted by love and pity, to relieve that misery. Let them take of their time and their substance to strengthen the hands of those who are caring for the little outcast members of our great human family, and they may say with Mr. Bent, as Job did of the days of his prosperity, "Because I delivered the poor that cried, and the fatherless, and him that had none to help him, the blessing of him that was ready to perish came upon me."—*Manchester Courier, January* 6, 1885.

A RAGGED PICNIC.

> "Oh, had I but Aladdin's lamp,
>   If only for a day,
> I'd strive to find a link to bind
>   The joys that pass away,"

Is a wish that happily finds an echo in many a human breast in this our city of Manchester. But, unfortunately, there exists in all large cities a large number of people, young and old, to whom the word joy is an unknown quantity—people who, if left to their own devices or resources, would pass their days from year's end to year's end with scarcely a ray of sunshine breaking in upon the cheerless monotony of their existence. It seems to me, sir, as one who knows some little of the dark side of life in this rich city, that, notwithstanding the large amount of philanthropic effort which is daily put forth there is a greater quantity dormant, but not from any unwillingness on the part of thousands to take part, either by subscriptions or work, or both, in the various organisations that have for their object the amelioration of the distress and physical suffering of our fellow-citizens. There can be no doubt of the truth that "God helps those who help themselves;" but, unfortunately, we have in our midst very many poor creatures who cannot help themselves. It is to this latter class that I am about to refer, viz., that large number of little waifs and strays who, from their very appearance belong to nobody; children who from their cradle (if they had one), have known nothing but starvation and want, who have never received that comfort and nurture so requisite to the due development of their little tender bodies; but instead of these absolute necessities have been reared in filth, fed on infamy, and had their little ears filled with vile oaths in place of the Divine supplication; children who, when they grow up, instead of being a credit and a profit to the State will become a disgrace and a loss, and live in Millbank or Pentonville gaol instead of some decent cot, or perhaps mansion.

I believe that Manchester is entitled to the credit of being the only place in the United Kingdom where the police, or rather that portion of the county police just outside the city boundaries, have taken upon themselves the great and much-to-be-commended duty of, in the winter, providing at least one good hot meal a day for all who care to tramp to Old Trafford Police Station for it, but also in the summer almost empty the back streets, courts, and alleys of the city of the most destitute of the children for one day at least. That day came round on Saturday last, a gloriously fine day. Early in the morning close on 2,000 little ones, some of whom had walked over three miles, assembled at Old Trafford Police Station, where, as a preliminary, they were fed with buns and milk, and then marched four deep at eight o'clock to the Bridgewater Canal Company's landing-stage at Pomona, where they embarked on several large boats for conveyance to Worsley. As I watched the process of packing these little folks, hundreds of them without shoes or stockings or hats, by the *posse* of stalwart policemen in plain clothes, who had volunteered to assist Mr. Superintendent Bent, after being on duty all night, or would have to go on duty when they returned home, I wished that every father who will take his family to the various sea-side resorts, or those well-to-do personages, called bachelors, who a worthy friend of mine says ought to be heavily taxed, could have witnessed the scene. To have heard the shout that rent the air, as the boats moved away, and the band struck up a lively tune, was worth travelling some distance to hear. I have heard the shouts and cheers of political partisans in the adjoining gardens, as Mr. Disraeli, Mr. John Bright, and Lord Randolph Churchill have at various times appeared before the surging mass, louder and stronger of course, but not more spontaneous, or heartfelt than the "hurrah" that arose from those boatloads of little throats on Saturday morning. How the three hours which were occupied in reaching our journey's end were passed away would not only occupy more of your space but take me longer to tell than I have time to. Suffice it to say that almost every popular air, music-hall or Salvation Army, had full justice done it.

By permission of the Earl of Ellesmere we landed in his grounds on the spot where the Queen landed in 1851, and after walking through the beautiful grounds, which are now resplendent with all the colours of the rainbow, and a few others, we arrived in a field adjoining the rectory, and were received by Earl Mulgrave, who quite unexpectedly gave every child present a bun and a bottle of ginger beer. The Misses Kate, Mary, and Florence Egerton, daughters of the Hon. Algernon Egerton, M.P., entered very zealously into the work of distributing the food. (Great cheering.) If ever they were happy in their little lives it was now. Glorious sunshine, a full stomach for once, grass to walk upon that did not hurt bare feet, wheelbarrow races blindfolded which resulted in collisions innumerable, to the great delight of the crowd; biting at buns dipped in syrup treacle and suspended by strings (no touching with hands), which so "transmogrified" the would-be biter that he would have made his fortune as a fly-catcher. Even this had its advantage, for many a lad had his face and hair washed at the pond who looked cleaner than when he started from home. Sack races, hurdle races, greasy pole climbing, tug of war, which to the uninitiated means a long strong rope, with an equal number of lads pulling in opposite directions. Our tug of war on Saturday was between Manchester and Salford, and I am bound to admit, to the lasting disgrace of Manchester, that Salford was completely victorious, which will no doubt be "tidings of comfort and joy" to my friend Mr. Alderman Bailey.

The domestic history of a number of these little folks is a scandal to our boasted civilisation. Idleness and drink are the two demons which are at the bottom of a majority of the cases. Of course there is a percentage due to misfortune, sickness, and death. One curly-headed little chap, aged six, with a little sister about a year younger, informed me that his mother was away—went out of where they lodged last Sunday, and hadn't come back yet—and his father was in Belle Vue. "What for?" He didn't know. "What does he work at?" "He hangs paper on walls." "Does he ever get drunk?" "Aye, when he has any work." "Does he ever beat you?" "Sometimes; but he punches my mother most." Noticing that he had a decent pair of clogs on, he quite confidentially informed me that Master Bent gave him them. I may here say that about 400 of those present have been clothed from head to foot during the last few months by Mr. Bent, each article being marked inside with the word "Police," to prevent their parents selling or pawning them.

The above is only one out of dozens of youngsters whom I interrogated during the day. That some severe remedy will have to be applied to the scoundrels who thus punish their innocent offspring goes without saying. They will have to be made to feel that they cannot outrage the public sentiment and inflict untold misery upon helpless little children. The garrotter gets the lash. Why should not the brutes who are responsible for the naked, filthy, hungry children which abound in our midst have a taste of it after due warning? I make bold to prophesy that, if condign punishment of this description could be meted out to a few dozen of them it would do more to put an end to this shameful state of things than 50,000 sermons. But to return. At four o'clock the commissariat department was again in full work, when mountains of buns and seas of new milk disappeared like magic. Soon after six o'clock we again embarked, and, after requesting each other and the people who lined the banks of the canal, to "Shout, shout the victory, we are on our journey home"—the victory, I suppose, referring to the complete annihilation of the before said buns—we reached port a little after nine, with no worse disaster than one little barefooted fellow treading on a piece of glass, which a good Samaritan quickly extracted and bound up the wound with a pocket-handkerchief. A number of new "threepenny bits," given by Mr. Roscoe, formed the prizes which were offered to the successful competitors in the sports. Before leaving the field the children were called together, and a photograph of them was taken by the Rev. A. W. Turner, St. Peter's, Farnworth. When we arrived at the police station again each little one was presented with another bun and more milk, after which we gave three cheers for Mr. Bent. The band played "God Save the Queen," and so came to an end a day that will long be remembered by many when the author of the outing shall have received his reward in another world. Of course, boats, milk, about 8,000 buns, band, &c., cannot be obtained without considerable cost. If any lady or gentleman who reads this will fancy they were present and send a donation towards it, to Mr. Superintendent Bent, Northumberland Street, Old Trafford, they will have an inward satisfaction which cannot but be comforting. Will 10,000 mothers send an old little frock or petticoat, or little jacket or trousers? They may rest assured that Mr. Bent and his stalwart assistants will see that some little naked creature is benefited thereby.—*Frank Hollins in Manchester Courier, July* 13, 1885.

CHRISTMAS DAY AT A SOUP KITCHEN.

"Whilst shepherds watched their flocks by night,
All seated on the ground,
The angel of the Lord came down,
And glory shone around."

This is a theme that has again made itself familiar to thousands of good Christians, both young and old, during the last few days. The angel of the Lord, who "came down" nearly two thousand years ago, was the harbinger of a little child, born of lowly parents and laid in a manger, and as we paced the yard of the Old Trafford Police Station on the evening of Friday last (Christmas Day), and saw the crowd of little children there assembled, our thoughts naturally gravitated to that child whose advent was being celebrated from pole to pole.

For days previous, in the streets, in the clubs, on 'Change, and every other place where two or three were gathered together, the stock phrases of "A Merry Christmas." "The compliments of the season," &c., had been on every one's lips. Turkeys, geese, and prize beef and mutton had been disposed of by tons. Santa Claus, that good fairy who revisits the glimpses of the moon on each succeeding December 24th, had filled numerous little stockings with toys, more precious to the sleeping innocents than "Rich Peru, with all her gold." The great god Bacchus had showered upon thousands of homes innumerable hampers of the products of Ireland and Scotland. The postman had completed his weary task, and hundreds of thousands of good wishes for the coming year had been exchanged. On every hand in the select and aristocratic region of Old Trafford thousands of gaslights, shining through dining-room windows, were indicative of the mirth that was going on inside, not only in Old Trafford, but all over the civilised world. Yet in the very midst of all this feasting and luxury, within hail almost of a district where scores of thousands of turkeys, &c., had been offered up on the altar of Christmas festivities, there shivered in an open yard, roofed by the canopy of heaven, and lighted by a single gas jet, about 1,000 poor little creatures, waiting their turn for a bowl of soup.

"Alas for the rarity of Christian charity under the sun," has been well said by a poet whose life on this earth was all too short. As we walked through this army of ragged, barefooted, bareheaded, unwashed little folks, the thought would involuntarily arise, that before we send missionaries abroad we ought to "pluck the beam out of our own eyes."

We establish missions for the conversion of the Jews; we send at great cost good and valiant men to the uttermost ends of the earth, to preach the glad tidings of great joy which we are all celebrating now; we have established amongst us a thousand and one societies for the propagation of innumerable fads, the net result as a rule being a good fat salary for the secretaries thereof; and we leave to Mr. Superintendent Bent and a very few others the task of practically dealing with the want and misery and ignorance that exists in our midst.

To most of your readers it will be known that Old Trafford Police Station is about two miles from the Infirmary, yet I find that many of the poor creatures who attend this soup kitchen walk from Ancoats and other places on the opposite side of the town, a many of whom assemble two hours before the time for distribution. The sight that may be witnessed any evening is a disgrace to our common humanity, and must be seen in order to understand the enormity of the trouble. This providing for the helpless at Old Trafford is unique. It is, I believe, the only charity where every penny subscribed actually reaches the bellies and the backs of the poor little people for whom it is given. Not one penny is paid for rent or services rendered by any person.

But, on the contrary, here may be found a number of brave fellows who at duty's call think no danger too great to encounter; men who have faced with the greatest possible courage the infuriated and senseless mob engendered by a colliery strike; men who have stood like martyrs and received the stones and bricks, and other marks of affection that have been showered upon them at an election time, without striking a blow in return until they received the word of command. Veterans like Inspector Halston, Sergeant Cameron, and others, who strip off their uniforms, put on the aprons, and for the time become the tenderest of nurses. The Old Book tells us that the sacrifice of Abel arose as a sweet-smelling savour; could anything be more sweet than to hear from 1,000 to 1,600 little shivering hungry throats sing with cheerful voice—

> "Be present at our table, Lord;
> Be here and everywhere adored;
> Thy creatures bless, and grant that we
> May feast in Paradise with Thee."

As we looked upon the hungry, ravenous little crowd, who thus wished they might feast in Paradise, there was one fact sure, viz., that before next Christmas a many of them would be feasting in Paradise. God grant they may.

Questioning a few, we received the following answers: One little girl, aged six, with two little ones younger than herself, said her dada drove a lurry, but he was out of work now, and they had "a likkle baby besides us three." Another little skeleton said her father was dead, and her mother had bad legs. She had two sisters and three brothers, and one was dead and buried. We thought the latter was to be congratulated. Another: "Father does neawt." Didn't know how many brothers and sisters she had, but they'd eight children. Another little fellow said they had eight children. His father had been dead above two years, and they had a baby about nine months old. This intelligent-looking little chap was naked, with the exception of a filthy petticoat and frock. I need not say that he went home properly clothed from head to foot—

every article marked inside with the word "Police;" and I pity the pawnbroker in whose possession they may be found by Mr. Bent. Another sweet-looking little lass burst into tears as she told me that her father was "drownded in Liverpool," about five years ago, that they had four children, and that her mother went out washing, but she had only three days' work, which would mean about 6s., wherewith to pay her rent and keep four children. Yet another little girl was interrogated as follows: "Have you a father living?" "Yes, sir." "Does he work?" "Sometimes, sir." "Is he teetotal?" "No, sir. Please, sir, he gets drunk many a time, sir." "Does he ever hit you or your mother?" "Yes, sir; he punches my mother many a time, sir. Please, sir, we had to sleep under some railway arches many a time, sir."

And we send missionaries abroad! We critically discuss the relative merits of Heidseick and Pommery, of 47 port, as compared with later vintage, and little Tommy and Polly trudge for miles, often carrying another less than themselves, and wait in an open yard for a basin of soup and a piece of bread! Fair matrons, "clad in silks and laces," surrounded by bright, healthy, happy children, preside at tables that groan under the weight of the good things placed upon them, whilst within a few yards numbers of their less fortunate sisters, clasping to their bosom some miserable little creature, patiently wait their turn for a basin of soup. There is no deception, no humbug about it. People who will walk a considerable distance for a bowl of soup and a piece of dry bread, and eagerly devour it on the spot, are hungry.

One old man, who had been a labourer in an ironfoundry, informed us he would be 68 in January; that he had walked from Edinburgh, trying to get work on the road. Poor old fellow! With a deep sigh, and in a strong Scotch accent, he said, "When ye begin to show the white feathers (alluding to his hair) ye canna get work sae easily. But I'll nae trouble anyone long. I'm aboot at the end, an' I dinna care how soon it comes." What " A merry Christmas," what a prospect of " A happy New Year," for these hundreds of guests of the police at Old Trafford, who nightly sit down to this simple banquet, with appetites keen as razors, as it is to many of them their only meal.

Reader,—I need not say that to feed 1,000 and more of these poor creatures every day, Sunday included, requires a very considerable amount of money. I appeal to the large hearted generosity of the opulent of this rich county of Lancashire. I ask every person who partook of a good dinner on Christmas Day, and have made merry in a good old-fashioned way, to open their hearts and their purses, and help Mr. Superintendent Bent in his noble undertaking. Encourage by your pecuniary aid his stalwart assistants, who show by their unwearying devotion to these helpless little ones that even under the blue coat of a policeman there can beat a large and sympathetic heart. No sauce or seasoning ever invented will give greater satisfaction or a finer flavour to your New Year's Day dinner than the fact that you have, according to your means and the fulness of your heart helped on this good work, not forgetting that the child who was first cradled in a manger, when He became a man, took the little children in His arms and blessed them.—*Frank Hollins in Manchester Courier, January* 1, 1886.

SUNDAY EVENING AT A SOUP KITCHEN.

When returning on a recent Sunday evening from a visit to Superintendent Bent's soup kitchen at Old Trafford, pondering over the never-to-be-forgotten scene just witnessed, the bells of various churches and chapels began to call aloud that the time for evening service was at hand. "Ring out wild bells to the wild sky, the flying clouds, the frosty light, ring out the want, the care, the sin, the faithless coldness of the times," naturally suggested themselves at such a time, and that the Laureate's wishes might instantly be granted was the fervent desire of the writer.

Yes, sir, it was a frosty night, and there was a keen wind blowing from the north, one of those biting, piercing winds that laugh to scorn the stoutest overcoat, and freeze one's very marrow. As we wended our way to town, and met from time to time, hurrying to some place of worship, ladies not "clad in silks and laces," but in garments much more adapted to so cold a night—as we noticed the lights gleaming in almost every parlour window, indicative of the warmth and creature comforts within—that one great query would keep intruding itself, why should so much misery and suffering be?

That a very large amount of it is directly due to preventable causes there cannot be the slightest doubt. But what is to be the agency to bring about the change is not for me to discuss now. "The poor always ye have with you" is as true now as when it was uttered by the Master, and if any of your readers want to see a sample of them—the genuine unadulterated article—let them go to Northumberland Street

Police Station, Old Trafford, any evening (Sunday included), about 4-30. If the sight there to be witnessed does not melt a heart of stone, I shall feel ashamed that I am a human being.

Here in this police drillyard, roofed with the "wild sky, the flying clouds," assemble every night, an average of about 1,000, miserable, starving fellow-creatures, the majority under nine years old, who wait patiently for the only meal many of them get during the day. For a basin of hot soup and a piece of bread that do not cost 1d., they tramp miles. Polly, aged nine, carrying little Billy, aged two or three, with another or two between those ages, clinging to what she calls her frock. Frock forsooth—rag, sir, is the proper word to use. No peripatetic vendor of sand and rubbing stones would give 6d. for the entire clothing of the whole four. The desire for food is daily illustrated by these little ones arriving an hour before the time for distribution. Some of the hardiest try to keep themselves warm by running races in the yard; but the great mass of them, bareheaded, barefooted, plenty with only a thin frock on, and entirely without underclothing of any description, huddle together against the walls and vainly endeavour to keep out the biting blast. It is a sight almost without parellel to watch them when they have been passed into the shed, and each one duly installed opposite a steaming basin of soup. Like magic each basin is eagerly pressed by two little hands, almost dead with cold—hands that could scarcely hold a spoon When at length the first 300 are seated, and that unique army of waiters who daily divest themselves of their uniform and without money, and without price, in their own time, put on garments of wrappering, and in the most humane manner minister to the wants of their little guests, when some stalwart representative of the majesty of the law has led off the supplication, "Be present at our table, Lord," and 300 little throats have joined in with only that fervour that little children can sing; the attack is electrical in its rapidity. Then is the time to see the warm side of a policeman's heart. Six feet of manly vigour and strength feeding some shivering mortal, either too little or too cold, or both, to feed itself. What a volume of heartrending incidents could be culled from the frequenters of this soup kitchen. Here are a few:—

1. A sharp-looking lad of 10. "What does your father work at?" "He used to work at th' exhibition, but he got sacked." "How long ago?" "Before Chrisemus." "Has he done nothing since?" "No, only sweepin' some snow up with a lot of other chaps as wus out o' work when it snowed. An' we have five children—us four, an' one as has got a bad leg a-whoam."

2. A girl about 12. "Father works at a croft, but he only get's fourteen shillin' a week. An' he has to pay a chap some money every week as he went bound with for another chap, and they have it to pay, or else they'd fetch us things." "How many children have you?" "Please, sir, there's me and these two little lads, an' a little baby as we had last Monday, an' it's another little lad; an' some women as lives aside of us is mindin' mi mother. No, sir, father doesn't drink only tea, an' he teks it wi' him in a mornin' in his can."

3. A lad of 10. "No, sir; we've had nowt only this soup to-day." "Why, how's that?" "Please, sir, father's got th' inflammation in his belly an' someat else, an' he's been in bed

about a month." "What does your mother do?" "Hoo looks after mi father and cleans th' floor, an' fetches some clooas from a shop, and weshes um a-whoam. We've five children, us four an' a little un; but a woman as knows mi mother says hoo'll have him while mi father gets better."

4. A lad of 9. "Father is a labourer, an' he's been out o' work five weeks." "Does your mother do anything?" Bursting into tears, he replied, when his sobs would permit him, "Oh, please, sir, mother was very bad a long time, and died before Christmas, and is put in th' cemetery now, and we'st never see her any more. We've nine children. Our Alice an' our Jane is in service. Our Joe is buried in Preston, an' there's us four, and two a-whoam."

5. A bad case from Salford. "Please, sir, my father's dead, and my mother goes out washing, but she's only two days a week, and we've six children. There's only one working; she's fourteen. She keeps herself, and gives mother two shillings a month.

These are only a very few instances out of thousands of children. But this benevolence of Mr. Bent's is not confined to children. Any adult, male or female, who present themselves before five o'clock are also supplied. Upon that portion of the Lord's Prayer (which thousands of people repeat daily, but don't all practise), viz., "Forgive us our trespasses, as we forgive them that trespass against us," Mr. Bent builds his charity. He considers that any poor fellow or woman who will walk from Manchester or Salford, and stand in the yard an hour, for what does not, as I have said before, cost 1d., is hungry, and though he or she might only have "come out" last week, common humanity cannot allow them to die in the gutter for want of food. But, sir, there are hundreds of poor creatures (adults) attend, who have never seen the inside of either workhouse or prison, who whilst they can help it never will, who through stress of weather, &c., are out of work, and are driven to this soup kitchen in order to keep body and soul together. I will give a few instances —

1. Worked at a coalyard in Salford at 2s. per week and one halfpenny per cwt. for taking coal out. When he was fully occupied he could earn about 10s. per week. (Splendid situation.)

2. An intelligent man had walked from London—a very clean, intelligent fellow. Produced his card of membership of a Gospel Temperance Society in Aldersgate Street. Thrown out of employment by circumstances over which he had no control, yet here he was on this bleak Sunday evening in a strange city without a friend or a penny.

3. A woman with a baby at the breast, which she was vainly endeavouring to keep warm with an old rag of a shawl. "Yes, sir, I have a husband, but he's out of work. He's a stone cutter, and used to work for Bobby Neill, and he's a good master, too; but the job is finished, and he has not been able to get another job yet. He's on the tramp looking for work."

> "'Rest thee, my babe, rest on! 'tis hunger's cry.
> Sleep, for there is no food, the fount is dry.
> Famine and cold their wearying work have done;
> My heart must break; and thou!'—The clock strikes one."

These are only a few, very few, samples of what anyone who chooses may see and inquire into themselves any night they like.

> "Oh, it was pitiful!
> Near a whole city full,
> Home they had none."

Now, sir, these crowds of people, large and small, cannot be fed every night without considerable cost. Every penny subscribed goes down the throats or on the backs of the poor recipients. There are neither pensions nor salaries attached to this fund, and I ask every good-hearted fellow, married or single, every loving woman, especially mothers, when they see their own loved ones at home, well cared-for, well fed, and clothed, to think of those hungry, starved fellow creatures who stand shivering in an open yard on a Sunday night, for the only meal many of them get, and out of the fulness of their hearts to send Mr. Bent, at Old Trafford, their mite towards feeding the hungry. Every sovereign will gladden the hearts and fill the stomachs of over 240 people. Could a sovereign be better spent, or a cheaper banquet provided?

Old Trafford is going to be the scene of great festivities and glorification during the forthcoming exhibition. Let it not be said that in close proximity to all this wealth and grandeur there is another exhibition of an opposite character, where little children will have to be sent empty away because funds for providing them with this most frugal of meals and a pair of clogs to warm little bare feet were not forthcoming in this Jubilee Year, and in this deservedly famous and generous city of Manchester.—*Frank Hollins in Manchester Courier, February* 24, 1887.

SUPERINTENDENT BENT'S CHILDREN'S TRIP TO WORSLEY.

Amidst the sounding of trumpets and shouts of war in connection with the election campaign it is pleasant to turn aside for a little to a heart-stirring sight of a very different kind—a sight such as seldom meets the eye, but one that once seen can never be forgotten. At five o'clock on Saturday morning, groups of poorly-clad children of all ages, with clear bright faces and joyful looks, might be seen hurrying along from all parts of Manchester and Salford to one common centre—Old Trafford Police Station. They were the waifs and strays of the streets, and the magician's wand by whose potent spell they were drawn to Old Trafford was Mr. Superintendent Bent's "Children's Trip to Worsley." One can imagine how the hearts of the half-starved little ones would leap within them as the magic words passed like wildfire through their little world a few days previously—"Mr. Bent's picnic is on Saturday."

By 7 a.m. about 2,000 children were busy in the large police drillyard putting out of sight buns and milk as fast as they could be served out by the sergeants and constables who had volunteered their services for the occasion, while Mr. Bent himself actively superintended the whole, taking care that no little one was jostled out of its place and done out of its breakfast by bigger lads or girls—in fact here, as on other occasions, the police motto appeared to be the Scripture injunction—"Do everything decently and in order," for each of the 2,000 children were marched up in procession one by one to receive his or her bun and milk, and then "move on" to make way for others.

Precisely at 7-40 a.m. the whole vast procession filed out of the police yard, headed by Mr. Superintendent Bent and the Ardwick Green Industrial School Band, with colours flying, one large banner (presented by Miss Ellis, of Blackley) especially catching the eye by its beauty and the inscription on it—"God bless our generous friends." Having reached the point of embarkation at Cornbrook, and all having safely been hoisted aboard by the strong arms of the stalwart policemen in attendance, the "canal fleet," provided and fitted up for the occasion by the Bridgewater Navigation Company, was soon seen making rapid headway up the canal, followed by the hearty cheers and "God bless yous" of hundreds of mothers, who had confidently committed their treasures to the care of the kind superintendent.

It would take a long summer's day to tell all the happy experiences of the voyage and the subsequent proceedings of the day. Suffice it to say that on arrival at Worsley the children were allowed permission to march four abreast through the beautiful grounds and flower gardens of the Right Hon. the Earl of Ellesmere, to the field where, by the kind permission of the Rev. the Earl of Mulgrave, the picnic was to be held. Here a plentiful supply of cakes and mineral waters was provided by the generous joint liberality of Lady Ellesmere and Lord Mulgrave. Buns and milk were also served out throughout the day, these latter having been conveyed by Mr. Bent from Old Trafford.

On the field, mixing with and interesting themselves with the children, were many lady and gentlemen friends from various places, among whom were the Rev. Mr. Harland and Mr. Upjohn, of Worsley, who took a very active part in promoting the children's enjoyment; Mr. Roscoe, Mr. Temperley, Mr. Noden, and others, small sums of money having been handed to Mr. Bent by the three latter gentlemen to be distributed among the children in prizes.

After a day of most thorough enjoyment, enlivened by juvenile games and races of all descriptions, interspersed with various airs by the band in attendance, the children were again marshalled down to the four large boats waiting to carry them home.

The return journey to Old Trafford having been accomplished in safety, the children were again marched to the police station, Old Trafford, where a supply of buns and milk were again served out, and the children, after making the walls of the drillyard ring with their songs, and cheers to their kind benefactor—whose chief happiness consists in making others happy—were dismissed to their several homes, to wander again, in their dreams, in the green fields of Worsley, and breathe its bracing air, and think they again hear Mr. Bent call them round him for milk and buns. Alas! many of these little ones, as they waken up with empty stomachs and empty homes, will sadly think, if they do not say it—"I awoke, and behold it was a dream."—*Manchester Courier, June* 28, 1886.

MR. SUPERINTENDENT BENT'S SOUP KITCHEN.

Very striking was the scene witnessed on Saturday at the soup kitchen of Mr. Superintendent Bent at the Old Trafford Police Station. The occasion was also remarkable in several respects, for not only did the 1400 children who assembled receive their usual allowance of soup and bread, but during the day about 3,000 buns were distributed among them, and, most important of all, they were clothed from head to foot. Inquiries had been made into the circumstances of each family whose children attended the soup kitchen, and in every instance in which the investigations proved satisfactorily, and where they showed that distress existed through no fault of the parents, each child received a ticket which entitled him to receive a complete suit of clothing on Saturday. On Friday there were about 2,000 children dealt with. They had their soup and bread, and on leaving every one of them was presented with an orange. During the day also a new feature was introduced, with the view of affording as much pleasure as possible to the poor youngsters whose life and surroundings, outside Mr. Bent's kitchen, are pitiable. A series of games were organised, into which the children entered with such gusto that they showed unmistakably that they had for the time forgotten and become oblivious to the sad scenes of misery to which it was their melancholy fate to return. But, as we say, no thought of the dark prospect which awaited them apparently entered their minds. All for the present was joy and gladness, which was enhanced when they learned that they were to come next morning to be donned in warm and comfortable clothing. In the morning an extraordinary incident occurred. The children were told on Friday night to present themselves at the police station at eight o'clock on Saturday morning, but so early as five o'clock large numbers of the ragged and starving waifs were huddled together at the gates of the police station, shivering in the cold until such time as the doors should be thrown open to admit them. The numbers increased, and at half-past nine, when admittance was given, about 1,400 children, as already stated, swarmed in with an eager rush. Then a grand transformation took place. Nothing like it or approaching it was ever seen in a pantomime. The drillshed was divided into two compartments, one for the boys and the other for the girls, and here and in other quarters of the yard the work was at once commenced of stripping them and arraying them in their new attire. The scene was as pathetic as it was interesting, the great majority of the poor children being so wretchedly clad that they excited the deep compassion of those who saw them. The operation of removing their garments—a palpable misdescription—went on through the morning, and as the weather was bitterly cold, being a repetition of that of which we have experienced far too much this last winter, and as the children were rather starved in the transition process, they were supplied with a bun. About one o'clock the operations were totally suspended for the customary meal of soup and bread, a resumption being made as soon as the feast was over. A great change was soon effected. Early in the morning the yard of the police station was crowded from end to end with a large mass of small humanity, whose appearance betokened abject poverty, and now, as if by a magician's wand, the same mass appeared to the public gaze clothed, not exactly in fine linen, but in good and durable attire. What made them still more pleasant to look upon was that all the little ones—an experience new to most of them—had clean hands and faces, the condition of a washing having been imposed upon the parents as necessary for the admission of their children to the participation of what was provided for them. We must not omit to state, that in this labour of undressing and dressing the children, a number of charitable ladies and gentlemen lent their assistance. Amongst those who by their presence showed their sympathy with Mr. Bent in his philanthropic efforts were Mr. and Mrs. Benton, Mr. J. Galloway, jun., Captain Cardwell, Dr. Bowman, Mr. H. Bowman, and Mr. George Bowman, deputy-chairman of the executive committee; Mr. and Mrs. F. Hollins, Mrs. Grassham, Mrs. Crossley, Mrs. Bruce, Mrs. Bent, Mrs. Street, Mrs. Cameron, Mr. Woollaston, Mr. S. Redfern, Mr. Hanlon, and Mr. Clemmitt, of the Minnehaha Minstrels, whose invaluable services on behalf of the kitchen are beyond all praise; Mr. Gibson, chairman of the executive committee; Mr. J. Moxon, Mr. Cochrane, and others. Another gratifying occurrence must be mentioned. Some few weeks ago Mr. Benton entertained 1,632 poor men, women, and children to a dinner of roast beef and potatoes in the yard of the Old Trafford Police Station, defraying the whole of the cost, and giving also a 1d. to each child as it passed out, and 3d. to each adult. A further instance of generosity is shown in the gift of Mrs. Benton during the past season of 85 yards of calico and two pieces of flannel. These were made up into articles of clothing for the use of the girls by Mrs. Street and Mrs. Cameron. Eight hundred corduroy suits were distributed among the boys, each receiving also a cap, collar, necktie, shirt, stockings and clogs, and a handkerchief. To the girls were given a skirt, dress, shawl, hat, stockings, and clogs, and also a handkerchief. As their dirty and tattered clothing, and their old clogs and shoes—all that was left of them—were taken from them, they were piled up in two separate heaps, and served as another reminder—and a very forcible one—of the hardships to which their little wearers had been subjected. It was unfortunate, but so it turned out, that from some cause or other fifty of the lads had to do for the present without clogs. Mr. Bent, however, hopes to be able to furnish them this week. Mr. Bent had an extraordinary reception. The worthy superintendent had been detained elsewhere by his duties, and it was rather late in the afternoon when he drove into the yard. His appearance was the signal for a remarkable ovation. As soon as the children saw their benefactor a great shout arose from their little throats. They pressed round him with outstretched arms, and it was with some difficulty Mr. Bent succeeded in extricating himself from his enthusiastic and youthful admirers.

A few figures relating to Mr. Bent's work during the season may not be without interest. Since the opening of the institution in January last about 155,000 meals have been served, making a total from the time of the commencement of the movement in 1878 of 1,257,198, surely a noble record. Mr. Bent is grateful for the assistance in money and new and cast-off clothing he has from time to time received; but we regret to say that he now has to face a considerable deficit. This has arisen to some extent from the greatly increased demand for clothing, which Mr. Bent, with the resources at his disposal, has been unable to meet. We refuse to believe that the benevolent public of Manchester will allow that incubus to remain, but that it will be promptly cleared off, so that Mr. Bent may be enabled to resume his generous mission with an unfettered hand.—*Manchester Courier, April 23, 1888.*

A HAPPY NEW YEAR.

The above stereotyped phrase has, during the last week, been on the lips of countless thousands of all those who profess and call themselves Christians, wherever they may dwell and to whatever nationality they may belong. If wishing one's friends a happy New Year would bring so desirable a blessing about, the potency of Aladdin's lamp would become a matter of indifference, and charms and soothsayers things of the past. But, unfortunately for us, whatever we may wish has no effect in fact, unless we by active industry endeavour to bring our wishes to a practical issue. Such were our thoughts as on the evening of New Year's day we stood amongst a crowd of little, aye, and big, fellow-creatures, to whom the festivities of the season have been but a hollow mockery. For millions of our fellow-countrymen the Yule log has burnt brightly; the mistletoe has hung in thousands of homesteads as well as in the baron's hall.

Father Christmas has once again bid us eat, drink, and be merry, and millions have, like true devotees, obeyed his mandate to the best of their ability and the utmost of their capacity; but alas, notwithstanding the noble efforts put forth by numerous bands of workers in the city of Manchester and our neighbours surrounding, there are a large number of human beings whose only portion has been to look on and shiver.

And so it came to pass that at the police station, Old Trafford, we found ourselves amongst as motley a crowd of God's creatures as ever wrung pain from a sympathetic heart or disgraced a civilised country. Here, gathered together from all parts of the city, &c., were over 1,500 starving children, standing in the police drillyard, with heaven's canopy for a roof, whilst—

> "Like a pall, the unstarr'd sky
> Hung o'er the city like a shroud; and the wind,
> Shrieking and hissing like a curse, went by,
> Leaving a fitful, solemn pause behind."

To paraphrase poor Tom Hood—

> "Was it not pitiful,
> Near a whole city full,
> Food they had none?"

So the poor little mites had tramped here, some of them for miles, to partake of the bowl of excellent hot soup and large piece of bread provided for them by Mr. Superintendent Bent and the men under his command at Old Trafford; and, despite all warning to the contrary, the little things begin to assemble a couple of hours before the time fixed, and though in a many cases without shoes and stockings, they stand like Spartans until this, to a many of them, their only meal is prepared. When at length 500 basins have been filled with soup in the shed, the first batch are marched in. Instantly, 500 pairs of cold hands clasp the sides of the basins to warm the little human frames almost perishing with cold, and, amidst a great steam, the large-hearted, though stern disciplinarian, superintendent, with head uncovered, leads off with the grand invocation—

> "Be present at our table, Lord;
> Be here and everywhere adored;
> Thy creatures bless, and grant that we
> May feast in Paradise with Thee,"

in which he is joined by 500 juvenile throats, who, at the top of their voices, express their gratitude to their Creator for the food provided; then, like a flash of lightning, 500 spoons are brought into active operation, and 500 little souls feel comforted. And so the whole are fed. Questioning a few, the following answers were received:—

A miserably-clad girl said she was nearly thirteen, and there were five younger. Father ran away to America three years ago. Her mother got four days "charing" a week, and got 2s. per day, and they paid 3s. rent. Let every well-to-do mother of six children ask herself what she would do with 5s. a week to keep six children.

A good-featured woman, with poverty and want stamped upon her pale face, yet her few clothes scrupulously clean, said her husband was in the hospital with consumption. She had seven children, all present, the eldest twelve. She did some washing, but could only earn 6s. or 8s. per week. They had had a two-pound loaf that morning which a neighbour, almost as poor as herself, had given her (God bless that neighbour), and the soup they were about to have would put them on till to-morrow. "What then?" we asked. She answered with her tears. Need we say that a good Samaritan who overheard the conversation, with a big lump in his throat, settled the bread question for several to-morrows?

A blue-eyed girl, no hat, shoes, or stockings, a chemise and thin old frock, who was shaking like an aspen leaf. "What is your name?" "Please, sir, Maggie Wilson, an' we lives in Salford. Please, sir, father's dead, sir, in Liverpool. Please, sir, there's only me an' this here little lad, sir, an' another little lad, sir, as ull be three in a month. Mother works at rag pickin', but she's got a 'fustion' in the end of her thumb, an' hasn't done any work for above a month. Please, sir, some folk in our street sends us a twothri taters an' things in sometimes." "Where do you live?" "Off Ancoats Lane, sir." (Over three miles from Old Trafford.) And then the little maid confidentially informed us that her and Billy (aged eleven and nine), when they growed big enough, were going to work, and Billy was going to be the father, and mother would stop at home and mind the house and their Joey.

A little fellow, minus cap and shirt, and barefoot, said his father was locked up for "feightin' an' bein' drunk." "Oh, aye, sir, he thumps mi mother many a time. We have a baby at'll be three week old in th' mornin'. Please, sir, owd Mary, as cleans some offices, and some more women as lives aside of us, comes in an' looks after mi mother, what's been bad since some day as they fotched us the baby. We never hardly has any dinner." This lad, aged eight, had carried his sister, aged three, out of Salford, because she likewise was barefooted, and had a sore toe, through being cut with a piece of glass.

These are only a very few instances out of the crowd that came under our notice. Out of work, sickness, death, and last, but by no means least, drink, are the causes that are responsible for this daily congregation of helpless, innocent children.

Although we know we are treading upon tender ground, yet we feel constrained again to say that it is almost monstrous to collect and send out of the country the immense sums of money we do annually for the benefit of some other nation or nations thousands of miles away, who are nothing and don't want to be anything to us. Surely charity begins at home, and the writer confesses his inability to comprehend the reasonableness of any organisation or society of men who think more of the natives of, say, Central Africa or China than they do of their own kith and kin at home. What we want in this and other cities is a staff of, call them missionaries if you like, men or women who, when they find an ill-fed, apparently destitute child, will trace the cause of its destitution to its source. If found to be a genuine case of misfortune or sickness, assist it; but if, on the other hand, it is proved to be a case of parental neglect and drunkenness—that the inhuman brutes have poured down their own throats the money in the shape of alcohol, and little Pollies and Billies have cried their eyes up for want of bread in consequence—then there is only one remedy, a drastic and sure remedy. It is composed of a piece of wood about two feet long and say nine lengths of whip cord, to be applied outwardly and well rubbed in. Men who systematically abuse children are cowards of the lowest type, and a coward dreads nothing so much as the lash.

That this great work of feeding from 1,000 to 2,000 children every afternoon, Sundays included, for several winter months, entails great labour and cost, goes without saying, though each meal costs less than one penny. Unlike many other philanthropic institutions there are no paid professional, philanthropic secretaries, or salaries of any kind whatsoever. Every penny received reaches those for whom it is intended. The police officers stationed at Old Trafford, in their own time, become cooks and waiters. They lay aside the truncheon and the handcuffs for the big rough apron and the bread-cutting knife. They prove that under the blue coat and metal buttons there beats a warm and sympathetic heart for the unfortunate offspring of some of those people with whom they deal elsewhere. These men have, during the summer, extended the shed accommodation by about 200 seats.

We feel quite sure that in this great city there are scores of people who will give a helping hand. We ask all mothers and fathers to contrast their own children's happy faces and their comfortable fireside with the wretched children and the cold drillyard at Old Trafford, and then, out of the fullness of their heart (not forgetting that every sovereign sent to Mr. Bent, Old Trafford, Manchester, will feed about 300 children), to at once decide, and in a practical form, that as far as these children are concerned, "A Happy New Year" shall not be an empty sound, but a grand reality.—*Frank Hollins in the Manchester Courier, January 4, 1889.*

Lightning Source UK Ltd.
Milton Keynes UK
UKHW050716081221
395281UK00003B/87